BLESSED BY *Joy*

THE TRIUMPH OF FAITH

*From the Pages of Joy's Journal
and the Heart of Her Mother*

Joyce Behm Harris

I John 4:16

By Joyce Behm Harris

With J. Gordon Harris

Foreword by Calvin Miller

HARRIS-BEHM PUBLISHERS

BLESSED BY

THE TRIUMPH OF FAITH

*From the Pages of Joy's Journal
and the Heart of Her Mother*

Copyright© 2007 by Joyce Behm Harris, Author
All rights reserved.

www.gordonandjoyce.net
blessedbyjoy@gmail.com

ISBN 13: 978-0-615-15713-9

Printed by Sisson Printing, Inc., Sioux Falls, South Dakota.

Dedication

Joy described her relationship with you, Mike Sauers, as a "spiritual connection." You loved Joy unconditionally and brought completion to her life. Joy wrote:

My best friend
The man who accepts me as I am
Encourages me in all I do
Challenges me to grow, to risk
Comforts me in struggles and pain
Prays with me, "Thy will be done."
Him I will honor.
Him I will trust.
In his hands, I place my heart, my love.

Respectfully lead one another,
   Support one another,
      Hold accountable one another.

May nothing on earth come between
   The love and commitment to one another.

Until death brings parting.
   Forever blessed.

Joy

June 4, 1997

Mike, in honor of you, your lovely wife, Ruth, and precocious son, Luke, we dedicate this book. Joy believed she would never know the love of a husband. God has been faithful to you with another family that honors Him and lives under His LORDSHIP. Your family has been and will continue to be a blessing to us and to future generations.

Jami, I dedicate this book to you acknowledging the close sisterly bond you share with Joy. That relationship cannot be severed easily and will always be a part of your life. You faithfully loved Joy not fully understanding all of her needs as we devoted a major part of our time and efforts to Joy's health care. We recognize your patience and tolerance as you gave preference to Joy during those childhood years. You are God's gift to Gordon and me. We love you. You have honored us with your life and devotion to God.

Gordon, as my helpmate, my partner in ministry, and the father of our children, I dedicate this story to you, my husband of 40+ years. In addition to your remarkable ministry and legacy, you faithfully and unselfishly went beyond the second and third mile to support our family. You chose to enthusiastically enter into the care of Joy not forgetting Jami. Your positive spirit, your hard and tireless work, your love and strong faith were the glue that inspired and made possible not only this book but Joy's incredible life. Your leadership allowed our family to endure and to soar regardless of the challenges of life. I love you and thank God for you.

This book, finally, is written with God's hand. The intent of this book is to honor God and to be a witness to those who struggle whether physically, emotionally, or spiritually and have discovered a renewal of faith, a new found faith, and a meaningful faith. The beginning and the end testify that God is faithful, God is love, and God is omnipotent. Joy understood that, and God became first in her life. God gave back to Joy His blessings, a ministry, and years of life. We dedicate this story of Joy's life to God to be used for His purposes.

To God be all glory, total love, and forever honor.

Joyce Behm Harris

Foreword

Many years have passed since I first met the Harris family, but the impact they made on my life has been nothing short of remarkable. Mine has been an odd and sad, memorable and glorious, splendid and wrenching affair with this band of warriors, who learned as a family the art of fighting a common demon which had set out to destroy them, but ended up only making them stronger.

From the moment their daughter Joy was diagnosed with cystic fibrosis, her ordeal became a unitive force in their lives. As you will see in the story that is about to unfold, Joy herself writes beautifully of her faith and struggle. I seldom read the footprints of a martyr without feeling the impact of their faith. I could not read this book and not feel the impact that Joy's faith has made upon me.

It is a surreal testimony of a young woman who fought it out on this planet with the never-ending battles of edgy medicine and point-blank hopelessness which she would never allow to wear the name. Cystic fibrosis is a child killer. It stalks the little ones and the determined youth with a growing weakness which makes it difficult to breathe or even hope without facing the darkness that covers sunlight and breathes forth the threat of loss over every happy moment.

But as Joy fought, ever day girded for battle, she found that her faith in Christ was a chain of manganese steel, binding her to her family. And her mother became her counselor and friend through endless hospitalizations and years of drugs and medical regimens of all sorts. And the miracles of madonnas and children are just the stuff of cold and drafty cathedrals. They are the flesh and blood of two souls that says once the fleshly umbilical is clipped, another is born. And the new umbilical is a lifeline, strong enough to bridge not only the generation gap but also the large gulf that separates heaven from the crying world which often precedes it.

But I offer you a warning: do not read this book unless you are prepared to abandon the work-a-day items that fill your agenda. Here is a book that will make you weep and laugh, pray and cry with such consuming power, you will have no choice but to go on reading while the world around you falls apart. But, that's alright. The world around you is not all that important anyway, as you are shortly to discover.

Calvin Miller
Beeson Divinity School
Birmingham, Alabama

Preface

Everybody loves a good story – stories that illustrate life with its struggles and nuisances, its unique mysteries, and its triumphs or defeats. These stories connect us to people and to the real world. This book is a story about one person's life and her family as they wrestle with God for answers that are not immediately forthcoming. It graphically demonstrates that an honorable and upright life does not guarantee any earned inheritance of blessings or realized dreams. This book and story will prove to readers that, ultimately, there is meaning, there is joy, there is fulfillment when life is lived beyond the interest of one's own desires and under the Lordship of God the Father.

Such is the backdrop of the story this book unfolds about our daughter, Joy. No section of this story is made up. It is not a scary story. However, it is a story of mystery that begins with love, dreams, hopes, then without warning develops into a crisis of unfathomable portions. Life unintentionally takes a dramatic plunge into the depths of despair and sorrow. Hopes for a happy family, for quality of life, for meaning and purpose are lost in the struggles and emotional pain of a death sentence pronounced upon our beautiful and precocious daughter, Joy. There seem to be no answers to the questions put before God.

As time evolves, God begins to take our family beyond the "why" questions to reveal a greater purpose than just living out one's days. God provides beyond all our expectations to ensure that Joy's life has meaning. Her life will bring honor to Him. It will be a beautiful and inspirational life. God will use the life of Joy to illustrate to the world that He loves us, that He has immeasurable gifts for His children, and that He desires no harm to come to them. Joy returns to Him her love and devotion and her desire to follow and obey Him until He calls her home.

We have lived this story and can attest to the fact that God is indeed faithful. The scripture, **Romans 8:28 and 38-39**, we discovered to be totally true:

28 And we know that in all things God works for the good of those who love him, who have been called according to his purpose.

38-39 For I am convinced that neither death nor life, neither angels nor demons, neither the present nor the future, nor any powers, neither height nor depth, nor anything else in all creation, will be able to separate us from the love of God that is in Christ Jesus our Lord.

– Joyce Harris

Joy – Eight Months Old

Joy – Three Years Old

TABLE OF CONTENTS

TABLE OF CONTENTS

TABLE OF CONTENTS

TABLE OF CONTENTS

I. INTRODUCTION

Witness to a Life

God is good, God is love, and God is faithful – three simple, yet profound biblical principles which, when applied to the Christian's daily walk, have immeasurable impact upon one's life and future. Such was the example of Joy Harris Sauers. My daughter, Joy, illustrated to the world that God can give grace to one who walks with Him despite living a life of pain, suffering, and ultimate death.

The story of Joy is a rich and complicated one. As Joy's parents, Gordon and I were brought to our knees when our beautiful and promising 4-year-old daughter was diagnosed with cystic fibrosis. This is a genetic disease accompanied by lung infections and digestive tract malfunctions. There is no cure. On that day, so many years ago, we were confronted with two undeniable facts – we would be living with cystic fibrosis and the knowledge that our child would die young. Gordon and I were consumed with chronic grief and conflicted feelings. The diagnosis tested the solidarity of our family. We engaged in that human error of asking, "Why." The questioning, pleading, and protests tortured our spiritual and mental sanity.

For a family that was used to taking initiative in solving problems, who had pat answers for the problems of others, who spoke eloquently of God's purpose and plan for one's life, we were stopped in our tracks by this turn of events. We were totally at the mercy of God. As time advanced, it became evident that God was in control. God's presence existed not for a moment in time, but evolved from the past, moved into the present, took control of the unknown future, and finally triumphed over health struggles to promised rewards.

Yet this book does not paint a picture of glorified struggle or martyrdom. Joy's story is about God working in the life of one who, despite her illness, could give a witness to others of His love, grace, and forgiveness. Toward the end, God observed Joy's struggles and perpetual decline of health. He saw beyond the diseased, frail body that was absent of hope for the future. He also took note of her commitment to ministry and her passion for living. He saw a life that could speak and live His message of redemption. God defined for Joy her purpose in life. Joy responded to God's call, and she discovered a reason for living and dying as she shared her life with and for others in His name. Ministry became her passion. Enthusiasm, joy, love and devotion were her trademarks. God reciprocated by providing Joy the energy to persevere. He could not remove the "thorn," but Joy understood, "His strength is perfect." This child of the Father possessed an indomitable spirit, a heart of sensitivity, and an ability to achieve in spite of health limitations.

Gordon and I have been left behind as a witness to the life of Joy. We nurtured our daughter in our home, we observed Joy as she matured to a young adult, and then stood aside as God began to work in her life. I thought I knew Joy. After all, I did birth her. I treasured her from the moment of conception. I nourished her, and I lived intimately with her. But as observers, Gordon and I could not comprehend the depth and heart of Joy's soul. The spiritual journal she recorded during the last five years of her life, and which we found after her death, was a revelation to us. It is the testimony of God's work in one life. The discussions she had with God as reported in her journal revealed Joy's heart.

Her greatest desire was to serve God completely and totally. In that close, personal relationship, Joy addressed God as *Abba, Daddy, Closer than a Heart Beat.*

On June 10, 1999 Joy wrote:

> *LORD, I need to soak in you, to take in your Spirit and grace. I need the strength of your right hand and the gentleness of your healing touch. I love you. I love life. I love Michael. I love others so much. Restore me, my body and spirit that I might serve that much more my God, my LORD. Hold me close to you that I may hear your heartbeat.*

In her own words, Joy speaks honestly throughout this book regarding:
- her struggle with life and death issues.
- her love and marriage commitments.
- her proof and evidence that God answers prayer.
- her personal feelings regarding her gifts and her struggle with self worth.
- her love for others and deep devotion to God.
- her critical health decisions.
- her regret and sorrow that loved ones must accompany her on that difficult road.
- her complete joy while participating in ministry and impacting lives.

Joy's story cannot be told without including family history. After all, this entire saga impacted our lives both positively and negatively. The title, *Blessed by Joy*, denotes that irony. What initially seemed a *curse* ultimately climaxed as a blessing – a blessing not only to us, but to those who knew Joy and who shared her life. As we could not understand the infamous "why" question, so we could not comprehend "why" God would choose us to parent and participate in the life of someone directed by God. This account of Joy's life will hopefully give meaning and inspiration to others who desire an explanation to the mysteries of life.

We tell Joy's story with her permission. Joy often wrote of her desire to use her life as evidence of God's work.

Joy penned on August 18, 1996:

> *God has continually kept his hand – his healing, and gracious touch on my body. This is part of my story and my testimony. It is now time to decide – how and in what form can I use my life as a witness. LORD, my life has always been a witness to your providence and will. How can I best vocalize that?*

October 28, 1996:

> *I want and look forward to all the opportunities I will have to share with people God's faithfulness and God's story of my life.*

That opportunity has been handed down to us, her parents. Many people have requested and encouraged us to tell Joy's story through this book. Joy's husband, Mike Sauers, also shares in this testimony, and other witnesses lend authenticity. But much of the story is told in Joy's own words.

The unique lessons that emerged through the life and experiences of Joy opened our hearts to a personal understanding of God, His greater will and how He works for good. For those reasons, we are compelled to tell Joy's story. We hope and desire that Joy's message will inspire, teach, and challenge you, the reader. As Joy's parents during those brief thirty years, we have discovered blessings and inspiration intermingled with that of pain and sorrow.

The story begins with Joy, the child, and ends with joy as she receives the "Good and Faithful Servant" reward. We invite you into Joy's life. Welcome to her world.

Joy's Prayer

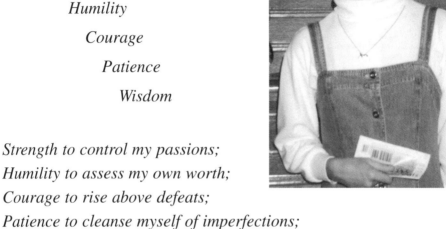

I need Strength

    Humility

      Courage

        Patience

          Wisdom

Strength to control my passions;
Humility to assess my own worth;
Courage to rise above defeats;
Patience to cleanse myself of imperfections;
Wisdom to learn and to live by the teachings of my heritage.

Let me not be discouraged, O God, by my failings.
Let me take heart from all that is good and noble in my character.
Keep me from falling victim to cynicism.
Teach me sincerity and enthusiasm.

Endow me with the courage to proclaim Your name,
To serve You by helping to bring nearer the day
When all humanity will be one family.

O God, be my guide and inspiration!

II. IN THE BEGINNING

Isaiah 40:31

If one must define a starting point, it begins with God's love and His grace. Gordon and I were introduced to this faith in the homes of our childhood. We were blessed with parents who lived, preached, taught, and modeled for us the Christian faith. They were not perfect homes, but we learned early in our marriage that the two of us could glean the best from our heritage and establish our own family values. We operated from an idealistic dream that ensured a perfect future for our home and our children. But then reality threw us a curve. We soon learned that we were inadequate to deal with the trauma of a child diagnosed with a terminal illness. We did not have the benefit of a road map to steer our course. We were at the mercy of God. Emotionally, spiritually, and physically, we were forced to depend upon God.

Gordon and I learned to lean on each other and to work and survive as a team. We both took responsibility for the care of our child. When one stumbled, the other took the lead. There were times when our patience wore thin. We endured frustrations, exhaustion, and sadness. But we did not complain. We did not accuse. We did not give up. We did not lose faith. Well, I take that back. Initially, upon news of the diagnosis, I suffered with episodes of depression. My faith was like a teeter totter, going up and down as I tried to maintain a balance between hope and despair, but that discussion comes later. Gordon always met the challenges with a positive spirit, a can-do attitude, and encouraging words. His support and never-give-up disposition kept our lives centered, forward looking, never wavering. I realize now in hindsight how blessed we were as a family by Gordon's leadership and wisdom. Most importantly, God was always present. He even went before us.

Our adopted scripture assured us of God's presence as daily we walked through uncharted paths.

Isaiah 40:31. . . those who hope in the LORD will renew their strength

they will soar on wings like eagles

they will run and not grow weary

they will walk and not be faint.

God was faithful, and we now can tell the story, *Blessed by Joy.*

The Story Unfolds

Gordon and I had been living in Louisville, Kentucky since our marriage two years earlier. It was 1969 and Gordon was in his final year of graduate studies at Southern Seminary. Our vision, now, was to start a family and live happily ever after. We were excited. I had already decided on a name for our first born, Donna Joy, as well as future children, Jami Ruth, a third, Jordon, if a boy or Jordyn, for a girl, and, who knows, maybe a fourth, if God so blessed us. I became pregnant and the baby was due August 9, 1970.

Gordon's major professor, Clyde Francisco, returned from a teaching sabbatical at the Philippine Baptist Seminary in Baguio. (His name will come up again four years later.) Upon his return to Louisville, he brought news to Gordon that the seminary in Baguio would need an Old Testament (OT abbreviated for future references) professor the following year. He suggested that we consider this ministry position. Both Gordon and I were open to mission service. Years before, we each had committed our lives to Christian service including missions, if that was God's will.

Gordon contacted the Foreign Mission Board (now known as the International Mission Board). We were instructed in the procedures of application. After all of the extensive paperwork and interviews were completed, approval was granted, and we were commissioned to serve in the Philippines.

The wheels were in motion – birth baby in August, attend missionary orientation in the fall, travel by ship to the Philippines, reside in Manila for one year of language study, move to Baguio City (located in the mountains of Northern Luzon), and teach Old Testament at the seminary.

Gordon completed his doctoral dissertation and final oral examinations in the spring of 1970. Rather than sit out the summer months in Louisville separated from our families down south, Gordon and I decided to move to Fort Worth, Texas where his parents resided. My parents lived in Louisiana, a five-hour drive away. Our decision to move was crucial in the events that were yet to unfold as we awaited the birth of our baby.

We had our lives neatly planned with or without God's help. A lady commented to me shortly before our baby's birth, "Your life and home will never be the same again." Mentally I disagreed with her. In my self-assured attitude, I thought, "We are who we are and that will not change." Her words, as it turned out, were prophetic.

The pregnancy was basically uneventful until the last month. The week of the anticipated birth, the doctor expressed mild concern. The baby was in breach position. He very gently manipulated her into head down position. The next week at my doctor's visit, baby had flipped back to breach. The doctor again commented, but in a more concerned voice. I reported this to my mother-in-law. With confidence, she announced that ninety-nine percent of babies experience no complications at birth. I accepted her reassurance, but nagging doubts invaded my thoughts.

Meanwhile, my baby was in no hurry to leave the warm and safe environment of the womb. It was already two weeks past the due date. My impatient mother-in-law faithfully took me on daily walks to speed up this blessed event. Finally, on Monday morning, August 24, 1970, our baby announced her intentions to greet this world. Such excited anticipation! Let's hurry. I want to see and hold my baby.

The Miracle Baby

The following morning about 2:00 a.m., I began to toss from side to side. I could not understand why I was in such pain. The nurse approached and asked me to rest easy. She explained that our baby had been delivered as an emergency caesarean birth at 5:00 p.m. the previous evening. Bewildered, I wanted to know why but could not form the words. I was confused. The nurse finally returned when I was alert. She explained that, during labor, the baby could not descend into the birth canal. They had charted the fetal heartbeat with each contraction using a new technology recently installed at the hospital (standard procedure today). When the heart beat went dangerously low without recovery, they rushed into surgery. The nurse also informed me that surgery was performed on my baby three hours after birth. They termed it "meconium ileus," whatever that meant.

Before I knew it, my mother and father were there by my side. They looked very concerned. They had traveled at a moment's notice from Louisiana to be with me and Gordon and our baby. My mother's worry could not be consoled.

The pediatric surgeon, Dr. Richard Ellis, met with us later in the morning and explained our daughter's surgery. Our baby's intestine had clogged, and nothing could pass through the bowel. Consequently, she had a very large distended stomach that they first had to pump. Surgery followed. More than half of her intestine had to be removed. Dr. Ellis estimated that our baby would be in the hospital approximately four to six weeks.

At 4:00 a.m., the nurse asked if I wanted to see my baby. "Of course!!!" They wheeled me down a long hall on the hospital bed, Gordon walking alongside. As we approached the intensive care nursery, we slowed down and stopped by a large window reinforced with chicken wire between the panes. The nursery was a rectangular room with many babies in their isolettes. Far in the back of the pediatric nursery was our baby with a large patch over her stomach. Although her head had been shaved in front and on the sides, her black hair was still plentiful. Tubes were coming out of head, arm, and feet. I recognized my baby immediately. I knew her! Her large black eyes were bright and flashing back and forth. She was busy and impatient – identical to that constant movement and kicking I experienced in the womb. Yes, she was "special" from the very beginning. Even though she was in a critical state, I was very proud and hopeful for our baby.

We were not allowed in the nursery and could only watch from behind the distant wire reinforced windows. Gordon, in frustration, brought binoculars from home, and we watched our baby – through binoculars.

We discussed the name for our baby. It would be Donna Joy. True to southern tradition I wanted to call her by both names. Gordon advocated for Joy. When his mother declared it would be "Joy," I surrendered. My family liked the Donna Joy, because Orville "Donald" was her grandfather and Don her uncle. But, alas, "Joy" won out. As time took its toll, that was who she was – Joy. It fit, and it was the name she preferred, as did I.

After a week in this hospital, Dr. Ellis telephoned to announce that he was moving Joy to Cook Children's Specialty Clinic. He asked us to meet the nurse at the hospital ICU to take Joy to this children's hospital. Gordon was not available, so his mother agreed to accompany me. I eagerly anticipated holding my baby. When we met the nurse, she had in her arms this little bundle wrapped in a blanket from head to toe. We got into the elevator, the nurse pulled back the blanket, and I saw my baby close up for the first time. Her eyes were big and dark, we looked at each other, and our gaze locked. My heart went out to my precious baby who looked perfectly healthy to me. I wanted to take her home but understood the gravity of the situation. The nurse asked if I would like to hold her. Before I could speak up, my mother-in-law announced with swift voice, "Oh, no!" My arms ached, but I, in shyness, would never refute my mother-in-law. When she recounted the events to Gordon's father, he spoke on my behalf, "Maybe Joyce wanted to hold her baby." I felt exonerated. I have since learned to be more vocal in protests that I feel are warranted.

Gordon's father was the pastor of University Baptist Church in Fort Worth. Subsequently, word of our baby's medical needs spread far and wide. So many people were praying. God heard those prayers .

Welcome to Joy's Life and World

Dr. Ellis suggested that I stay at the hospital three days prior to Joy's discharge to become comfortable and confident in her care. I looked forward to time with my baby. The first evening, the head nurse approached me and commented that I could return home. In other words, "You're in our way." You can imagine how well that set with me. I was there with the doctor's blessings, and I intended to stay and finally care for my daughter.

On a Sunday morning four weeks from the day of Joy's birth, we were excited to finally bring Joy home with us. No longer would we drive from the hospital with empty arms. Gordon and I met the nurses. We dressed Joy in a little gown, wrapped her in a light blanket, and walked with her to our car. She sat on my legs looking up at me as we drove through the streets of Fort Worth. I was happy. I remember just smiling at her and continuing to smile. We were going home with our precious baby.

The doctor had prescribed a special pre-digested formula which came in powder form. Once home, I carefully and nervously mixed the formula following as best as possible the verbal instructions from the nurse. Why weren't they written down? Why didn't I ask? In the middle of the night I awakened in a panic. I feared I had mixed it incorrectly, harming my baby. I went to the kitchen about 2:00/3:00 a.m., emptied the entire case of twelve bottles of formula down the drain (and it was expensive stuff), remixed it, and set the controls to sterilize twelve more bottles of formula.

Caring for Joy became a two parent responsibility. We took turns every other night setting the alarm to feed her every three hours. If she slept too long between feedings, she would awake ravenously hungry and crying hysterically. Her cry was so desperate that she could not purse her lips to suck from the bottle. I learned to take her into my arms, hold the bottle in my left hand, walk with her, and rhythmically pat her with my right hand. Then, and only then, would she relax to accept the bottle. Before her birth, I had observed on a pharmacy shelf, a nipple that was fashioned with ribs/wings on either side to fit comfortably into an infant's mouth. I described this to Gordon and sent him on a mission of mercy to purchase those nipples. He returned with the exact ones, and they fit perfectly for Joy's inexperienced sucking reflex.

Getting Joy to burp was extremely precarious. If she cried too much and swallowed air, everything would shoot out her mouth in projectile fashion. We could not trust anyone to feed her because of her sensitive digestive system. It was a labor of love for us. I simply could not get enough of our precious Joy.

For Joy's first professional picture at six weeks, I chose a pretty pink dress. When I finished dressing her, I smiled at her and told her how pretty she was. She looked at me, smiled, and gave a little jiggle with her body. She understood. The picture was taken with her wearing the pink dress, lacy socks, booties that swallowed her tiny feet and a Mohawk hair style (compliments of surgery).

The Philippines

Still recovering from the birth and in the hospital, I mentioned to Dr. Ellis that we had been commissioned as missionaries to the Philippines. The expression on his face was that of surprise. He was silent for a moment. He just looked at me with a furrowed brow, but said nothing. He did not caution us or try to dissuade us from missionary service. He knew that Joy's health would determine our future. Although Joy was quite fragile, she continued to gain weight and strength. We presumed that our future plans would only be delayed. Missionary orientation that had been scheduled for fall would simply be postponed until January of '71. Joy still required follow-up by our pediatrician and needed our full care and attention.

In January we traveled to beautiful Callaway Gardens in Georgia to attend the orientation with newly appointed missionaries. Petite Joy was the center of attention during our three month stay. Valuable classes on culture adjustments, Philippine history, language study, resources for problem-solving, cooking, hygiene, basic car mechanics, testimonies from seasoned missionaries, etc. were carefully planned and executed. We met wonderful friends, but the time became long and drawn out. We were anxious to be on our way. It was stressful trying to feed and care for Joy in a cold, dark, one-room, A-frame cabin.

In April, we finally departed for the Philippines by ocean liner. Saying goodbye to family in Louisiana, Texas, California, and Hawaii was exhausting. When finally we boarded the ship, I was a proverbial *basket case.* I welcomed the time alone with Joy and Gordon. I was starved for rest, sleep, and emotional healing. It was a wonderful respite. We were ten days on the seas. I never realized how much of our planet is covered in water. Along the way, the ship docked in Japan, Hong Kong, Taiwan and finally the Philippines.

When the shipped docked on the shores of the Philippines, we were overwhelmed by the welcome of missionaries who quickly became our family. They took charge of our luggage and crates. Nora Stanley immediately went to Joy, changed her diaper, and managed her needs. I lost sight of Gordon in all the flurry of activity. At last we felt we were home, in an unfamiliar land, yet where God had placed us for ministry.

That is not to say there were no adjustments. The first shock was the heat and humidity that enveloped us as we left the comfort of an air-conditioned cabin and sea breezes. The next surprise was the unbelievably congested traffic, the constant roar of buses, the belching exhaust of diesel fumes, and the continuous symphony of bleeping horns. Traffic in the Philippines has its own unique system.

The right and left lanes exist but only to indicate the direction for the flow of traffic. At intersections the lights are observed – red and green. However, as each vehicle approaches a red light, the driver maneuvers his vehicle into whatever space is available, no matter how small, which gives him the edge as he anticipates the green. I have seen intersections where cars, buses, and jeepneys are all meshed together in unimaginable contortions, looking like a puzzle with each vehicle neatly and tightly fitted next to the other. When green pops up, amazingly, all vehicles roar their engines, move on, and are gone. It is fascinating to watch! In our culture it would be hours before such a traffic jam could possibly unravel.

To the untrained American driver, the scene appears disorderly and chaotic, but the system actually works well in their culture. As long as the driver does not acknowledge another driver vying for his position, he justifiably has the right of way – sort of a game of bluff. Our mission organization wisely gave old, beat up cars to new missionaries. I will admit, Gordon had three fender-benders our first year. After that, we were seasoned drivers. My defensive driving is still evident to this day.

We settled in a home in Quezon City, a suburb of Manila. We lived there during eleven months of language school studying Ilocano, the language of the mountain people. It was a five half-day intensive tutoring process. I had to leave Joy in the care of our helper. It was difficult being separated from my nine month old baby. My thoughts were distracted and my enthusiasm waned. It takes total concentration to learn a new language, and I confess that it was not easy for me. This time in Manila was critical for us as we adjusted to a new culture. We attended a little church on the outskirts of Quezon City. It was an open air building that was built as a lean-to attached to an outside wall of the pastor's home. We had many memorable and enriching experiences during this first year of our missionary service.

Before we left the United States, my sister-in-law had recommended a Filipina (female gender) pediatrician who had trained in the U.S. We looked her up and, amazingly, she lived in the same residential complex – a little more than a block from our home in Quezon City. It is incredible considering that the population of Manila numbers in the multi-millions. Doctora Minerva (Eva) Cruz also took care of Joy after we moved to Baguio City. Her services were instrumental in the health of Joy. God had provided.

As early as July, 1971, I expressed concern in a letter to my parents regarding Joy's constant stuffy nose and lung congestion. It was especially aggravated by the small air conditioner we had in our bedroom. Joy slept near us in an adjoining bedroom. Doctora Cruz attributed Joy's congestion to either allergies or changes between hot and cool temperatures. She prescribed a medication to help clear it. We continued to care for Joy in our usual way assuming this health issue was related to allergies. Gordon had suffered from allergies all his life. In spite of that stuffy nose, Joy continued to do well physically – growing and gaining weight.

After almost a year in Manila, we moved to Baguio City, approximately five-six hours of travel north from Manila into the mountains of Luzon. Here Gordon continued language study with a private tutor. In addition, he began his teaching at the seminary and also worked with pastors in the lowlands – in the province of eastern Pangasinan. Incidentally, on the shores of Pangasinan is the Lingayen

Gulf where General MacArthur returned during the liberation of the Philippines at the close of World War II.

And Baby Make Two

After Joy's first birthday, which we celebrated with missionary friends, I began to feel "babyless." Joy was beginning to walk, and my arms felt empty. Gordon and I were so in love with Joy that we thought, *let's do this again.* I became pregnant at Christmas and our second child was due in September of '72. During my pregnancy, it often occurred to me that God surely would not allow a second birth to be critical. But I refused to let those fears distract me from the joy of birthing another child. Little did I know of potential health risks. We had no knowledge that Joy's health problems were due to an inherited genetic factor. All of our unborn children would be at risk.

In August 1972, Gordon, Joy and I, along with our helper, Carmen, traveled to Manila to keep appointments with my doctor in anticipation of the scheduled delivery. We stayed at the Missionary Kids' (MK) dorm. On August 24, Joy celebrated her second birthday – a joyous event. Her birthday photo showed a robust, fat-cheeked, smiling little girl. The happiness was short-lived. In a few days, she became sick with diarrhea – a very common occurrence in the Philippines and not to be taken lightly. I called Doctora Cruz several times. She gave instructions, but Joy's condition worsened. She lost weight and dark circles formed around her eyes. When all efforts failed, I told the doctor that we had to bring Joy in. When Doctora Cruz saw Joy, she was alarmed at her loss of weight and frail appearance. X-rays were taken and, to the doctor's shock, bilateral pneumonia was evident. Joy was hospitalized for two weeks in Manila. Doctora Cruz attributed the pneumonia to a form of childhood tuberculosis that was common in the Philippines, but manageable. She prescribed an oral medicine that we administered for a year. It would, in effect, ensure immunity to TB.

Jami Ruth came into our lives on September 26, 1972. We named her after "James" Gordon, her father, grandfather, and great grandfather. Ruth was biblical and my sister Jeannie's middle name. I now fully realize that, had we been living in the States, we would have learned of Joy's diagnosis, and the gift of a second child would have been denied. That makes you, Jami, exceptionally special.

Unlike today's parents, I did not adequately prepare Joy for her baby sister. Joy had been discharged from the hospital about one week prior to Jami's birth. After Jami was born, Gordon brought Joy to the hospital to see me and the baby. She sat beside me on the bed and looked and looked at this little person in my arms. I put my arm around Joy and invited her into this circle of love and family.

Upon our discharge, Gordon brought us *home* to the MK dorm. I will never forget the welcome we received. Joy, Carmen, and two German shepherd dogs came running to greet us. With Jami in my arms, I waited for Gordon to open the car door. As I turned in the seat and placed my feet on the ground, there, standing in front of me, was Joy with two panting dogs on either side – all three the same height. Joy spontaneously extended her arms to carry her little sister into the house. Of course, I put my arms under Joy's, and we made our way inside. Joy, from then on, assumed the elder sister's right as protector of younger sister, Jami.

One of my most precious memories occurred a few nights later. I was nursing Jami late in the evening. I was lying on my side toward the edge of the bed facing the cot on which Joy was sleeping. Joy awakened, her eyes big and curiously watching. Our eyes met and focused for a moment. I lifted myself upon my elbow, leaned over toward Joy and kissed her. I said, "I love you." Joy gave a body jiggle, closed her eyes, and was back to sleep – assured of Mother's love.

We had *helpers* in Baguio who were a part of our family. Carmen became Jami's surrogate Mommy and Charine, Joy's. It was interesting how they paired up. Charine was the cook. Of course, food was Joy's most important activity of the day. At the evening meal, Joy first ate with us, then made her way into the kitchen, stood on a stool between Charine and Carmen, and ate again. She followed their style of utensil – fingers. Joy scrunched the rice so that it stuck together, balled it between her fingers, dipped it into the fish sauce, used her thumb to push it into her mouth, and enjoyed. I am sure that she also consumed a wide sampling of their menu, which often included fish.

Years later there's a secret we harbored as a family: As a young person in her teens, Joy would regress to the finger method of eating rice if she thought we were not looking. After all, this method was more efficient. She never dropped a rice kernel, and it was served without gravy, so no messy fingers. It generally occurred toward the end of a meal. I never reprimanded Joy, but I did call her attention to it. It would not have been acceptable outside the walls of our home.

Rice and a high protein dish remained Joy's common meal throughout life, even for breakfast. Her system lacked the necessary enzymes to digest proteins and fat, and she craved nutritious foods. Junk food was never her preference. The one sweet that she loved was angel food cake topped with cherry pie filling. The cake was fat-free, egg whites were her protein, and cherries the fruit. It was interesting that Joy's manners at the table were impeccable, even as a very young child. Her grandmother was impressed whenever she sat at the table with Joy. Every bite went into Joy's mouth – not a crumb wasted. Seldom did we have to clean her up after a meal.

In the morning, I gave Jami her bath and, in the evening, Joy. Jami napped after her bath and, upon awakening, busily searched for Carmen, who was the housekeeper and lady of the laundry. Carmen always talked to Jami and watched her carefully. It was obvious that Jami loved Carmen and vice versa. Then Carmen applied to work in the States as a nanny and housekeeper. She was accepted.

After Carmen left our home, Jami became very "clingy" and "whiny." She would not allow anyone outside the family to come near her or hold her. We had one exception. On a Sunday morning the seminary choir sat together waiting to perform their musical at a church in Baguio. The girls were with me – Joy beside me and Jami on my lap. With no prompting, Jami climbed off my lap, walked across the aisle to another pew, and climbed into the lap of a young lady within the choir. That was totally out of the ordinary, and we were mystified. We shrugged our shoulders. Typically, Jami clung to me and rejected anyone who approached her. Then it dawned on us. This young girl looked like Carmen. Jami felt safe and loved, and the young girl was proud to have been selected. Filipinos love children.

Jami's timidity followed her throughout childhood, even into high school. Both separation from Carmen and our move to the States – first Fort Worth, then Sioux Falls – contributed to her shyness. Jami could not communicate her feelings, and I now wish I had been more sensitive to her needs. Even so, Jami has found her place in the adult world. I, as her mother, consider her well-adjusted, confident, independent, socially sensitive, an exemplary adult, and a solid Christian. Her gifts and accomplishments as an artist are amazing. She has become assertive in making choices and seeking a successful career. God has been good to her. I thank God everyday for her.

Joy never completely recovered from the effects of the pneumonia at two years of age. She, at times, would cough and wheeze to the point of losing her breath. There were other disturbing health concerns. Joy continued to have frequent bowel movements – about six daily. With the short intestine and voracious appetite, her loss of weight became a pressing issue. Joy also suffered two rectal prolapses. During the spring and summer months of '74, Joy began to run a low-grade fever for which there was no evident cause. I was concerned. There had to be an explanation. I brought it to the attention of a doctor in Baguio, but there was no satisfactory answer.

In June of 1974, all of the Philippine missionary families gathered at the seminary in Baguio for the annual mission meeting to conduct business, sing, and worship. It was a time of renewal and fellowship. Of course, there were many children. I brought Joy and Jami to the quadrangle of the seminary campus for a group picture with all of the children. The children were all running around in play and laughter. I observed Joy as she stood aside from the children. She silently watched them play, all the while smiling. I knew she wanted to join in the fun, but did not have the physical stamina. In one disturbing, unwelcome moment, I suddenly knew. Joy was slowly failing. Alarms went off in my head.

My knees became weak and wanted to fold. She would never be the healthy child I had envisioned.

Twenty eight years later, in June of 2002, Gordon and I traveled to Texas to attend a reunion with our Philippine missionary family. Jim and Mary Slack were at the reunion with their family. They had driven from Virginia for this time together. Mary was a nurse. During her college years of nurses' training in the early 1960s, she had taken care of a little boy with cystic fibrosis. Ten-plus years later, in 1973, we were in the Slacks home in southern Mindanou where they were stationed. I was director of the seminary choir on tour in that area. Unknown to me, Mary observed Joy and recognized in her all the symptoms of cystic fibrosis. She confessed it was then that she started praying for Joy. She decided not to mention this to me. She was wise. I would have panicked. Mary was very perceptive, sensitive, and a spiritual giant. It gave me great comfort in these latter years to know that someone was praying for Joy, although we had no clue to solve the mystery of Joy's health concerns.

That summer of 1974, Gordon and I made the decision to return home before our four year assignment was up. Arrangements were made to fly to the States in October after three years and four months in the Philippines. We asked Gordon's parents to schedule an appointment with Dr. Richard Ellis, Joy's birth surgeon. Joy was now 4 years old and Jami, 2.

A Farewell Memory

On a Saturday in late September we were scheduled to leave Baguio for our furlough in the U.S. But Gordon had another agenda. In the early morning hours around 3:00, Gordon got up, walked to his office across the seminary campus, and worked at his manual typewriter to complete a book he was writing for TEE (Theological Education by Extension). On our way to Manila, the seminary choir would accompany us as far as Clark Air Base where we were scheduled to give one last concert at the Baptist Church. We had toured with the seminary choir throughout the Philippines for more than a year performing the Skillings musical, "Love." On Sunday after our performance and following lunch, we met outside with these wonderful young people for our farewell good byes. We shared hugs expecting to return after eight months of furlough. As we turned to walk to our car, the students picked up their guitars and sang their parting song to us, "We Are One in the Bond of Love." It was a moment etched in my memory. And so, although half way around the world, we still feel and cherish that bond of oneness and love in Christ.

Joy – Four Years Old

III. THE SPIRITUAL STRUGGLE

The Diagnosis

The long flight half way around the world was very hard on the girls, especially Joy. By the time we arrived home in the States, Joy was sick again.

October, 1974, Fort Worth: Gordon was out of town for a speaking engagement when Joy and I met the scheduled appointment with Dr. Ellis. Gordon's mother drove us to the doctor's office, but waited in the car during our consultation. Jami, now two-years-old, was sitting on my lap unquestionably robust and healthy. Joy was on the examination table, very petite, with dark circles under her eyes and coughing that awful chronic cough. Dr. Ellis sat down across from me. He alarmingly fired one question after another, shifting focus from Jami to Joy and comparing their differences. Suddenly he blurted out, "Why she could have cystic fibrosis!" I flinched, but said nothing. He arranged for us to go immediately to Cook Children's Hospital. Joy would undergo a simple and fairly painless sweat test to measure the salt content in her perspiration. The results would, presumably, tell us why she was not thriving.

When we returned to the car, I did not mention the potential diagnosis to my mother-in-law. I did let her know that Joy was scheduled for a lab test at Cook Children's Hospital, but that I would, first, take her home, then continue with Joy and Jami to the hospital. The sweat test took only a few minutes. We waited for the results. They brought in the lab report and showed me the graph which peaked on the measure of salt content. They explained that this indicated positive for cystic fibrosis. I had no inkling what cystic fibrosis meant, but, at least, we had a name for Joy's physical problems. Now, we could treat it. I actually felt relieved. After all, just look at the myriad of miracle drugs available; Joy would soon be as healthy as other children. As the saying goes, "Ignorance is bliss." My world would soon be enlightened.

The doctor arranged for Joy to be admitted on Monday to Dallas Children's Hospital. This hospital had a reputable cystic fibrosis (CF) clinic and the sweat test would be repeated there to confirm the validity of the diagnosis. If confirmed, they would instruct us in Joy's care. An added bonus was the availability of an active parent support group. This was beginning to sound serious.

My Aunt Lottie and Uncle Bob, who lived in Dallas, volunteered to care for Jami during those days Joy was hospitalized. I would be with Joy day and night. Gordon was in and out between commitments to speak at various churches. Bob and Lottie brought Jami to the hospital during the day for short visits. They reported that Jami appeared happy and did not suffer separation anxiety, for which I was grateful. She was on the heels of Bob the entire time. He had a workshop in his garage and Jami, at the young age of two years, was fascinated by all of his tools. Her creative gifts were already evident.

Monday morning at Dallas Children's Hospital: After all the admission procedures, Gordon, Joy, and I followed a staff person toward the room assigned to Joy. It was impossible to ignore the sound of loud and vigorous popping as we made our way down the hall. I looked toward the sound and saw a staff member beating on the back of a child. Will this be required for Joy? I didn't think so.

Joy was now in her room. The nurse arrived with an IV bottle, a pole on wheels, and, of course, needles. Joy knew about needles and began to cry. She folded her arms and held them tightly refusing to release her grip. After prying open her arms with words of empty reassurances, the nurse finally finished the dreaded procedure. Needle trauma would remain a constant throughout Joy's life.

Next to arrive was a respiratory therapist. He introduced himself and explained his role. He showed us a mask which was attached to a small cup into which he squirted a vial of medicine. It had an elastic band he stretched to fit around Joy's head holding the mask over her nose and mouth. A compressor was turned on which forced air through tubing into the mask creating a mist. With each breath, this mist entered Joy's lungs. Upon completion of the mist, about fifteen minutes, the therapist turned off the machine and started clapping on Joy's back. This is what I had witnessed earlier. He called it percussion. The therapist explained this was to free Joy's lungs of accumulated mucus. Joy should be encouraged to cough and cautioned *never,* never suppress a cough. He then asked me to come over to Joy. He explained the cupped hand position and instructed me in the techniques of chest percussion. I thought, "You mean I have to do this? At home?"

As I watched, I noticed that the pinky finger on one of his hands was misshapen – crooked, as if previously broken but never splinted. Without realizing it, as I began the percussion, I stuck out my pinky finger and tried to crook it. He courteously corrected my hand position. At least I could still laugh. I learned that one does not use a straight hand, *slap,* in this percussion. The cupped hand palm traps the air which cushions the blow to the child's body. Indeed, I would continue this therapy once we were home. That's what they meant at Cook's Hospital when they said I will be instructed in the care of Joy. But I still had no clue as to what was going on or the seriousness of this disease.

After a few days in the hospital with Joy, I began to harbor dreadful fears. I had unanswered, unspoken questions. I was not fully informed about cystic fibrosis – that there was no cure for the disease or the prognosis. I dared not ask. I didn't want to know, and denial was helping me along.

One evening, I finally mustered the courage to ask the respiratory therapist. Very timidly, with great hesitation, in a hushed voice I asked the dreaded question.

"Is Joy going to die?" He stopped the hand percussion, paused, and not looking at me answered gently and softy with two words, "Many do." That was it!! Doom's day. That night, as I lay in the cot next to Joy, I cried uncontrollably.

When word got out about our daughter's illness, well-meaning friends told us their cystic fibrosis stories. The worst story suggested that our 4-year-old daughter might live to be 8 years of age or, if fortunate, to age 13, the projected odds of CF averages. The main point was that Joy would die young. It was a diagnosis of death. My world stopped.

Starting Over

Life took a sudden turn around for Gordon and me. We first had to learn about this disease. Then we had to adjust our lives for Joy's daily care. Finally, we were forced to consider how it would impact our future. Simultaneously, we wrestled with our emotions and our faith.

We were in the mid-1970s when we learned the ugly fact that CF was the #1 genetic killer of children. The advances in medicine through the last three decades have now projected life expectancy into young adulthood. Presently, one half of all individuals with CF live to the age of thirty-seven; however, one half do not. The Cystic Fibrosis Foundation published these facts:

- *Cystic fibrosis is a genetic disease affecting approximately 30,000 children and adults in the United States.*

- *CF causes the body to produce a thick, sticky mucus due to the faulty transport of sodium and chloride (salt) within the cells that line organs such as the lungs and pancreas. This abnormal mucus clogs the lungs and leads to life-threatening lung infections.*

- *CF is inherited – passed from parents to their children. One in 31 Americans (one in 28 Caucasians) – more than 10 million people – is an unknowing, symptomless carrier of one copy of the defective CF gene. A person must inherit one defective gene from each parent to have CF. There is a 25 percent chance that the child will have CF; a 50 percent chance that the child will be a carrier; and a 25 percent chance that the child will be a non-carrier.*

- *CF occurs in approximately one of every 3,200 live Caucasian births (in one of every 3,500 live births of all Americans). There are about 1,000 new cases of CF diagnosed each year. Most individuals are diagnosed by the age of three; but nearly 10 percent of all newly diagnosed cases are age 18 or older.*

(Summarized from the CF Foundation's National Office at 6931 Arlington Road, Bethesda, MD 20814. www.65roses.cfforg (866) 347-2345.)

The facts of this disease produced shock waves in our lives. We had to learn to live with its reality. We didn't know it then, but it would have enormous consequences for our family. It affected our relationships with one another, our activities of daily living, and our unknown future, not to mention its implications for Joy's life. At the same time, our mental, spiritual, and emotional health suffered. We were confronted with a situation for which we were unprepared and left with few answers. It was literally a *one day at a time* existence.

Living with Cystic Fibrosis

As an infant, Joy's hunger was rarely satisfied. Her enormous appetite was compounded by two factors: a short intestine and the absence of enzymes to break down food for digestion. Often, we would need to feed her in the middle of the night. She awoke every morning crying because of hunger. It was always a rush to prepare breakfast. The dietitian at the Dallas hospital told us that Joy's diet should be low in fat. Enzymes were prescribed to help her digest and absorb nutrients. It came in the form of a powder which we mixed with applesauce. Eventually, Joy learned to swallow the large capsules. Never again would she put applesauce into her mouth.

Once the diagnosis was made and the treatment started, we began to see immediate improvement in Joy. The supplemental enzymes, high protein diet and limited fat diet were doing their work. For the first time in four years, Joy slept through the night and awoke in the morning without desperate hunger and crying. Thank you, LORD. Her appetite was still voracious, but the frequent bowel movements diminished. Weight gain was obvious. She now played and she was happy.

But I was not happy. Although Joy showed improvement, I experienced a pain so deep it defies human explanation. There are no words that can match its description. The dream and plan for another child would not be realized. Thank you, LORD, for Jami. Had we lived in the States and learned of the diagnosis prior to conceiving Jami, this child would not have blessed our lives.

The hospital in Dallas sent us home with a compressor and the equipment to continue Joy's respiratory treatments which had to be administered two to three times a day. We did not have a treatment table, so I did the treatments on the floor. Gordon walked into the house one afternoon while Joy and I were on the floor engaged in the treatment. I was vigorously pounding on Joy in what we called *pop-pop*. Gordon watched for a moment and then said, "Let me try that." I briefly demonstrated the cupped hand position and the various front/back/up/down/side positions. He started the treatment and willingly took over from there.

Gordon and Joy became a team. Joy cooperated and responded to her father's approach better than she did mine. He was direct and matter of fact but positive. And he always interspersed their sessions with humor and fun.

Gordon often traveled on business. When he did, it was my turn. This was not something I looked forward to as Joy would always be up to her old tricks with that strong-willed resistance of hers. Somehow we managed, but it was with effort even though she knew she felt better after a treatment.

Gordon: "The times I spent doing Joy's respiratory therapy was personal time with our daughters. I watched the cartoon *Wonder Dog* over and over. *Sesame Street* was our favorite TV show. I was able to parent my daughters beyond what I would have done if there had been no physical crisis. Though I focused on Joy's therapy, Jami always joined in the moment, and we enjoyed time together during the treatments."

Wrestling with God

Gordon's Point of View: "God seemed absent from our lives. Where was help when we needed it? I was angry that this disease was threatening our family and the life of our older daughter. I vented my anger on a chaplain who came to visit our room in the Dallas hospital.

"A world of cystic fibrosis specialists opened up God's touch in new ways. The medical personnel loved the children with CF and also our daughter. The thought of death of any of these lovely children was hard to live with. Doctors at the CF clinic introduced us to respiratory therapists, pharmacists with multiple antibiotics, compressors and mist tents. We met parents who volunteered to work with families of new diagnoses. An active parent support organization operated in the Dallas/Fort Worth area. We learned that these parents gave assistance from a different point of view than did the people at the clinic. They shared from the heart, talking from the practical edge of experience and knowledge. They lived with the day-to-day reality of caring for their children who were born with this devastating disease.

"These parents somehow put aside their despair and shared with us practical advice especially in regard to eliminating the thick mucous that threatened health. They demonstrated to us, through their lives, that parents can have a positive impact upon the chronic conditions of CF. Their conscientious efforts result in longevity of their children's lives. They also helped us recognize the grief process triggered by the diagnosis. These parents and their compliant children were the true heroes in our early days of living with cystic fibrosis. The parents in the support organization taught us to focus on life, not death. We then were able to treat the chronic issues of CF as a normal part of life. I admired my wife, Joyce, for the way she scheduled our family life around respiratory therapies and Joy's need to eat often, nutritiously, and on time."

My Turn: Gordon mentioned that *we* were able to treat the CF as a normal part of life. His use of the proverbial *we* pronoun did not apply in my case. I was personally entering a period of depression, guilt, and anger – a lot of anger. I could only see a deep dark pit from which there was no escape. I was confused and unable to make sense of life. I had a few questions for God, unrealistic to one who professed great faith.

"Why, God? I thought we had a miracle baby. Is this your idea of a cruel joke? Why would you allow such devastating cruelty to an innocent child?" My thoughts fluctuated irrationally. Why would my child be any different than children around the world who suffer unjustly? I tried bargaining with God. "Is this your punishment for my sins?" I felt guilty. "I'm sorry. Please, just heal Joy. I promise to be a better missionary." "Where are you, God?" "What about our future?" My faith was shattered. I was totally at loss. I prayed for healing, yet I felt there was no hope. My feelings and thoughts did not make sense. I so loved Joy, but, in despair, I no longer saw the beautiful miracle baby. I saw our precious Joy with the diagnosis of *death*.

No one seemed to recognize my grief – not family, not friends. They all went about their lives and business as if all was well with the world. I cried. My whole world was ripped apart and in disarray. Romans 8:28 was certainly no comfort. Please, do <u>not</u> quote that scripture to me. What good can possibly come from a diagnosis of death? God was silent as I railed at Him.

God Was Silent

As irrational as it may sound, I felt that God was displeased with me. I felt as though my service as a missionary was not good enough. In fact, my entire life lacked spiritual devotion, and I was full of sin. I was guilty and Joy's illness was God's punishment. One may reply, "How juvenile." But growing up in a legalistic, intolerant, God-fearing *religious* culture, it seemed perfectly logical to me. My hopeless situation had to make sense some how, some way. Where, when, and how had I gone wrong? I painstakingly reviewed my many sins.

God did not speak to me audibly. At some point, I remembered a particular New Testament scripture. I looked it up. The account is recorded in John 9:1-3 (NIV translation). The disciples approached Jesus and asked for an explanation about a man who had been blind since birth.

> **John 9:2 – His disciples asked him, "Rabbi, who sinned, this man or his parents, that he was born blind?"**

Jesus answered, not with a rebuke, but with an explanation that contradicted the beliefs that were taught by the religious leaders of that day.

> **John 9:3 – "Neither this man nor his parents sinned," said Jesus, "but this happened so that the work of God might be displayed in his life."**

To further back his authority as the Son of God, Jesus spit on the ground, mixed his saliva with the dirt, made mud, placed it on the man's eyes, then instructed him to go and wash in the Pool of Siloam. Still blind, he walked with mud on his eyes into the pool and washed. The blind man had faith to believe and acted on Jesus' words. He went home with sight.

Such a revelation to me!! It brought comfort as I struggled with my faith. I reasoned: God does not carry a big stick to whack one down when already down. He is a God of love, grace, and forgiveness. That's the whole point of the gospel! He sent His Son to refute the legalistic practices of the religious leaders – the belief that a life lived by man's rules inherits God's favor. Jesus was the fulfillment of the law. Here I was with a seminary degree, yet legalism had raised its ugly head.

Still, the "why" question bothered me. As a child, I had asked my father if it was wrong to question God. My father answered unequivocally, "Yes, it is wrong. One never questions God." Here I was in God's face with that unapologetic question, "Why?" Somehow I felt it was a valid question and deserved an answer. But God was silent. In one of those epiphany moments, approximately two years after Joy's diagnosis, it occurred to me that Jesus had asked the "why" question on the cross of crucifixion when he cried out in a loud voice:

Matthew 27:46 – "My God, my God, why have you forsaken me?"

But God was silent. I did not need to flagellate myself for asking the "why" question. I could not know the future – that in time, the works of God would be evident in Joy's life.

Earlier in the day Jesus had asked three of His disciples to accompany Him into the Garden of Gethsemane to pray. They walked a short distance, then Jesus asked them to stay back and to watch and pray. Jesus went further into the garden alone. He was overcome with sorrow and fell on His face to the ground and prayed:

Matthew 26:39 – "My Father, if it is possible, may this cup be taken from me. Yet not as I will, but as you will."

He returned to His disciples who were asleep. Jesus again went off by Himself. In great torment He prayed again, then a third time. And God was silent.

The part – "not my will, but yours" – was difficult for me. In spite of my questions and limited faith, God had amazing plans for Joy's life and her witness. Over time we would all come to recognize God's touch upon her life and to understand that we were indeed *Blessed by Joy*.

IV. GOD HAD A BIGGER PLAN

The Father Knows Best

God was not absent from our daily needs. During those eight months of furlough in Fort Worth, God was working out His plan for our future. Whether it was denial or naiveté, we went about planning our return to the Philippines. We actually believed that we could care for Joy in that environment. Even with all of her medicines, daily respiratory treatments, and anticipated hospitalizations, we thought we could manage. It was not in our heart to *abandon* that ministry. We loved our missionary families, our Filipino friends, our work, our calling.

In April of '75, Dr. Fowler, the physician consultant for the mission board, visited us in our home. I do not remember much about our conversation. But I will never forget when he cautiously and gently advised us not to return to the Philippines because, "It would not be wise for the health of Joy." The reality could no longer be denied. We knew he was right. We just had to hear it – to face the truth. Now what??? That conversation was on Tuesday.

On Thursday of the same week, we received a phone call from Dr. Gerald Borchart, Academic Dean at North American Baptist Seminary in Sioux Falls, South Dakota (currently named Sioux Falls Seminary). We did not know about this Baptist conference, but Gordon's father did. He mentioned that they were small but strong in missions, and that their giving, in comparison to that of Southern Baptists, was greater per person. They were solid in their theology. He had nothing but praise for their heritage and theological stance. The timing could not have been more perfect. Could this be God's doing?

How did Gerald Borchart get Gordon's name? Gordon's major professor, Dr. Clyde Francisco from Southern Seminary in Louisville, Kentucky, was in Fort Worth. Francisco was aware that one of his former students was home on furlough from the mission field. He doubted that Gordon would return because of his daughter's health. In a conversation with another OT professor who had been contacted by Borchart back in January, the connection was made and Gordon's name was submitted to the Sioux Falls Seminary. It's amazing how God works.

Gordon agreed to travel to Sioux Falls for the interview process. It included the presentation of a paper before students and faculty and a question/answer interview with the faculty. The school was very positive toward Gordon. After Gordon came home, Borchart called to inform him that the faculty vote was unanimous. It would be a major change for us. We would move away from family and friends.

Our history and roots went deep within Southern Baptists (SB). My father, Orville Behm, was a SB pastor as was Gordon's, James Harris. Gordon's grandfather and great-grandfather from years back had also been pastors. We would be out of the mainstream of Southern Baptists with whom we had long-time friendships. Gordon and I were always rather adventurous people. Nevertheless, it was a difficult decision, and Gordon wrestled with it most of the night. The most deciding factor for Gordon was that it was a small seminary similar to the one we had left in the Philippines, and the relationships were close among faculty and students.

Another major consideration was the availability of health care for Joy. We needed a clinic with physicians informed and experienced with the complex health needs of cystic fibrosis patients. Where would we live since we had minimal financial resources to purchase a home? How can the Seminary salary support us? What about health insurance? It would be a year before Joy would be covered for a preexisting health condition. Her medications and hospitalizations came at a tremendous cost.

I can tell you now, that all of those needs were met. God provided down to the last dollar. We did struggle, but we managed, much to God's credit and Gordon's resourcefulness. We did not complain, although I did worry.

God Provided

From the small rental house in Fort Worth, our furniture was loaded onto a moving van. We had only beds, appliances, and a few dishes. All other belongings had to be freighted from the Philippines. We drove from Fort Worth to southeastern Arkansas for one last visit with Grandma and Grandpa Behm. Our journey took two days. The map led us northwest through Arkansas where we spent the night, then straight north to South Dakota. The longer we drove, the more remote our destination seemed. We left the metropolis of Fort Worth and Dallas and drove endless miles along sparsely populated, flat terrain. The distant horizon seemed to stretch forever and continually heightened our anticipation of the future.

Upon arrival, we were welcomed with warm and hospitable greetings from Gerald Borchart and seminary friends. They helped us unload our burdened car and move into a temporary apartment. Our first task was to find a home in which to live. I had in mind a split level house, three bed rooms on one level, a fourth for Joy's treatments and equipment, a kitchen, living room, one full bath, a half bath, and an additional room for an office. Price could not be more than $35,000. We searched all week. That type of home and price simply did not exist. The homes were very small and priced beyond our budget. On Friday of that week, the realtor told us of a house located on Riverdale Road that had been on the market for two years. It was in poor condition due to destruction by dogs. He said it was **very** smelly. The price had been lowered to $40,000. We decided to look, anyway. Maybe the owners were in a negotiating mood.

When we drove up, I was encouraged. It was split level and had an over-sized, two-car garage. The realtor warned us of the smell before he opened the door. I still wanted to look. Oh, my goodness!! You could have knocked us over. The smell took my breath away. It was a quick tour during which I realized that it was laid out <u>exactly</u> as I had imagined. We decided to make an offer of $34,500. The owner agreed to the price if we would pay the last six months of taxes, $500. That brought the price to $35,000. Gordon's Aunt Josephine Harris loaned us $2,000 for a down payment, which we repaid a few years later. Yes, LORD! Thank you. You have provided even down to the last dollar. It was up to us now. We were more than willing to put in the sweat equity.

We spent the summer throwing away carpet, sanding floors, painting, wall papering, cleaning, etc. It was hard labor, but it became our home in a neighborhood full of families with children, a hospital within a half mile, a quality school within walking distance, and wonderful Christian friends. Thank you, LORD!

One more hurdle – the health insurance policy of the seminary stated a one-year exclusion for new clients with pre-existing health conditions. Joy's care would be an enormous expense, and our seminary salary simply could not cover it. A social worker at the clinic introduced us to South Dakota's Children's Comprehensive Health Care. Our situation met all the criteria for supplemental health care. All costs of Joy's medications, hospitalizations, and equipment would be covered that first year. The seminary health plan would pick up the insurance the following years. God cares about the large and small details of our lives. Most of all, He cares for our children.

Unfinished Business

There were many details and changes in our life that kept me working, occupied, and distracted. During the day I buried my grief in busyness and denial. But at night I was weighed down by unbearable, unmentionable, painful feelings for Joy. I cried and continued to cry. I was overwhelmed and confused. There was no answer to this hurt and no hope for the future. It all boiled down to unfinished business with God. It came to a head on a Sunday morning in the fall of 1975.

In the Philippines, I sang this little chorus to Joy many evenings as we snuggled in the big overstuffed recliner rocker before bedtime.

> *I've got the joy, joy, joy, joy down in my heart,*
> *Down in my heart, down in my heart.*
> *I've got the joy, joy, joy, joy down in my heart,*
> *Down in my heart to stay.*

Of course the *joy* of which I sang was our precious, beautiful miracle baby, Joy. The evenings were our time to read books, to "sing" books when my voice gave out, and to just love each other. She would resist sleep as the evening stretched from one book to another.

That was 1971. It was now 1975, a totally different set of circumstances. I could no longer sing that little jingle, "I've got the joy . . . in my heart." This Sunday I sat with Joy and Jami on about the fourth/fifth pew from the front. Dr. Lee McDonald, professor of New Testament, was the guest preacher substituting for our pastor who was out of town. Gordon was also away on business. Lee spoke from the text, "The joy of the LORD is your strength" (Nehemiah 8:10). I sat there wishing I could quietly slip out. Such irony! I could no longer postpone the truth. I had no joy. I had no strength. I had no hope. I felt betrayed by God and isolated spiritually. The last year had sucked the life out of me. Silently, tears filled my eyes, ran down my cheeks, and dropped to my neck. I was embarrassed, but could not stop.

This was a pivotal point in my life. There were some feelings and issues I needed to address. I realized that I had neglected to love Joy with depth. In my twisted, tortured mind, I had allowed Joy's illness and my grief to blind me to sensitivity for Joy. My anger and blame had also pushed aside God. He had His hands full trying to get my attention. His loving grace simply would not let go. God turned my head around so that I could see Joy for the precious, precious child that she was. I spoke to her in the evening, "I love you, Joy," and the expression on her face was that of returned love, peace, and comfort.

I re-discovered a full and complete love for Joy. However, I also had to do some repair work on my relationship with God. God had not betrayed me, or Joy, or our family. I had betrayed God. For some reason I believed I was immune to the hardships that came from living in a fallen world. The fact that I professed Jesus as Son of God did not make me special or protect my children from harm. What Jesus did for me was forgive my sins, His greatest gift and His eternal gift. It was up to me to be obedient to His word, to nurture that relationship, and to love Him with all my heart, soul and strength, found in Deuteronomy 6:5 and known as the "greatest commandment". It became my own personal life verse. I realized that when God's love is applied to life, His purposes come into alignment with all of living, thinking, and doing. This love relationship has become an on-going process with God and me, a work in progress and continues to this very day.

My prayers for a miracle healing for Joy did not cease, but those requests were limited in scope. God saw beyond Joy's physical needs and answered those prayers on His own terms. In His time, God granted to the world His adopted child who rose above the limitations of a diseased body to proclaim His promise of eternal life to others. God captured Joy's heart and set her on a mission of spiritual magnitude.

Devotion to God

March 21, 1997

> *LORD, You are above any matter.*
> > *Your glory far outweighs anything I can imagine.*
> *LORD, Your grace is overwhelming*
> > *That you would love and redeem a sinner such as I.*
> *LORD, Your caring touch sustains me,*
> > *Your outstretched arm carries and holds me when I am weak.*
>
> *You alone are my God.*
> > *You alone are my heart's desire.*
> *In you I trust,*
> > *I am healed,*
> > > *I am strengthened*
> *To face another day,*
> > *To live in you and for you.*

Hope Supersedes the Goal

Gordon and I had a choice. We could pamper and protect Joy, or we could allow her to experience the growing pains of life. We did not want to dwell upon her limitations or illness. We had observed this style of hovering parent in another family and did not believe it was healthy for the child. It was our choice to focus on life. As an example: My mother sent Joy a children's book on the meaning of heaven. It was a well-written book, illustrated beautifully, and biblical, and I am sure my mother wanted to reassure Joy. But I could not bring myself to read it to Joy. We did not speak about *death* to Joy. It seemed to be fatalistic. I wanted Joy to believe in her dreams and reach for *the moon*.

Although Joy's health could go wrong at any time, we allowed Joy to experience as full a life as possible. We were well aware of the threat of pneumonia – her constant enemy – which seemed to perpetually stalk us. This *enemy* could overpower us, defeat and rob us of all hope if we gave it freedom and permission. But we took a proactive approach. We defined our goal on several levels: by the schedule we followed each and every day, by keeping Joy's lungs clean and clear, by ensuring her tummy was satisfied with high protein food, and most of all by the faith we lived and our trust in God's love and faithfulness.

Although our schedule never varied, we did not project a hopeless lifestyle. In fact, as I think about it, Gordon and I seldom said the word *cystic fibrosis* in our home. We would not deny Joy fun, happiness, or a future. Joy grew up feeling that there was another tomorrow for her. As a result, Joy developed a sense of purpose and achievement for herself and for life in general. Joy was determined and independent. Her limitations, rather than weaken her spirit, became a driving force that strengthened her resolve to live each day to its greatest potential. In fact, she was always seeking to reach beyond her age skills.

And then, an incident occurred in high school that left Joy with lingering doubts about her future. She came home very angry. How the conversation developed, I do not know, but a student mentioned to Joy that she would die young because of her disease. Joy was in disbelief. How could someone have the nerve to say such a thing? She had dreams for her future. Knowing that her life might be cut short, Joy was all the more determined to excel. Go Joy!

V. OUR LITTLE WORLD ON RIVERDALE ROAD

We made the Riverdale Road house our home. It was located in Kidsville, USA, a neighborhood in the style of a Norman Rockwell painting. It was a safe place for children to play, to walk to school, to enjoy the freedom of going in and out of homes. We were fortunate to have happened upon this little community to raise our two girls.

The Neighborhood

During our last year in the Philippines, Joy could not sustain the energy it took to engage in physical play. We had happy times, good memories, and meaningful relationships, but it was difficult for Joy to play actively as children do. She felt isolated from the group. When we moved to South Dakota, this void was apparent to me. I sensed that Joy was lonely. We enrolled her in a private kindergarten in the fall of 1975. Her teacher explained to me that, daily, she greeted each child by name; "Good morning, Roger," "Good morning, Julie." But Joy would never acknowledge the greeting or respond in kind.

As we were driving down 26th Street one afternoon, Joy asked me how to make friends. I said, "You make friends by being a friend." That was all she needed. After Christmas, Joy suddenly started talking and greeting her teacher with, "Good morning, Mrs. . . . . ." By first grade, Joy was chasing boys around the playground in pursuit of a kiss. There was great hilarity in that chase! She found numerous opportunities, the first grade teacher reported, to visit with her friends using the ploy of sharpening her pencil. She'd sharpen her pencil, alright, and then visit with her friends as she sauntered along, slowly making her way back to her desk. I was pleased. She was growing socially.

In 1974, upon our return from the Philippines, one of our first purchases was a trampoline. We had saved some money gifted to Joy when she was born. The doctors agreed that the trampoline would be good exercise for Joy. It would encourage deep breathing, and shake loose some of the congestion in her lungs. That trampoline, however, had more value than just health. It became the social gathering for children in the Riverdale Road neighborhood. This was especially good for the girls. All of the changes in our lifestyle since leaving the Philippines had been difficult for them, too.

In Fort Worth, a friend had offered us the runt of toy poodle puppies. Joy accepted this puppy with open arms and named her Sparky. I have no idea where she picked up that name. Sparky was a small bundle of wiggly black fur – so cute and most appropriately named. Joy proudly carried Sparky around precariously perched on her shoulder. Sparky fell off that perch more than once and soon developed an aversion to being lifted off solid ground. Sparky, Joy, and Jami were constant companions around the Riverdale neighborhood.

Joy was a take-charge person. She organized the neighborhood kids in different activities. One afternoon, she directed her friends in choreographed movement to a tape featuring Evie, a Christian recording artist from North Dakota. When Joy discovered Easter egg hunts, it became her self proclaimed honor to organize and invite the neighborhood to a hunt in our yard. Birthday parties were always a big event.

The Home

We ran a *tight ship* in our household. We structured our life around the care of Joy. It was the accepted practice, and Joy, for the most part, cooperated. However, true to Joy's strong will, resistance surfaced from time to time. She had no options. Joy's treatments, meals, and bedtimes were always on schedule. Survival ruled and she trusted us. During those years, Jami was the child in the shadows, but not forgotten. We made every effort to include her. Jami accepted Joy's needs as a part of daily life and never resented the attention devoted to Joy. At times their relationship could be adversarial.

Gordon looked forward to evenings with his daughters. We instinctively created a system that was like clockwork. I prepared the girls for bedtime and supervised their baths. By this time, we had an adjustable treatment table that was fashioned by the Optimist Club at no cost to the family. Gordon would do Joy's treatment, which consisted of an aerosol mask followed by hand percussion. We had Joy lie on her back, then chest, on each side, alternating with her head up and then down. During Joy's treatments, I sterilized and rinsed the equipment, then prepared a snack for the girls to eat before they were tucked into bed.

Gordon read their favorite book to them, or he'd entertain them with his embellished interpretations of Bible stories. He prayed with them, kissed them good night, and always concluded with, "I love you." Before going to sleep, Jami routinely had Gordon check under her bed and inside the closet for monsters, then tightly close the closet door. In the morning, I often found Jami sleeping on the floor between the twin beds. She must have thought that the beds protected her. Gordon often answered to Joy in the middle of the night. In the morning, I prepared breakfast, the mask, the medications, and school lunches as Gordon repeated Joy's respiratory treatment. Sterilization of the equipment was last on my morning agenda.

Gordon: "Bed time always came early. Joy's need for rest brought us together for prayer and a story every night. Joyce got the girls ready for bed, and I managed the rest. I showed the girls pictures from a children's Bible and told Bible stories with imagination and enthusiasm. I assume that Joy's love for the Bible started there. I certainly cannot complain about either daughter's behavior as they passed through school. Bedtime was a fun time and a fitting end to the day.

"One evening at bedtime, Joy and Jami told me of their salvation decisions at a "backyard Bible club" and their desire to be baptized. Joy was 10 and Jami, only 8, but they understood clearly their decision. Their baptism confirmed God's presence with us. Parenting was my greatest surprise and pleasure. I cannot imagine why some fathers do not assume their part in the care of the children. Our daughters' confessions of faith and baptisms confirmed that I invested in the best things."

The School

Because Joy was not a physically active child, her books became prized possessions. She found great pleasure in reading – discovering the world of fun in her imaginative world of stories. She hoarded those books. In elementary school, Joy discovered another resource of books – the library. The school she attended was close enough to walk with her friends to and from home. Those were the days when it was safe to do so. One afternoon during the beginning year of first grade, I waited in the driveway for Joy. All of the other children were walking home. I looked up and down the street. Joy was missing. I grew concerned and got in my car to trace her steps. The school was quiet; no activity, no parents or cars. Panic was building as I went up and down the streets. Still – no Joy. Finally, circling back to check at home, once again, there I spotted Joy walking casually home. She must have taken a different route. I literally screamed at Joy, "Where have you been?" Very innocently, she said that she was in the library looking at books. My thought, after such a dramatic outburst, "She'll think reading books will be cause for punishment."

When she was in third grade, Joy started private piano lessons from Janice Houts. She had a slow start. It wasn't until the third year that Joy suddenly discovered that fingers, together with piano and written notes, make beautiful music. Even her teacher was amazed at Joy's spurt of musicianship. She excelled in piano through high school and continued taking lessons for one semester in college. Music was one of Joy's greatest enjoyments.

I introduced Joy to music early in her childhood. We had fun reading and then singing books and stories. At three years of age, Joy spontaneously joined the seminary choir in song. In her high little child's voice, we heard from the front pew, "Love Can Work a Miracle," from Otis Skilling's musical, "Love". She was carrying a tune! The choir broke up giggling. Sacred music became one of Joy's most personal ministries, especially during physical and spiritual struggles.

Passion for Football

Joy's love for football was not inherited from the mother gene. We can thank her father for that. Actually, it does have a history. During our early years in

Sioux Falls, we drove home to Fort Worth and Louisiana to spend Christmas with our families. These were joyous occasions. We would have felt isolated and lonely separated from family during Christmas.

One December, we traveled south accompanied by perfectly beautiful weather. After the Christmas festivities, dinners, and gift exchanges, we prepared to return to Sioux Falls. The skies began to appear ominous and hovered lowly. Misting rain began to fall as we drove from northwest Louisiana to Dallas. Our plans were to spend the night with my Aunt Lottie and Uncle Bob, get up at 4:00 a.m., resume our travel to Sioux Falls, and arrive home late that night.

We watched the weather report at 3:00 a.m. and discussed if we should delay our return home. I mentioned that if we did not leave now, I feared we would not get out. We decided to continue with our original travel plans. As we pulled away, it was still raining and getting colder by the minute. By the time we reached the Oklahoma state line, our car was encased with ice and the highway treacherous. We traveled slowly all day only to get as far as Salina, Kansas. Fortunately, we found a vacancy in a motel that was almost hidden under snow drifts. The next morning, we got back on the road, and our speed did not exceed 30-35 miles an hour. The blowing snow created blizzard conditions the entire trip home. Thankfully, we arrived safely. The national news reported the devastation of Dallas. The ice storm held Big D hostage for an entire week.

After only one such experience, we decided subsequent Christmases should be spent closer to home. We vowed, however, to make it special. Why not Minneapolis with the Vikings? They always had a big game the day after Christmas. And so it was. We had such memorable and fun experiences at those exciting games. (Fortunately, the Vikings won all the games we attended.) I will never forget that first game as Joy explained to her football challenged mother all the plays and rules. She was in her element, but totally embarrassed because her mother wore a red sweater – the color of the opposing team – not purple for Vikings! Major blunder! Years later, when Joy traveled to Minneapolis for clinic appointments, she coordinated the two events. On Sundays in Sioux Falls, she would immediately rush home from church to catch the Vikings game. I would attempt to take my Sunday afternoon nap while she and her dad loudly cheered or booed the Vikings.

Middle School

Joy finished her six year elementary education at Horace Mann in May, 1982. The elementary years had been wonderful for her with the same kids, great teachers, and gifted students. She loved school and dreamed one day of being a teacher. With the close of those years, Joy anticipated a smooth transition to higher education. Middle school was daunting, but conquerable. With her strong will and intellect, she would soon be in charge.

Joy never shared with us what was happening in the environment of middle school. She dutifully went to school, but as the school year progressed, Joy began to withdraw. Still today, this is difficult for me to tell. By January, it was apparent that all was not well. Joy was not happy. Previous years, she cried if she had to stay home from school. One morning she cried because she *had* to go to school. At the end of the year I told Gordon that I would not allow Joy to return to that school. We would send her to Sioux Falls Christian even if I had to "dig ditches to pay tuition." I learned the following year, by way of our dentist who had a son at that school, that kids were mocking Joy's cough, talking behind her back, and teasing her. I regret now that I did not report to the administration our daughter's unhappiness. In recent years the public school system has successfully initiated a program to promote the acceptance of diversity among students.

The next two years at Sioux Falls Christian were happy for Joy. In college, Joy did a semester of supervised teaching with middle school students. Ironically, her absolutely favorite age to teach was middle school students. She excelled in teaching methods, behavior management, and creative subject matter. I believe that Joy had some good role models. One was Mrs. Baar, Joy's eighth grade English teacher at Sioux Falls Christian. At one of the conferences, Mrs. Baar graciously and gently informed me of Joy's giftedness, her wisdom, sensitivity, and maturity. She mentioned that Joy possessed a depth not seen in children. I had never taken notice of those characteristics, but I was happy to be informed.

Joy and Politics

In 1984, Joy was concluding her eighth grade year. After school late in May, she informed me that she had invited Senator Tom Daschle to our home on such and such a date to be interviewed by her. "What? What do you mean?" Joy again explained to me that she had called his office and arranged an interview. I was stunned. "Oh, Joy. What have you done? Please, no. We can't have him here at our house. You will have to call his office tomorrow and arrange a different place. Ask him to come to Daddy's office." Joy agreed and it was done.

The shock wore off and arrangements were made for Senator Daschle to meet us at Gordon's office Sunday afternoon of seminary graduation. Joy and I waited in the office. At the appointed time, we went to the entrance to welcome him. I was a nervous wreck. Joy was cool, really cool. Senator Daschle came walking up the sidewalk accompanied by one of his aides. He sat down in the office, and Joy, with pen and pad, began to ask questions. She was in charge. Senator Daschle was very professional as if engaged in an actual news conference. Joy never wavered. I was proud of my daughter and her confidence as she sought to interview those in the highest government. As their time together came to a close, Senator Daschle commented that Joy asked very good and probing questions. I knew that she loved politics. I was not aware, however, that she was so well informed. Senator Daschle stayed for the reception following graduation, and the visit was warm and gracious.

On a different occasion, Joy traveled with Gordon to Washington, DC. She visited the office of Tim Johnson (now Senator), met Congressman Johnson and had her picture made sitting in his chair, behind his desk and also with him. She worked for Bill Clinton in his first presidential campaign, met him, and got his autograph. Those days were exhilarating for Joy. I am convinced that, had God not placed his hand on her life and called her to greater service, she would have set her eyes on public service. She loved to debate politics and, on one occasion, unapologetically and enthusiastically took on one of the seminary trustees. I was stunned. I held my tongue and breath as they verbally duked out the pros and cons of government and politics.

High School

Joy transferred to Lincoln High School in 1985. She played the oboe in concert band and took advantage of the advanced courses in history and math for which she received credit toward a college degree.

In high school, Joy experienced a traumatic turn of events in her health. It was spring of 1986, Joy's sophomore year. Gordon had given Joy her evening respiratory treatment. We never skipped those treatments – morning, noon, (when possible), and night. I was a sound sleeper. Gordon often got up to assist Joy when there was a need. It was shortly after 1:00 a.m. when I awoke to a strange, abrupt, loud gurgling cough not typical of Joy. I sat up in bed and spoke audibly, "Something's not right." I went into her room and turned on the light. Joy was unconscious with blood running from her nose and mouth. I screamed for Gordon. Gordon appeared at the door, went immediately to Joy on the bed, picked her up from the pillow, moved behind her, wrapped his arms around her torso, and gave a quick Heimlich maneuver. Blood gushed from her nose and mouth saturating her hair, her face, the bed and floor. Joy was drowning in her blood. I yelled for Jami to call 911.

Gordon sat Joy on a chair and told me to keep her head upright while he changed clothes. I tried to support her and steady her head, but her body was limp, leaning, about to slide off the chair. Her head flopped from one side to the other with her eyes floating in opposite directions. When Gordon returned, he said, "I told you to keep her head upright." I tried, just could not. He picked her up and laid her across the end of the bed on her side. I instructed Jami to turn on the outside porch light and open the door for the ambulance to recognize our house.

Meanwhile, Joy's jaw began to lock. I put my thumbs into her mouth while her jaw slowly closed with amazing power. "It's okay, Joy," I said. She relaxed the jaw, then slowly closed again with a vise gripe. I reassured her each time, and unconsciously Joy would relax her jaw, then start all over again. I just wanted to keep her conscious. She almost bit through my thumbs which damaged the nail beds and now cause my nails to split vertically, then break or peel horizontally. I never told Joy about those nails. For me they are a visual symbol of Joy's life and struggle. I'm proud to bear those injuries. It's the unseen wounds that never heal. Those lie deep within my heart.

When the ambulance crew arrived, they immediately hooked Joy to oxygen, and she began to regain consciousness. From that time on, Joy had to be on oxygen, first only during the night and eventually, for twenty-four hours a day. We learned from the EMTs (Emergency Medical Technicians) that, if this should happen again, we were to lay Joy on her side. Gordon had unknowingly performed the protocol action.

I have often considered the fact that I awoke rather than Gordon. I was a sound sleeper. If there was a problem during the night, Gordon would instinctively get up to take care of Joy. I can only say thanks to God for sending his angel to alert me to Joy's gurgling attempts to breathe and cough. God sees the fallen sparrow. How much more he cares for his children. If only we knew all of the times God has intervened to protect us from harm. It is our responsibility to be sensitive and alert to God's presence, walk in His steps, listen for His still, small voice.

In her later high school years, Joy became more self-sufficient. It relieved a terrific burden from full responsibility for Joy's care. We, as parents, had probably taken our responsibilities too seriously. Joy could finally make healthy diet choices, manage her own schedule, and often cook her own food. A hand-held percussor allowed her to participate in treatments without constant parent involvement. We still were available at a moment's notice. When Joy requested, we were more than happy to assist. It was perfect timing for us to consider a housing move that would accommodate Joy's needs and allow her greater independence.

Because of frequent hospitalizations, Joy's graduation was in jeopardy. She had accumulated many absences, within two days of being disqualified despite excellent grades. Her grandmother from Fort Worth had booked a flight to attend this momentous event. It would have been a tragedy had Joy been eliminated from the graduation ceremonies. Joy was worried, but completed the year with no more absences. She proudly walked across the stage for that coveted graduation diploma as her beaming grandmother watched with the rest of us.

Joy and Jami

VI. FAMILY TIES

Sibling Issues

Joy was two years older than Jami. One would surmise the two-year age difference assures a congenial and happy co-existence – the sisters would play together and their lives would parallel one another. This assumption proved true only to a point. During preschool and early childhood years, Joy and Jami lived in beautiful harmony with one another. A subtle change began to filter into their relationship after Joy's diagnosis.

Our lives took a dramatic and abrupt change during the short eight month period during which we made two major moves. In addition Joy was diagnosed with cystic fibrosis and subjected to daily respiratory treatments. She was hospitalized two times within one year and both were extremely traumatic. Most disturbing, Joy felt my depression – a silent, but foreboding entity. In Joy's childlike thought processes, she felt at fault for her illness and responsible for the changes in our lifestyle. She never directed her frustrations at us. In fact, she cooperated with our expectations and rigid schedule. Joy could only express those misunderstood feelings at her younger sister – the vulnerable one. Gordon and I were constantly negotiating between the needs of our daughters. We could not expect them to comprehend the tensions that existed within that close sister relationship – one healthy, the other chronically ill.

Circumstances dictated how we, as parents, managed the demands placed upon our time – demands that could not be postponed or ignored. Thus we became legalistic in scheduling our lives, our activities, and our daily routine. Joy required our ever-constant care and attention while Jami's needs were less evident. She was the more passive, compliant child, and it was easy to see past her needs. She, in effect, was the child left in the shadows. This was not deliberate. We were in survival mode. At the heart of our home was concern for Joy's health.

Jami could not always express her frustrations. Temper tantrums were not effective with me, so she gave those up. On occasion, she would burst into tears. During one particular incident, Jami was in her bedroom sitting on her bed crying for no apparent reason. Gordon went into her room, sat down next to our daughter and pulled her toward him wrapping his arms around her. He held her lovingly and quietly until she calmed down. I remember being touched by Gordon's sensitivity. Jami felt loved and comforted. We did not know what triggered Jami's crying, but it appeared to us that the issue had been resolved. However, we as parents should have been more sensitive to Jami's needs. Although Jami was the quiet and healthy one, her feelings were affected by our family dynamics.

Joy and Jami were totally opposite in character, personality, and gifts. Each had her own strengths and needs. Jami was the happy-go-lucky social butterfly. She was the risk-taker – spontaneous and impulsive, but less confident, more dependent and compliant. She was a visual thinker and observer. Joy was the more serious, contemplative, independent, and studious child. She was cautious, sensitive, and practically always processed her thoughts before taking action. Jami had many friends; Joy had a few close friends.

As the older sibling, Joy became the more dominant personality. She was more verbally adept. She could control most situations and, ultimately, became quite skilled in managing Jami. This worked well during Jami's preschool and early childhood years.

I remember the time one summer when we were visiting my parents on their Louisiana farm. I had sternly instructed the girls to never go down to my father's ponds alone. He had three. I was outside puttering around, and the girls were tagging along with my father, who was working in his garden. Suddenly, I heard the girls screaming and my father yelling. My first feeling was that of terror. One of my children had fallen into a pond. I came running in horror, fearing the worst. To my surprise, they were soaking wet and laughing. Joy and Jami were helping my father water his garden when Joy instructed Jami to spray the water on Grandpa. Jami, the dutiful sister who always *obeyed* Joy, doused him good. Grandpa sternly admonished, "Now stop that." That was an open invitation to continue with greater enthusiasm. He rushed to retrieve the hose which both gripped in tandem and in defense of a feared reprimand. An all-out water war waged. It ended peacefully accompanied with laughter and an unforgettable memory.

Jami loved and idolized Joy. She modeled Joy's behavior and her dress. As soon as Joy outgrew her dresses, Jami claimed them for herself. Joy wore a uniformed jumper during her kindergarten year at a parochial school. As soon as Jami entered kindergarten two years later, she insisted that dress was required. I was washing it almost every day. Jami attached herself to another dress that had passed its usefulness and beauty. The hem line reached the ground, and it was torn and tattered with the side seam ripped halfway up. Jami could not be dissuaded. She wore that dress with pride, convinced that she was the princess of the neighborhood. Never mind my thoughts, she thought she looked lovely, and she was having fun.

In time, as Jami grew and claimed her place in the family, she learned to assert her will. Then one fateful day Jami announced to Joy, "You are not my mommy, and I don't have to do what you tell me to do." Jami had finally realized that she was not an extension of Joy. She was her own person. Nothing – no one could change that.

Joy had her flash points and both girls had short fuses. It was a constant give and take relationship as each carved out their place in our family. Joy claimed leadership by right of her age, but Jami refused to follow. Many confrontations resulted between the two sisters as they learned acceptable and appropriate social skills. This is what psychologists call experimental behaviors. Jami could not match Joy's verbal skills and vented her frustration through passive-aggressive behavior. She found Joy's level of frustration and pushed those buttons effectively. This made Joy even more determined to rein in Jami. On the other hand, there was obviously a great deal of love between the sisters. One evening, in particular, both girls were laughing and goofing off when Jami spontaneously wrapped her arms around Joy and exclaimed, "I love you, Joy." In spite of their differences and spats, they did love one another.

The events during one particular hospitalization illustrated the dichotomy between Joy and Jami. Both were in the children's playroom of the hospital. Joy sat quietly hooked up to an IV pole for administering drugs. She did not feel well; her eyes were sunken and dark. Jami played games and jumped around in oblivion – not to aggravate Joy, but simply to have fun. I watched Joy as she glared at Jami. Joy's patience finally exhausted, she declared, "I wish you were sick and not me!" Joy had never in the past nor ever again made a comment like that. Her tolerance level had simply reached its limit. I was not surprised at Joy's outburst, and I understood her feelings.

Their summers, as children in the Riverdale neighborhood, were filled with lots of friends, play, and laughter. The innocence of childhood had its place in the order of life, but the march of time created transitions as the girls moved beyond the security of our little family. As Jami and Joy grew into adolescence, they developed friendships that were more compatible within their different ages. As a natural part of this process, a disconnect began to develop between Joy and Jami.

Jami mentioned to us, on more than one occasion, that we, as parents, were too serious. She was correct in her analysis. Jami loved to have fun, and it barely existed in our home. She looked for opportunities to escape the cloud that hovered above our family. Jami began to withdraw from us during adolescence. She developed friendships among middle school peers and discovered a freedom and acceptance. Fortunately, her friends came from homes of devoted Christian parents. Those close friendships have survived the years and are still very precious to Jami. We were blessed to have an active and positive youth leader in our church. Kelly Lashly was a wonderful role model for Jami and Joy. She brought into their lives fun times, a positive and accepting spirit, and excellent Bible teaching with application. We could not ask for a greater blessing.

For many years, I prayed that Joy and Jami would become friends, appreciate one another and respect each other's lives. I knew that the future would eventually catch up with Joy. For Jami's emotional well being, she needed to make peace with Joy. That prayer was answered the last year of Joy's life.

As adults, Joy and Jami's past differences began to melt away. The first peace offering occurred at Jami's graduation for the Master of Arts degree. Gordon and I had traveled to Memphis by car and Joy by air, arriving and leaving one day apart. After graduation, we drove home to Sioux Falls, and Joy stayed over with Jami. Mom and Dad were out of the picture. The girls had the day all to themselves. Their time together was filled with sisterly fun – touring Elvis' home, sharing lunch and just enjoying one another's company. This is still one of Jami's most precious memories.

The weekend prior to Joy's last hospitalization was spent in Rapid City. Gordon had served twenty-two years as a chaplain in the Army National Guard. He held the rank of Colonel. Now retirement ceremonies and reception were in place. Jami flew from Memphis for this auspicious event. Joy, her husband, Mike, along with Jami, Gordon and I were together as a family. Before the ceremony, I observed Joy and Jami sitting together on the couch engaged in animated and humorous conversations. Thank you, LORD, for answered prayer. Little did we know that, in two short weeks, Jami would travel home to Sioux Falls for Joy's memorial service as a fallen warrior.

Distance... Does It Matter?

I have to admit that I felt sorry for myself living so far from family. The miles that separated us from our families took its toll on my adjustment to South Dakota. Most people in these parts are surrounded by their immediate family, their extended family, and even distant relatives. I envied them. As Joy and Jami were growing up, Gordon and I were "it." We did not have family near who could step in to give us support. A weekend retreat was out of the question. We once left for a two-night, three-day seminary retreat, but that did not happen again. To ask someone to stay overnight and assume the responsibility for Joy's treatments, meds, and food was asking too much. I told Gordon that I would never leave the girls again. Gordon had numerous travel commitments which I accepted as part of his job responsibilities. But one of us had to be there for Joy. I would be the one. I never regretted that decision. There were challenges, but the girls and I managed, and I was happier. When Gordon got home, he willingly took charge, and we resumed our various responsibilities. But enough of this self pity! We survived; the girls had a safe school and neighborhood, wonderful friends, and a church that fed our spiritual needs.

We always enjoyed those summer vacations down home with our parents in Texas and Louisiana. It was amazing, the love between grandparents and grandchildren. The bond with cousins was never in jeopardy. The distance of miles only heightened our anticipation for the next journey to our faraway, beloved home. Although separated for a year at a time, when we all got together, it was as if we'd never parted.

Grandma and Grandpa

My parents retired from pastoral ministry and built their little retirement home on a farm ten miles from the town where I grew up in northwest Louisiana. It is a beautiful part of the state with rolling hills dotted with pine trees. Their home was only a mile from the Sabine River/Toledo Lake and state park. The land was my father's greatest prize. God had provided that place for my parents during a particularly difficult time in their ministry. It was considered *holy land* to my parents. They would live there the remainder of their lives.

My father worked that farm daily and was able to develop it into an income-producing enterprise. He also continued part time pastoral ministries in the rural churches of that area. My mother was a professional musician. She had become quite successful and well-known in that part of the state as a piano teacher and children's choir specialist. Parents brought their children from miles away to be taught by my mother. Their life was secure and happy. We always looked forward to our annual summer vacation and occasional Christmas visits. Joy and Jami had many fond experiences with Grandma and Grandpa.

Joy learned to fish from the ponds that her Grandpa stocked. It was her first request upon our arrival. "Grandpa, can we go fishing?" Joy would pester him daily! Even the heat and humidity did not deter her. Of course, he loved to fish, but, when he took the girls fishing, he spent most of his time baiting their hooks with worms. Joy and Jami never quite mastered that skill. This love of fishing filtered north to Sioux Falls. On summer evenings, Joy eagerly waited for Gordon at the backdoor. "Daddy, can we go fishing?" Gordon always obliged.

In college, Joy penned a descriptive essay as a tribute to her grandparents and in memory of those childhood years.

A Bountiful Album of Treasures
D. Joy Harris
February 4, 1989

Grandma and Grandpa with their devotion and affection recorded for me an album full of life and admiration that I consider invaluable. The most valuable times for me did not result from typical toys or games. The best times were with my family and on the farm. Grandma and Grandpa always shared with me their time and their knowledge. Even though the chores, as many as there were, piled up, they always made sure we were entertained. Whether welcomed or not, the opportunities for learning were always there. Objects and memories represent those times, as they are so carefree and boundless in my mind. Grandpa's farm holds rich and hidden treasures that created my memories as a child.

The rich red Louisiana acreage, small as it was, held boundless excitement. The trees and forest were immense in size. Their limbs grew so high that they blocked almost all the sun as it fought to break through to the floor below. When it rained on the farm, the soil and land took on a totally new form. The ground changed from dusty brown to a muddy red clay which presented for us as children a wonderful opportunity for play and folly. The color of the soil crusted our clothes, much to my mother's dismay, as we pretended that the red creation was sent by God for our enjoyment alone.

As part of that acreage, the pond constituted its share of the land in weeds and plant life. We were given strict orders never to brave the pond on our own. We knew what lay in the shadows of the tall, thick grass was not an animal to play with. The height of the grass held in nature's secret threats as it so cunningly concealed the snakes, animals and dangers we had heard stories about. Around the farm the creatures told tales not available in books. The story of the fish that got away was not applicable in this case. Catching fish from the pond was as easy as catching the flu in kindergarten. In our case, we added some incentives or cheated just to make sure. Who would have guessed that dog food would bring the fish home like a dinner bell before an evening meal. They crowded and jumped in anticipation as we waited, ready to cast our poles into the thick mob. Their favorite meal, once the worms were finished, was the maggots. Never mind that to Grandpa the maggots were strictly throwaway. For us they were the prime bait.

The frogs also presented a rather unique challenge to us. They lived under the house, and their numbers were like the locust during the plagues. Catching them was the easy part. We caught them by the dozens, but unfortunately our efforts to preserve them alive failed. Their fragile, tiny, green bodies were not built at all durable compared to the adult frog. When Mom and Grandma began smelling our little victims as they rapidly deteriorated in the margarine tubs, our little experiment was over. Even without the memories of all the animals or silly antics that came with them, the house and its essential meaning could stand alone.

The farm house blended quietly into the outside scenery like objects enveloped in fog. Its inner character brimmed with classics and priceless relics. The kitchen held a big part of life for the family as the center of fellowship. The lamp above the dining table was where Grandpa always bumped his head in the rush to get to the food. The food, which was always homemade, from no recipe in particular, filled the house as we waited, anticipating a feast in the tradition of Thanksgiving. When the house was quieter, Mom and Grandma looked through the old chest and discovered classics they thought were gone. Amazingly, Mother's wedding dress appeared, and even an ornament from the wedding cake popped up.

Pictures and other old keepsakes recalled a past time and memories to be organized and arranged. The house's character and its furniture even represented the years. The big old soft chair was always occupied and anyone who left his place was never assured he would get it back. Even the old shag rug and worn couch represented a treasure of memories.

That little Louisiana farm holds an entire sea of buried treasure that my childhood revealed to me as I searched for it. The animals added to the beauty and roughness of the land to create a unity and peace that coexists there. The hard work of my grandpa paid dividends in that his home and place of shelter meant security for the body and heart. Every stitch and flaw, predator and prey came together forming a network of life and time. Hopefully the memories and happiness will continue through them and me if I can live up to their legacy.

Grandmother and Papa

Joy and Jami had another set of grandparents – Tunis and James G. Harris. Jami was named after Gordon's father, James. Tunis was proud of her name. She said her father learned about the country Tunisia and decided that was a pretty name for his newborn infant. It was a unique name and indicator of a special and unusual lady. Tunis was a brilliant lady, always with a book in hand. Her manners and correctness were impeccable. Physically, she was a beautiful woman and always dressed appropriately and fashionably. This defied her most hidden, yet, unbending trait. Tunis called herself Scotch; in other words, frugal, to the point of fault. We could tell many anecdotes, but that would not be fair. Here's one. Gordon still recalls that his mother limited him to only two slices of bacon per BLT sandwich. Of course, his appetite would beg for more.

Tunis was a very spiritual woman. She felt deeply her faith, her relationships, her family and her husband, to whom she was devoted. She did not flaunt her faith, flash her feelings, or share them freely. She was always the woman of tradition, courageous living, and proper behavior. She taught a women's Sunday school class as a young woman until age 90. She would never reveal her age, but, alas, we had to put a date on the tombstone.

Tunis was very perceptive regarding events, people, and circumstances. She had practical wisdom and a restrained sensitivity. It took only a short comment during an opportune moment to know that she understood the dynamics of a relationship or a situation. Tunis was quick verbally. At times, she was known to speak out of turn. Those stories became legends, and she did not deny them. She would occasionally, without warning, let out a quip from her Smoky Mountain roots. For instance, when I was pregnant with Joy, my appetite could not be satisfied. She said that I ate with a "coming" appetite. She had many such phrases not typical of daily conversation. The only person who could *best* her verbally was her husband. She always acquiesced to him.

Tunis was also very gifted artistically. She had a good eye, talented hands and a great sense of décor. Her home was her place of retreat and comfort. She expressed beauty through its design, color and modesty. Tunis was definitely the lady in charge at home. Her children knew that and were ever so respectful. Her leadership was unquestioned. She did not have to unleash anger. Her words and voice spoke volumes and were unchallenged.

Our girls did not know their grandparents when we returned to the States from the Philippines. They had met them as babies, but did not remember. They were introduced to our girls as Grandmother and Papa. Papa was expanded to Pawpaw, but he did not mind. I am sure that my girls broke all of Grandmother's rules, especially those involving manners. Jami was not one to be corralled. She was quite active and her body could not remain still. Our first restaurant event was one we soon desired to forget. Jami was out of the chair and gone! She went from table to table and enjoyed the attention and adoring eyes of everyone. To have strapped her in a chair would have been disaster. It simply would not have been worth it. So I just kept my eye on our active daughter the best I could.

It was unusual for Grandmother to freely express affection. I remember when we had just received the cystic fibrosis diagnosis. Joy was scheduled to be admitted to the Dallas Children's Hospital on Monday. We were driving home from church on Sunday afternoon, and Joy was sitting tall on Grandmother's lap. Unexpectedly, Grandmother said, "I love you, Joy." Although, we, as parents, were not yet informed regarding this disease, Grandmother was well aware of its devastating prognosis. Her heart went out to this beautiful, precious little four year old granddaughter.

Gordon's father was the beloved pastor at University Baptist Church in Fort Worth for twenty five years. Gordon was the fourth generation of pastors in that family. We could have no more children to carry on the tradition of pastor since the Baptist ordain only men for pastoral leadership. Yet our two girls were just as gifted and destined for a great ministry as anyone from that lineage. One can never imagine the wonderful plans God has for his adopted children, the children of His kingdom, regardless of gender.

Our first Sunday at University was the celebration of Gordon's father's tenure as pastor. We were sitting together as a family. Joy was on my lap, sitting tall watching as the choir processed into the sanctuary choir loft. Each member of the choral group stood erect. They were beautifully robed, perfectly spaced, and very reverent. Suddenly the brass instruments proclaimed the opening, the choir raised their folders in unison, and voices and ensemble rang out. It was electrifying. Joy turned to me and said, "Mommy, are those angels?" It made me wonder: had Joy heard angels' voices before? At that moment, we were experiencing God's messengers announcing the presence of God in our midst, and we were in awe.

Gordon's father had dedicated his life to God's call as pastor. He often said, if the church could not pay his salary, he would pastor that church without pay. He truthfully meant it. His wife was as involved in ministry as he. She also held down the home front. She accepted that call with as much dedication as he the pastorate. After the children were out of the nest, she accompanied James on every Tuesday evening visitation. I learned a lot from Tunis as a wife, a homemaker, and ministry partner.

Jami, Yent'l and Joy

This picture was a Mother's and Father's Day gift from the girls.

VII. BEYOND CHILDHOOD

In Israel

Joy graduated from high school in May, 1988 and planned to apply for admission at Augustana College. At the same time Gordon was granted a half year sabbatical from the seminary for the fall of '88. When Joy heard Gordon arranging to teach and study at the Institute of Holy Land Studies (now named Jerusalem University College) in Israel, her ears perked up. Typical of her grandiose schemes, Joy boldly asked to go with him. It would be an opportunity to travel in the Holy Land and also take classes from the Institute. Our biggest concern was that of health issues. It would be a risky venture for Joy. She would need oxygen. If there was a medical emergency, would care be available? But then we knew not to interfere with Joy's ambitions.

Gordon and Joy began to research the medical resources available in Jerusalem. They learned that cystic fibrosis was not uncommon in Israel. The Hadassah Hospital in Jerusalem was equipped and trained to care for CF patients. Also, the pulmonologist there was a US citizen, educated in Pennsylvania, and a trained specialist in cystic fibrosis. His name was Dr. LaFaire. We could only give our blessings to Joy. She trusted her dad, and Gordon was more than willing to shoulder Joy's care.

As soon as they arrived in Jerusalem, Gordon set up an account with a supplier of oxygen. Every few days, a short, muscled man lugged a heavy tank of oxygen to their second floor apartment. Gordon also scheduled an appointment with Dr. LaFaire to become acquainted should Joy need his services. All of our concerns were met. Gordon has always been resourceful. Arrangements were made for both of them to live in Israel while Jami and I stayed in Sioux Falls. We would travel to Israel in December to join Gordon and Joy and return home together.

The Institute of Holy Land Studies provided instruction and tours of Israel far beyond that enjoyed by tourists. Gordon and Joy worked in archaeological digs in Jerusalem with Gabi Barchai. Joy had the task of washing pottery. She got upset when Barchai threw away pieces of common pottery. She worked hard to wash all the pottery, not just the unusual pieces. Still Joy loved the experience of a lifetime, which also included investigating the tombs of Ketef Hinnom. She studied away from home, enjoyed wonderful friends, and developed her independence through the experience.

Toward the end of October, Joy fought the beginnings of an infection. The school had scheduled a trip for the students to the Negev desert in southern Israel. Joy decided to stay back to conserve her energy for the future trip to Galilee. Our daughter was absolutely in love with the Holy Land and eagerly anticipated the Galilee trip. She did not want any health problems to keep her home. On Friday morning, Gordon went with the group, then returned by bus to

Jerusalem that afternoon before the Sabbath. He faithfully kept Joy's treatments going through the weekend, but soon realized that she was losing ground.

On Monday morning, Gordon arranged for a student to stay with Joy while he taught his class. During his lecture, Gordon was interrupted. The student told Gordon that his daughter was having trouble breathing. He went to Joy immediately and, at the same time, instructed the school to call an ambulance. Joy was transported through the narrow, crowded streets of Jerusalem. She vividly remembered the continuous sudden stops, the blaring siren, and neck jerking accelerations. At one point, Gordon thought he had lost Joy. But, he spoke to her and she responded. Joy suffered a pneumothorax (collapse) of her right lung, her good lung. She could take in oxygen but could not exhale. Her lung was similar to a balloon blowing up but unable to expel the air.

I received the phone call from Gordon about 11:30 p.m. I had just drifted into a deep sleep and caught the edge of Gordon's message. He kept speaking, but my mind refused to process the information. I just blanked out. I was frantic fearing that Joy had died. "What, what, what," I repeated. He started over. I then began to comprehend. Joy was in intensive care and had been intubated for the ventilator (the insertion of a tube into the airway to allow the exchange of air by way of a ventilator). He reassured me that everything was under control, but I should have known. Joy was having a difficult time. She fought the ventilator as she tried to breathe on her own rather than let the machine breathe for her. I asked Gordon if I should come. He said, "Not at this time."

We kept in touch daily, and each time I asked, "Should I come?" Finally Gordon said Joy was asking for me. Immediately, I was on the phone with Educational Opportunities arranging transportation. EO graciously refunded the tickets Jami and I had previously purchased. I rebooked for the next flight to Israel. I arranged for Jami to stay with Jeanette and Alan Kostboth, who lived only a half block from Lincoln High School. It was a perfect match for both of them. Jami adjusted to the emergency circumstances and endeared herself to the Kostboths. Alan still mentions the graciousness of Jami and her sweet disposition.

The next day, I was on the plane. When I arrived in Tel Aviv, Gordon tried to prepare me for Joy's condition. No words were adequate to the reality of the shock. Joy was emaciated, she could not stand or walk, one eye was totally red with blood, and she had a serious bed sore that was open clear to her tail bone. It looked hopeless, and the days passed with no improvement. At night, Gordon and I took turns sleeping at the end of Joy's bed. Gordon took the first shift while I slept on a couch in Dr. LaFaire's office. Gordon would wake me about 2:00 a.m., and I would take the second shift. Before I arrived, Gordon had shouldered all those hours, never leaving Joy.

God has many wonderful "angels." A little lady who worked in housekeeping brought us a breakfast of boiled eggs, yogurt, fruit and bread each morning. She was a Middle Eastern Jewish immigrant who spoke little English. We thanked her each day. Her sweet spirit and beautiful smile melted any barriers that may have existed between different cultures and beliefs. It has often occurred to me that this world would be much safer and more peaceful if we considered one another as God's image of Himself. We all desire the same respect and fulfillment of basic needs. Where is God's love in this world torn asunder by evil?

Another angel was the father of a young soldier. He and Gordon developed a friendship in ICU as they both waited for the recovery of their children. His son had saved a mother and her children from a fire on a bus traveling near Jericho. Terrorists had bombed the bus. He suffered severely burned lungs. After I arrived and Joy was out of ICU, this father walked up twelve flights of stairs to invite us to join worshippers for the Sabbath meal served in the hospital. It was an honor, as Gentiles, to be invited to a Jewish Sabbath meal. Unfortunately, this man's son did not survive the injuries. In life and in death, this young man was recognized throughout Israel as a hero. (As a matter of explanation, the observance of Sabbath is taken very seriously within the Jewish faith. The streets are barren, the elevators do not operate, and worship is total. Any and all electrical devices do not operate because it causes a spark, the lighting of fire.)

As the days ticked by, Joy's condition continued to deteriorate. We were desperate. I told Gordon that we had to get Joy home. Our frustration was compounded by the fact that no airline would consider such a risk to fly one so ill. Dr. LaFaire could see my panic. He approached us about another medication, actually an older drug considered non-effective, obsolete within US medical ranks – Colymycin, an aerosol. It was hard to come by. As soon as Joy started that treatment, her condition began to improve.

During the hospitalization, Dr. LaFaire approached Joy about a lung transplant. He said it was a surgery routinely performed in England as a heart and lung transplant. This was the year 1988. Joy was not ready to consider such a radical procedure. She was wise in her decision, but the seed had been planted. It would be nine years in the future when that surgery would be a last resort in her fight for life.

It was now Thanksgiving. The Institute of Holy Land Studies was hosting their annual traditional dinner with all of the finest tableware, food, and decorations. Joy had been looking forward to that event. We consulted with Dr. LaFaire, and he agreed to allow Joy to attend the dinner. Joy was brought to the school by car, then carried from the car down the long driveway to the entrance on a locked arm-to-arm chair between Gordon and a friend with Joy's arms wrapped around their shoulders. It was a beautiful sight and such a joyous occasion. Joy was out of the hospital. What a wonderful Thanksgiving it was!! Joy ate heartily.

After dinner, Joy asked to stay all night at the apartment. We allowed her to sleep over and she was the better for it. She did just fine, and Dr. LaFaire agreed with our arrangement. We borrowed a car the next day from one of the faculty and drove around Jerusalem and Tel Aviv. Unfortunately, Galilee was off limits, Joy's only regret during her Israel expedition.

As Joy began to regain some strength, it was time to seriously consider a flight home. Dr. LaFaire took this responsibility upon himself. Primary in his efforts was his concern for Joy. It was a long flight, and he knew how fragile her health was. She had been in the hospital three weeks, and her recovery was on-going. He did not want to compromise Joy's health just to get her home. Dr. LaFaire made numerous phone calls. When he felt that Joy could withstand the strenuous travel, he wrote a letter to the airline asking for their assistance. At last, he came to the school bearing the coveted letters. At the same time, he visited with Joy and checked on her recovery. I could not change my flight schedule, and left the following day.

Gordon and Joy were going home. Gordon speaks of their travel: "We traveled with oxygen all the way from Israel to New York. Joy survived the long trip out of sheer courage to reward the confidence of airline officials. I got little sleep in order to keep her alert. Unfortunately, the only domestic ticket that had been available at the last minute was one with multiple stops. Once in the US, the landings and changing of airlines were difficult, but there was always a wheelchair and an airline official waiting to push Joy to the next plane. I got my exercise keeping up with them. When we arrived in St Louis for the final trek home, I gave a big sigh of relief. 'Thank you, LORD. It was your intervention and answer to prayer.'

"When we disembarked at the Sioux Falls airport, a group from Trinity Baptist was there to greet and welcome us home. They were a beautiful sight. They were also there to assist me with Joy. Their love and support will always be remembered. Joy was now home, but still not well. She loved being in her own room and her beloved bed. But she needed yet another two weeks of hospitalization.

"Joy's time in Israel was one of her most cherished memories. She loved the country and all its varied history. To live and study in the Holy Land brought to reality the life, work, and ministry of Jesus. She dreamed of an opportunity to go back, especially to Galilee, but that was not to be."

A Change of Seasons

The girls had graduated from high school. Joy was beginning her second year of college; Jami her first. Joy would continue to live at home. We had lived on Riverdale Road for fifteen years, and we realized that Joy needed her privacy and space. We considered our living needs and our finances. We contacted Rodney Fluth, a realtor, and started our search for a new dwelling place. It was fruitless. Finally I told Rodney, "You know our needs and our finances. If you come across anything, just give us a call." A few weeks later, one Saturday evening, Rodney called. A house had been on the market at least two years, but presently was owned by the bank. (This sounds vaguely familiar.) If it did not sell in the next week, the bank would move in, re-carpet, paint, etc. and jack up the price considerably. We had to make a decision by tomorrow, Sunday. Wow! Okay. "Gordon will be home late tonight and we'll take a look on Sunday afternoon."

The house was hardly visible from the road. Trees and bushes literally enveloped the house. We liked the configuration, but, alas, it needed a lot of work. At the same time that we were looking at the house, another couple was snooping around. Rodney advised that we put together a bid that evening and submit it to the bank Monday morning. It would take at least six weeks for a response from the bank. We followed Rodney's advice, and went home.

Monday morning, I experienced the proverbial *buyers regret.* I told Gordon that I had serious reservations about this major purchase. His response, "There's no way the bank will accept that bid." With that, I left for work. About mid-morning, Gordon called me at work. The bank had accepted our bid! I began to shake. Now what? Are we up to this again?

It was a wise decision. The downstairs became Joy's home. She could walk directly from the car into the house without climbing stairs or walking much distance. The walkout basement had an office, a living area, shower bath, a bedroom for Joy, and another for Jami when she was home from college. Joy's bedroom was large enough for her medical equipment. It had a nice size closet and an entire wall of shelves that reached the ceiling. It was perfect for Joy's books, mementoes, and sound equipment. As a bonus, the sliding glass doors to the patio looked out upon the large backyard. Joy loved watching the wild life. A small stream at the bottom of the hill with a huge weeping willow tree drew all kinds of critters. We accepted the challenge of the house. I was grateful and anticipated the move.

On a Friday afternoon, I went back to clean the Riverdale house and close it up. The packing and moving took all of a week during the hottest days of summer – July. I would not miss that house on Riverdale Road. It had constantly been in need of maintenance and repairs. I walked away from the house, got into my car, and looked back. Suddenly I was overcome with tears. Fifteen years! That was my girls' childhood – their birthdays, growing up days, school days, play days. Memories and sentiments flooded my thoughts. God had met our housing needs and finances during one of the most difficult times of our lives. We had poured our time and energies into that house, not to mention our family remembrances. It was small but it had met the needs of our family. This move became a symbol of our transition into a new season of our lives. Thank you, LORD, for taking care of us – in the past, in this present, and for the future.

Sun

LORD you are more precious
than silver, more costly
than gold
more beautiful
than diamonds
and I long
to worship
thee

LORD

moon

Every hill and mtn.
Every river and sea
Every man and woman
The sun, the moon, the
land, the air, the
LORD GOD made them all

VIII. MINISTRY

The Call

December 10, 1995

Father, God, you are "doing a thing" in my life, and I know that. Thank you, LORD. Move me, work within me, grow me. Your healing touch gives me peace and joy in unexplained ways.

Reading the story, <u>The Crippled Lamb,</u> in seminary chapel was a great step for me. Thank you for your presence in that and for the affirmation of my sharing. Use me and my story to effect and affect people for the Kingdom. I am excited about the possibilities, LORD, for the Kingdom and for my ministry. I can hardly wait. But I will. In your time, you will show me where I will be and how I can best minister.

Thank you, LORD. I give all the praise and glory to you, for your strength is glorified in my weaknesses.

My mother, Lois Behm, made an insightful comment about Joy as a child, "God is not finished, yet, with Joy." Truer words were never spoken. At any time, God could have said, "Okay. Come home. No more suffering for my child." There certainly were opportunities. But not yet. God saw her leadership potential, her strong commitments, her enthusiasm, her visionary gifts, her love of people, her willingness to work, her openness to His spirit and direction. How could he disappoint her by sympathetically bringing her home to Him? No, she asked too much of Him not to allow her to use those gifts. He could not deny her opportunities of ministry. Besides, her life would be an example to others – an inspiration to those who suffer, who are discouraged or lack hope. He wanted to give Joy that thrill and joy of service. He said, "My grace is sufficient." He would use her life, her witness, and her gifts to feed, inspire and nourish His flock.

January 9, 1996

There are some commitments I am going to have to make from here on: prayer, discipleship, Scripture memory, and a more active role in reaching unsaved people. I have been asking for stronger faith and more trust or signs. But what I need to do is <u>get up and get busy.</u> God is all the time working in my life. It's up to me to acknowledge it and go from there.

God's plan for my life will reveal itself in time. I need to be Joy Harris, a saved Christian in ministry, following God's will. He will take care of the rest.

February 2, 1996:

> *LORD, what are your plans for me and in what ways can I be most used for your kingdom and glory? If only I had a glimpse.*

Joy graduated cum laude from Augustana College with a major in history and a minor in math. Her last year was devoted to supervised teaching – first semester middle school history; the second semester, high school math. Joy accomplished more than just credit toward fulfilling degree requirements.

When Joy was growing up, first year middle school was very traumatic for her. Now, this present year, she conquered the fear and humiliation that had stalked her and left her crippled emotionally. Not to be undone, Joy discovered her gift of speaking, her creativity in organizing and delivering subject matter, her strong leadership qualities, and her ability to relate personally and professionally to others. She was in love with teaching. She would come home and enthusiastically tell us about her experiences with the classes. The trauma of that seventh grade many years past had been conquered and resolved. She could move on with her life in confidence and affirmation.

January 14, 1996

> *Now is where the action needs to begin. Joy, what are you willing to do for Jesus? You have enough faith. Get up and do something about it. God will be glorified. Prayer, sharing, relationships – these are my challenges. What about faith? Faith needs action. God takes care of the rest.*

February 5, 1996

> *I love the statement from this weekend: "God has not called you where He will not enable you to go." LORD, give me the patience and strength, the wisdom to be me and to know how to handle each incident, person and day that I meet.*

> *Here goes Spring! Kelly and I met today for our accountability contract. I think it will be a good experience and discipline for me to have to structure this in and be held responsible to do so.*

For Such a Time as This

July 7, 1997

> *Stop playing hide and seek, Joy. Let God hold you, calm you, and sing the sweet melody that you are so precious to Him. You mean the world to Him. The LORD has spoken and it's your responsibility to comply. It's also the same as when the Spirit prompted you as you read the book of Esther:*

"Surely you have come to this place for such a time as this." What an awesome faith and witness that such a young woman, an orphan adopted, Esther was.

Do I have the wisdom and commitment to prayer and seeking God's will and direction as I live my life? I need to truly seek what and how God is calling me and will use me. I am so special to Him. He has a plan to use me where I am, today.

Pray and seek His face. Allow the Holy Spirit to lead you. Your task is to seek. The LORD will reveal Himself and His will. Take the risk, the step of faith.

July 28, 1997

I am experiencing the heart ache of feeling useless, disposable. The attempts I make to try things fail. I am between school work and moving out of my church position. Between all these misses I am feeling useless, without a purpose. I haven't even factored in CF yet. Am I feeling depressed or just in an in-between stage?

I need to find a task, purpose, something to occupy my time. I also constantly need to return to the truth of God's love. In a world that focuses on product and success, to accept my worth simply for being Abba's child takes work and discipline. Remember, Joy, <u>it's the heart that matters that moves the heart of God.</u>

September 22, 1997

Deep thought: How difficult it is to be present at a non-Christian funeral. It is my goal then to reduce the number of non-Christian funerals, one man and woman at a time!

Opportunities for Ministry

After college graduation, Joy enrolled at North American Baptist Seminary in the Marriage and Family Therapy program. The next semester, she shifted to the Master of Divinity three year degree. That was her mission. Joy's primary strength was her commitment to a ministry to those less fortunate. She did not wait until a degree to begin ministry.

While still a student, Joy noticed an announcement that Indian Services needed a leader for its parenting program. The program worked with families who failed as parents and faced losing their children to the court and social services. It is amazing that this tiny, unmarried woman took on the most difficult parenting challenges without fear. Joy traveled downtown to teach parents the skills they had missed in caring for children. She joined the parents in court for the hearing that would determine if they could keep their children. She agreed to testify if needed. Her heart broke when the judge took the children away from their parents who loved but could not implement necessary parenting skills. Concern for the poor and those struggling, motivated her education.

March 13, 1996

> *I'm going to court this week and I just pray that my LORD will guide my thoughts, words, and spirit. I only want to be helpful and truthful to B and F and the magnitude of the decision that is about to be made. It is so heavy, so huge.*
>
> *Father of all of humanity and creation, guide my thoughts, words, and deeds that they would be helpful, truthful, and honorable.*

Jane Thibault delivered a series of lectures at the seminary in April, 2006. Dr. Thibault is a clinical gerontologist and the Associate Clinical Professor for the Department of Family and Geriatric Medicine for the University of Louisville in Louisville, Kentucky. One of her primary points struck close to our hearts. She spoke of the disabled using their suffering as the power to help others suffer less. Joy demonstrated this principle in her life and ministry. She loved deeply and gave all of her small frame in order to enable those who struggle to gain hope and meaning.

February 2, 1996

> *The more I talk to people, I realize that every person has some burden or struggle he/she deals with in life. Mine is my health. I need to give back to others the care, love, and support so many have given me.*

One of Joy's best friends, Liz, told Joy about a situation with her sister, Patti, and husband, Brian. Brian was stricken with spinal meningitis while in France as a professional jazz musician. He was left unable to communicate, dress, or walk, with Patti assuming total responsibility for his care. They first lived in Omaha, Nebraska, a three hour drive from Sioux Falls, then moved to Lincoln, a five hour distance. When Joy learned about their circumstances, she decided to give Patti some respite care. She drove those miles, first to Omaha then Lincoln, to sit with Brian to give Patti some free time just for herself – to jog, grocery shop, or do whatever she desired. Joy did this not once, but numerous times. At Joy's prayer service, Patti and Liz packed up Brian with his little dog in their van to drive to Sioux Falls. It was their farewell to Joy to express their love and grief.

September 24, 1996

> *Keep Christ always in view, not yourself,*
> *Others first with a basin and towel.*
> *LORD, keep me in your care and love.*
> *May I learn each day to become more like Christ.*

Creative Teacher

In 1989, Joy single-handedly started a Bible study for singles in the home of Marietta and Ted Faszer. Within six months, it had grown to a regular, faithful group. At its peak, it reached more than thirty participants. Later, it was reorganized into three groups and a separate group for single moms. Child care was provided by another group. Several in these groups came to know the LORD and to profess Christ as Savior.

After Joy and Mike were married, they hosted a couples Bible study and a second one on a different night. Joy also took it upon herself to organize home Bible studies within the body of Trinity Baptist Church. Most of this she accomplished via the telephone, her instrument of contact. That phone sometimes appeared to be a part of her ear anatomy. Joy had experienced the thrill of ministry. There was no stopping her.

As a master of divinity student at North American Baptist Seminary, Joy wrote a weekly column in the student newspaper, "Sem Times," edited by Bob Frye. Her mystery column was authored by the "Chapel Mouse" who ended his musings with a lesson for application.

> *In junior high you occasionally find a "kick me" sign on an unsuspecting student's back. As a junior, I am feeling what it is like to be at the bottom of the totem pole, again. It seems to be part of the cycle of life.*
>
> *Working with small group ministries, I prepare weekly Bible study lessons for our college and career group. At the end of the summer, 1993, college students were leaving for school while others returned from summer vacation. I adapted the "kick me" sign to illustrate my lesson.*
>
> *Everyone was given a sign, taped on their back, and a pen. Upon each others' signs they wrote comments according to the instructions on the sign, "encourage me." With so many new faces, we did not know every person we encouraged; we did not need to know them. The compliments and encouragements flowed naturally. As people removed their "encourage me" signs they read their comments, delighted at what had been written.*
> *This activity was more meaningful than I could ever have imagined. Recently, a friend opened her Bible and in the front was a small green sheet. It was her "encourage me" sheet. She encouraged me.*

Find time to encourage and build up one another. The blessings will be returned to you.

Hebrews 10:24 – ...let us consider how we may spur one another on toward love and good deeds.

Hebrews 10:25 – Let us not give up meeting together, as some are in the habit of doing, but let us encourage one another – and all the more as you see the Day approaching.

Future Considerations

As Joy continued to weigh the options for future ministries, she recorded the wise words of Mark Adams with whom she worked.

September 1, 1996

- *The more I pray, examining myself, the more I will know and see God. For it is only when I recognize both my sins and giftedness that I can know and understand God's grace.*

- *Form follows function. How I minister will be and is determined by how and who God has made me to be. Ministry must flow from who and what I am, not vice versa.*

- *Ministry is accomplished by and comes from individuals, not from institutions or programs.*

- *Worship should flow and focus on God. Blessings from that then flow back into us, a rejuvenation of our spirit.*

- *To be successful will be for your story to continue, not just in the concrete ways but in and through others.*

By Mark Adams, permission granted,
August 23, 2006

September 26, 1995

I have become somewhat uncomfortable with my position as a student leader and the way people hold me in high esteem. I just want to be Joy. I need to learn how to turn attention, praise, and leadership from myself and onto God. I, by myself, am totally inadequate. Only because of Christ's power do I succeed.

January 8, 1996

Church planting is very exciting to me. LORD, give me a vision and direction for my ministry. Comfort me, guide me, and love me Father.

Joy spent two years of supervised ministry at New Hope Church with Pastor Chuck Ashe and his wife, Pat. She diligently worked with the children's ministry.

June 4, 1996

Church is going so well. I love your work, LORD, for it is not I who am glorified, but you. Too often I feel good about what I've done when it's only by the movement of the Holy Spirit and your will and timing that people come to the LORD.

LORD, you take care of your children. Thank you for allowing me to have a part in that. I am who you have made me to be. I so want to bring honor to you, your power, your love, your grace. You are worthy, so worthy, LORD. I love you.

LORD, you alone know the future and for that I am thankful. I will attempt to live each day, making decisions within your will, knowing you will guide my actions and open the doors for opportunities where your purposes may be served and your name be glorified.

August 18, 1996

I still question where my life is going and what the future holds, but the most I can do is take it one day at a time. My life and future is and always will be God's to lead and direct.

October 4, 1996

School is going well though by the end of the week I am struggling. I am finding challenges in leadership and in engaging others in the business of leading. I have grown so much it almost scares me. I have been given the chance to tell my story at chapel in November though it freaks me out. I know it is something I need to do.

LORD, I pray that as I begin to formulate what I will say that you would give me the thoughts, images, picture of how best to describe your presence in my life.

October 17, 1996

It is good to be back in school with the opportunity to worship in chapel. We have had some good services and I have needed to be fed. I have committed to speaking in chapel. I will use II Corinthians 12:5-10 and the song, "His Strength is Perfect." I am hoping Matt Putz will sing for me.

LORD, I will struggle through this. I just ask for your guidance on what I will say. What does my life say about you, LORD? It's not about me. It is you who are my life source. Father, Daddy, give me understanding, a spirit to discern. *Joy*

God must have smiled on this adopted child of His whose greatest desire was to love and serve Him. But then He knew that in the future He would have to step in to save her from the physical body that would eventually fail her. He would be there in her finest hour.

Joy's car that gave her freedom to move to places of ministry.

IX. KNOWING JOY

happyjoy@iw.net

Who is this young lady, by the name of Joy? Those in her e-mail address book knew her as *happyjoy@iw.net*. So many have commented that we named her well.

But there were other dimensions to Joy's life. Some recognized Joy by her physical form: her height less than five feet, her weight seldom more than ninety pounds. Joy desired that no one identify her by an illness, "cystic fibrosis." Despite her petite body, Joy packed a wallop into that complex and deeply committed personality. Most would know Joy by her strength, but not of the physical sort. She allowed nothing and no one to stand in her way of living life. I will explain.

Her vocal skills became evident to us, her parents, during that infamous *terrible twos* stage. Once she discovered the *no* word, she put it to great and successful use. This voice also served Joy well as a young adult. She could more than adequately express her thoughts and ideas, political persuasions and views, feelings and beliefs. One would not want to debate Joy or, alas, cause her temper to flare. Furthermore, those verbal skills were useful as a speaker, as a spokes-person in her health and medical concerns, as an organizer, as a writer and academician, as an advocate for the less fortunate and those suffering.

We, as parents, knew Joy as a *warrior*. Yet this warrior was balanced by a unique spirit of love, sensitivity, and spirituality that could only be attributed to God. He placed His special hand upon Joy's life. All who knew her could recognize the undeniable touch of God.

Unrestrained, Spontaneous Laughter

A laugh from Joy was never a suppressed giggle or smile. She totally filled a room with vocals which produced volumes from deep within her lungs and gut. Her mother-in-law, Cheryl Sauers, spoke at Joy and Mike's wedding and recalled the first time she met Joy.

Mike Sauers brought Joy to a family picnic to introduce his new lady friend to the extended family. Cheryl harbored nagging reservations about this petite woman, perceived by them as cultured and astute. During the dinner, one of the little nephews started choking on a chicken bone. Everyone panicked. To the shock of all, the little boy simply reached down into his mouth and throat, extracted the bone, then held it up to display for all to admire. Everyone breathed a sigh of relief. But not Joy. She burst into spontaneous, uproarious laughter at the whole incident. Cheryl was amazed. How could one fit so comfortably into a family whom she just met? She was, after all, not unlike them. Really the same.

<u>March 18, 1996</u>

> *I met Mike's parents Sunday (and all family). They are so sweet, and they remind me a lot of the Behms (Mom's family). It was a bit chaotic at dinner, but they are a neat family. I wonder what they think of me. Mike's mom is going in for surgery on Thursday so this will be a stressful time for their family. She seems so great.* $\mathcal{Joy}$

A Place for Humor

Joy wrote this article for the "Sem Times" under the pseudonym name, "Chapel Mouse".

I'M LISTENING

Wow! What a bonus week. All my senses have been fine tuned. Though a mouse's vision is only black and white, it can always be refined. Sometimes a mouse can forget how great his God and community is. In the same way the eyes of God's servant, Elisha, were opened. Since God's prophet was blinded by an opposing army, perhaps there is hope for mice in a world of cats. Cats could definitely learn better manners. But a banquet for the enemy? That might be stretching it.

Wednesday morning, as I was cleaning my ears, my living quarters were rudely disturbed. My home became mobile as my van pulled out of the garage. I began traveling through territory that seemed foreign but inviting because of its vast corn fields. The retreat to which all the humans were congregating was worth the disruption.

A powerful message was given to Samuel and also to us as we listened. God will "do a thing" through just one who will listen and be open to his will. Who needs a comfort zone when God is leading you? Though I left my comfortable community to enter a foreign land (I heard it was Iowa), God blessed me through the message I heard.

How is your sight and hearing?

> *– The Chapel Mouse*

Joy totally appreciated the dry humor of Dr. Paul Rainbow, Professor of New Testament. Dr. Rainbow did his graduate studies in England. He possesses the distinguished intellect, recognizable good manners, and refined style of British culture. To his credit, he is also an accomplished classical musician. After sitting under his lectures, Joy would arrive home still laughing at his unintentional humor. The punch line often unrecognized in class, left Joy laughing solo. She loved his classes, style of teaching, and humor.

Appetite + Food = Cooking

An interesting development evolved from Joy's ravenous appetite and love of food. During endless boring days when housed within the walls of a hospital room and, in an effort to stay mentally occupied, Joy discovered the food channel while surfing the net – the perfect expression for her food fantasies. TV cuisine became her entertainment. Yet an adolescent, she began to put that knowledge to the kettle and developed into a fine cook. It became another step in her life toward independence.

Awesome Sneezes

To describe a sound in written word takes a lot of imaginative and descriptive language. Joy's sneezes filled the echo chambers of worship and classroom. They interrupted thoughts and the flow of lectures, conversations, and homilies. They defied the small stature of her body. One would ask, "Where did that come from?" Joy, of course. Unmistakably Joy! We miss those sneezes that required more than just a "Bless you" – more like, "Are you all right?"

Joy reading scripture.

Argus Leader photograph, December 25, 1998

X. THE SERIOUS JOY

Time for the Arts

Joy was always planning her next concert or theatre excursion. She never missed an opportunity for a quality Christian concert. She was one of the first to purchase tickets for Augustana's annual Christmas Vespers concert. For many years, she volunteered to turn pages for the pianist or organist as they accompanied Handel's "Messiah" performed by the Seminary Community Choir of Sioux Falls. Among Joy's papers, I found a Christmas wish list: tickets to Bette Midler, Kenny Loggins, or Celine Dion; tickets to an opera in St. Paul, "Porgy and Bess." One of the perks of her trips to the clinic in Minneapolis was attending a play at the theatre.

June 18, 1997

> *I just watched* "Les Misérables" *on PBS tonight. Sooo profound! "To love another is to see the face of God." They will know we are Christians by our love.*

Dr. Stephen Brachlow, the seminary history professor, directed an annual seminary drama. His performances were professional quality using volunteers from the seminary student body and the community. One year his choice was "Surprised by Joy," the story of C.S. Lewis and his wife. Joy recruited several of her girlfriends for the performance. They arrived early to get seats in the first row – practically in the face of the actors. It was total rapture by this small spectator group. Their response to the various scenes was laughter, awe, and finally sadness in the final scene. They lived the story as it was brought to life by the drama team.

Political Advocate for the Discriminated

Even with her strong intellect and ethics, Joy was deeply aware of those who were less fortunate and those denied equal opportunities simply due to difference of color or character. She was especially outraged by the culture that was created and forced upon the Native American. She spent her college years researching the history and reasons for such blatant discriminations. Each year, she delivered a paper at the annual state symposium sponsored by the Center for Western Studies at Augustana College. She was scheduled, one year, to read her paper. Just one problem: Joy was sacked up in a hospital room. She was determined that this would not interfere. She requested a pass, which was granted. She had me pick her up – oxygen tank and all – and deliver her to the building and the room. I sat with her. I asked if she needed her oxygen to read her paper. Of course not! She whipped off that canula and strode to the lectern. She read her entire paper, taking short breaths while I held my breath. No harm done, but pride was in evidence, especially by her mother. "That's my daughter!"

Once while visiting cousins in the south, Joy was appalled that the African American was still suffering injustices. I had grown up in the south. I tried to explain the history and culture of the south. My rationalizations were unacceptable. Her comment: "How could you let those things happen? How could you live under those conditions? How could you accept that kind of culture?" as if I could personally do anything about it. Indeed, why wasn't I more involved in seeking change in a culture that was so radically wrong? I had no answer.

The Sensitive, Loving Joy – To Small Creatures, Nature, Friends and Children

As a child, Joy re-papered her bedroom walls with animal posters. She had every kind of creature imaginable. Her favorites were baby seals, Bambi and colts. She had an aversion to fur coats. One embarrassing moment after church, Joy hung around, shifting from one foot to another, pacing restlessly. Finally she could stand it no longer. She approached Ginger Jones, who was wearing a rabbit fur jacket.

"Do you realize how many rabbits had to be killed for that jacket?"

Ginger quickly came back, "Oh, these were just road kill."

We all still laugh about that incident. Ginger, thankfully, was not offended.

April 10, 1995.
Yesterday I held a precious creation, Hunter Nicole. She was born April 9, 1995 at approximately 8:30 am. She is a beautiful baby girl and such an awesome creation! Mama Holly is doing well and, oh so proud and happy to have this new creation. To hold her was beautiful, and I feel honored to have had the opportunity. What a blessed miracle she is! Amen.

March 10, 1996.
Today was Joshua's shower and it was beautiful. I had the chance to hold him a couple times and feed him too. He fell asleep on my chest and shoulder. Lynne said he likes to listen to your heartbeat. He is so precious. To know that I will never have one of my own, the time and beauty of holding and cradling Joshua is especially meaningful. I wrote in his journal contemplating that by the time he is old enough to read it, I may not be around. I'm crying now.

Uncompromised Ethics

Joy held strong convictions which she carefully and meticulously worked through in her heart and mind. She lived by those convictions and had no trouble expressing them verbally or by written word. The final year of study at the Seminary required Joy to write her Statement of Faith, the perfect opportunity to express those beliefs. She produced an eighteen page, double spaced document. It was a beautifully written work that detailed Joy's commitment to God, to ministry, to scripture, to the church, and to Jesus Christ and His teachings. I have chosen to lift only one paragraph from the exposition. It was under the topic, "The Christian Life."

Statement of Faith, NAB Seminary, Spring, 1999.

Each individual is responsible to present an ethical witness to the world. Integrity and character are key components to maintaining a Christian witness in a secular world. Character traits include love for others, honesty, humility, servanthood, and righteousness. A Christian will be marked by higher character and actions. The Christian ought to be marked by a concern for all individuals and for all peoples. Part of that concern ought to include a concern for the lost, that every person matters to God and ought to have the chance to respond to the gospel. Therefore, both an ethical witness and a personal verbal witness are important. Because of a concern for all people, social concerns ought to be important to the Christian – poverty, justice, equality and the environment. The Christian is called to be different than the world, to care for it as God would, and to bring to all people the message of the gospel.

From when I wake I...

T rinity family
H ealing
s **A** l v ation and grace
u **N** failing love
K indness

Each
and
every
day

day

day

day

day

day

day

Y O U
H   O
H   L   T
W   Y   R
H   E
    A
    C
    H

are the
alpha, omega
king of kings,
bright morning star
lily of the valley
prince of peace

L O R D

– of my life
– of all living things
– of the universe
– of heavens
– of lords
– of church
– for all time

To when I sleep

XI. THE WARRIOR

Joy Struggled

<u>September 26, 1995</u>

> **II Corinthians 12:9-10 – ". . . My grace is sufficient for you, for power is perfected in weakness. . . . Therefore, I am well content with weaknesses, with insults, with distresses, with persecutions, with difficulties for Christ's sake; for when I am weak, then I am strong."**
> **(New American Standard Bible)**

My prayer tonight.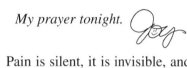

Pain is silent, it is invisible, and it is lonely. Many people do not understand the toll that physical pain takes from one's life. Joy could not share that pain with others. She never complained. Joy used her strong-willed character to compensate for physical limitations – to convince the outside world that she was as good as any of the best even though starved for breath, nutrition, energy and health. The reality of her health and the public image she displayed did not match up.

<u>Fall, 1994:</u>

> *I am sick again. I am exhausted, short of breath, tight and heavily congested. I am tired, in every sense of the word and in every way imaginable. I wonder if God tires of my pain and requests for healing. I am tired of asking. I am tired.*
>
> *I have healed again so it's just a matter of getting my strength back now. I hope to go a little longer this time before getting sick. I must gain back some of my weight.*
>
> *LORD, some days I am so tired and sad from the effort and expenses of my health care. You have given me so much. Yet, I struggle. I am very happy with myself and my life, but I tire too. Give me strength and wisdom. I love you LORD.*

Joy could fool most of those around her, but she could not fool her family. At home, Joy could let down that facade. She was safe, but alas physically and mentally exhausted. Her patience wore thin, and she lacked the stamina it took to endure frustrations. This became a point of contention between Joy and Jami. Jami has confessed she longed to be included in Joy's life, but felt shut out. She could not know that Joy was fighting her own inward battles.

July 3, 1995:

> *I am so afraid of being hurt and that if anyone really knew what I was like or what it was like to live with me, they would reject me. Not having to be vulnerable would just be so much easier and safer. I see that even with my friends and fellow seminarians. I am open, but still always hold people at an arms length from me. I am scared. It is so hard to be confident in myself sometimes.* Joy

As an adult, Joy summed up her feelings – this quote from one of her sermons based on Psalm 42:11.

> *Various hospital stays brought me to tears, tears of exhaustion, frustration, loneliness and just plain pain. I felt so many times that desperate need and thirst for life, the life that only God gives. Physical and emotional pain was a constant. I cried if the color of my jello wasn't what I wanted. . . . The Psalmist says in verse 5, "Don't be sad or discouraged little heart. Just wait patiently. Wait patiently, for I know I'll be praising God again soon. He will deliver me. That's my God." (paraphrase by Joy)*

The Healing Joy

Joy's theme verse for 1995:

> **II Timothy 1:6-7 – For this reason I remind you to kindle afresh the gift of God** *that is within you. . .* **for God has not given us a spirit of** *fear, but rather a spirit* **of power and of love and discipline.   (NAS)**
> (*Italics indicate Joy's words*)

Joy longed to be authentic. She recognized the rough edges of her survival mode. For her own spiritual and mental health, she had to make peace with this defensive posture. Joy unwittingly had built internal walls to protect herself from the outside world. To be effective in ministry, she knew that her relationships, leadership, and communication skills required fine tuning. Those walls had to come down, and it would be a momentous step for Joy. She excruciatingly began to open up, talk of her feelings and her fears. Joy could actually let in the enemy – that outside world. In that process, she discovered freedom, love, and acceptance.

Her honesty with God, the promises of scripture, and her dependence upon Him, created a safe environment for a metamorphosis to evolve in her life.

June 16, 1995

> *On Friday I went to Mom's summer musical. The story was on the "do not worry" passage of Matthew 5. I cried. Jackie encouraged me to do what was healthy for Joy and not just physically, but emotionally.*

I have built walls around my feelings, but this week I have started to take bricks out of those walls and, as of yet, have not been crushed or destroyed. I can let people in and not be hurt. People will bless in the process. Mike did. Randy and I talked this week, and he sent me flowers with a message that touched my heart, "You are too important." What a week has come together.

August 19, 1995

I am struggling this week with self-esteem issues. Who am I, really? Who do I want to be? I butted heads twice this week in conflicts that have left me feeling very put down. I am going to have to put behind me these incidents; evaluate them for what they're worth and what they've taught me, but put them behind me to move on with my life.

I need to be the most positive, loving, patient, and godly woman I can be. But I have to let God help me with that. Let go and let God, Joy. Love and Peace

August 24, 1995

I have come to the realization that I need to accept myself. Regarding the two previous conflicts: I did what I thought was right. If I was inappropriate, I am open to being corrected. But, what I won't and can't stand for is someone to treat me with disrespect. I want to learn from everything I do, but I want to be valued for the precious child of God that I am. If you cannot teach or correct me under those precepts and with that deserved respect, what you say, regardless of its truth, will mean nothing and only reflect poorly upon you. You, my friend, are that type of person. You "put people in their place." That is hardly deserving of my time. I cannot accept the kind of shame and demotions you so freely give. I will not be devalued.

LORD, it is such a fine line to walk between humility and servanthood; value and leadership; between being humble yet not walked on; a leader yet not a controller. Guide me best in your path. Amen

When Joy entered seminary for the 1995 fall semester, she faced head-on the private life she had created. Joy had developed this defensive posture to protect herself from emotional pain. She had been tormented by peers and abused by a disease that put her at a disadvantage. Joy felt vulnerable in the world. She feared that people would consider her less able, exclude her, make unjust conclusions. She carried those burdens every time she walked out the doors of our home. This way she would be in control, but it took a lot of energy to maintain those walls – to act as if all was well when, in actuality, all was not well.

September 9, 1995

Ready or not, school is off and running. This semester may be a difficult one. I pray your love and presence to be especially close to me. Thank you for what you teach me each day – to see the butterflies and beauty around me; how to come into your presence as I long for your comfort.

I need to know that God has empowered me to love, with power and a sound mind. At the same time, I need to be courageous in my work, relationships, ministry, and life. I know I will grow immensely this year. I am both excited and fearful.

Sometimes I feel alone and lonely, yet I am so afraid of letting myself be vulnerable and open – truly open – with people. This is the risk I will struggle with the most. I cannot allow myself to close off people to my feelings and to my ability to accept and give love. I think I have been lacking that, and I can't allow that to continue.

LORD, Daddy, Abba, Father, I praise and adore you. Amen.

October 17, 1995

I have a cold. I am on Augmentin and am doing better (so far). I wasn't ready for IVs yet, though I knew they were coming.

Homework is going well, but I'm just tired a lot. I have a lot I could be doing, but am doing what is most necessary for right now. I am needing to keep a check on my speech, attitude, and presence. I have caught myself in some pretty negative and critical moments, and I need to be more mindful of how I am coming across and how I'm being perceived. I struggle so much to accept myself and my limitations. I don't see how anyone else could accept them or me.

I am still using my Timothy verse and risk poem as my themes. As I read that verse tonight a couple of things strike me. Fear is not of God. (I also remember the verse that perfect love casts out fear.)

The second thing that hits me is that I have been given the spirit to love. Combining those, I want to focus on what logically follows. Concentrate on God and his love. Express love to others and fear will be overshadowed or leave. Could this really happen? Am I capable of this kind of love? I don't know, but I want to entrust that need and power to God. He will direct me and show me into paths of love.

LORD, show me how to love and give me the opportunities to do so. Prompt me to act, to love, to change, to become that quality that casts out fear and negativism. I am yours and willing.

December 10, 1995

> *I have survived one of my longest, most difficult semesters. Thank you, LORD. I give all the praise and glory to you, for your strength is glorified in my weakness. Thank you, LORD for renewing my body and spirit. Continue to hold me in the palm of your hand and care.* *Joy*

March 10, 1996

> *I hate myself when I get in these moods. I doubt myself, my worth, my decisions. I know I'm tired. Reading through my old letters and memories, I realize the power of the written word.*
>
> *Instead of being so analytical or critical of my life and events around me, I need to concentrate on the best memories and joys of my life. Terri said it well, "If you're too analytical, you can't enjoy the beauty." Well said.* *Joy*

September 12, 1996

> *I seem to be having a rather low self-esteem day today, but I'm not exactly sure why. Everything is going well in my life, but I think the issues getting me down are not those involved in my life. My spirit seems to be low. I have and am finding such refreshment in a renewed devotional life, and yet I feel so unworthy.*
>
> *Issues I thought had passed, have resurfaced. I find it difficult to be around my friend. When I see her, I am reminded of her words and her exclusion of me from her life. I find myself wondering if maybe I am all those things she said I am. I find myself very uncomfortable knowing that in her I have an enemy, in that to her I invoke anger and pain. Maybe I'm just being ultra sensitive.*

September 24, 1996

> *Six days ago, my friend apologized. I was absolutely stunned. But I feel relieved about the guilt and resentment vibes I felt. I love my friend. I will have to pray that our relationship will have a chance again. LORD, give me patience and an open heart.*

Joy's Heartaches

July 23, 1997

> *Sometimes I think my heart needs to hurt, even to break before I can get back to what is really important. I want so much to be liberated from my failing body. I want to feel whole physically. I want to be able to share all my life and leisure with Mike. But I know right now there are things I cannot do and that hurts. It makes me angry, jealous, sad, and frustrated. It makes my heart hurt.*

I know in my head that I just need to be patient, and I will have the health and strength in God's time, but my heart longs to be free and able to join in those things that I am not able to do. Someday I will be able to camp, dance, and slide the water slides, travel, hike, bike and all the activities I dream about.

Right now, though, I need to wait. I need to be thankful for how God has blessed me. I need to do His work according to how He has gifted me today.

Petition to God

Heal my wounded soul, LORD.
   Heal me morning,
      Noontime, Evening.
Hold me close to you.
   Show me your grace.
My heart will still ache,
   But you comfort me daily.
I need you so desperately. Hold me, please.

Joy Speaks to You

Each of us has a heartache. Some days your heart will hurt more than others. Though for each of us, it is for different reasons. God is there in the midst of pain, and we will be whole again. Our heartaches make us who we are as we see God's presence and hand in our past, our thoughts, our heart.

There will come a time when our heart hurts less, when we can again come to God with praise and thanksgiving. Though you cannot understand some-one else's heartache, know and search your own. See what God has done. See the hope. If you do not understand your own heartache, you will not be able to help another.

Joy lived a life of contrasts – one within the world and its demands, another controlled by health and medical needs, and yet a third dedicated to God's plan and will for her future. The God-focused spiritual life was the critical component to maintaining balance between the forces of survival.

Joy dedicated to the LORD her needs, her health, her cries, her hopes, her pressures, her loves and disappointments. She discovered that only in God's hands could she trust her life and future.

So, who is this little "warrior" of whom we write? As parents, we continue to discover the depths of Joy's thoughts, commitments, and life. She certainly was human and flawed as are we all. Joy's story exemplifies how God can use one committed life with its physical limitations, take it to incredible and undiscovered lengths, and bring it to completion for His honor and glory.

XII. In The Hospital

Beware

One warning all should heed: "Beware!" Joy's in charge. Joy could interpret her lab results, she was efficient in the operation of IV therapy, and she understood the battery of medications. Joy had a team of doctors and respiratory therapists. She was familiar with their personalities and their style of doctoring. Most of all, Joy knew her body. She could make her own decisions and did not hesitate to voice any concerns, questions, or explanation of prescribed treatment. This confidence grew from experience. It had a history.

Early in the fall of 1975, less than a year after Joy's diagnosis, Joy was admitted to the hospital in Sioux Falls. This would be the pattern for the rest of her life. Sometimes, she could go two years between hospitalizations. Due to a number of reasons, which I will not go into, this first hospitalization in Sioux Falls was difficult for Joy. It was also hard on our family, the doctor, the hospital, respiratory therapists and personnel. After several days of frustration and lack of communication, a very understanding doctor visited us and Joy. He asked the right questions, and he knew how to listen. He had impeccable bedside manners and the ability to relate personally one on one with patients. However, the damage had been done. Joy would not soon forget the trauma of that difficult hospitalization.

There would be a next time, and so it came to pass two years later. Joy was sick with pneumonia. There were no alternatives. Hospitalization was it. Joy was <u>not</u> going to that hospital and that was final! I have not failed to mention that Joy was the strong-willed child. In this particular case, stubbornness and resistance ruled. She would not be moved and force was not an option. The hospital had since employed a nurse advocate, Diane. She also was the coordinator of the CF Clinic which Joy regularly attended. Joy absolutely adored and trusted Diane. Diane called me to ask if she could come to our house and visit with Joy. Of course. She and Joy talked for about twenty minutes. Diane reassured Joy that it would be different this time. Diane later mentioned to me that she had never encountered a child so traumatized. Joy's fear was not going to fade away. No amount of persuasion, bribery, threats, counseling, or promises made a difference.

I went into Joy's room the next evening when it became obvious that Joy could no longer postpone the inevitable. Joy and I talked. I asked her, "If there was a friend for you in the hospital, would that make a difference?" She indicated yes. "Let's pray about it and ask Jesus for a friend." We prayed. It was a short, simple prayer, but earnest. Joy accepted that prayer and cooperated. I did not know how God could answer a last minute prayer.

Wouldn't you know – a young boy, a little older than Joy, was on the same floor and wing. They got along famously. They played games, hung out together, ran the halls, played foosball, and Joy was happy. God answers the most simple of prayers. How can He turn away a prayer based on the faith of a child? Thank you, LORD!

The outcome of that experience created ripples for the future. Joy discovered that she had power, and she used it to her advantage. This was no joking matter for Joy. She learned the hard way to make her needs known. On the other hand, Joy became her own best advocate in health care. She watched every move of the nurses and technicians, and if there was any question about how or what they were doing or going to do, she did not hesitate to voice her concerns. The end result was that medical professionals began to respect Joy and great friendships formed.

Joy never got used to needles. We had memorable experiences. This particular incident occurred in Joy's early childhood. On a Sunday afternoon, the nurse on duty came into Joy's room with her *tools*. She stated that the IV needle had to be replaced. The present one had worn out. She confidently mentioned that it was a simple procedure; there would be no problem finding Joy's vein. We began the sticks. None could access the tiny veins. Besides, they would roll. The nurse tried the other arm. After about five sticks, I said let's get someone in here from lab, Joy cannot take any more of this. Soon, a young man arrived from surgery. It took him only <u>one</u> puncture. From then on, Joy allowed only surgery to hook up her IVs. Never again would she tolerate such torture. When she asked for lab from surgery, she got it. No questions asked.

During a hospitalization in college, one of the physicians in pulmonology approached Joy about an angiogram to determine possible heart involvement. Joy agreed and called me at work to let me know. I was a little surprised that Joy would agree to such a procedure. Hesitantly, I said okay. I trusted her judgment. If there was any question, Joy would certainly ask it.

A little while later, Joy called again. "Done already?" I asked.

She said that she was back in her room and explained: The technicians took her down to x-ray by wheelchair, and she was laid on the treatment bed. They introduced themselves and engaged Joy in friendly conversation to ease any fears or anxiety. Before beginning the procedure they explained to Joy the steps that would be involved.

Joy announced, "No, you are not going to do this. Please take me back to my room." The technician said, "But the doctor has ordered this." Joy repeated in no uncertain terms, "Take me back to my room." They tried to talk her into it and the purpose of the angiogram. This time Joy's firm voice left no doubt of her meaning. Sternly, she repeated, "Take me back to my room!!" They wheeled her back to her room. Even the doctors had to learn the hard way. Keep Joy informed. She demanded respect and nothing less.

Dr. Rodney Parry was Joy's doctor for many years. Joy loved and respected him. But he had to earn that respect. As a child, Joy was under the care of a pediatrician and, when hospitalized, was admitted to the pediatric wing. She knew the staff and nurses. She felt comfortable there and the staff had gotten used to her idiosyncrasies. But time advances and children grow up.

Dr. Parry was head of the pulmonary department and also Dean of the medical school. He visited Joy from time to time when she was hospitalized in the pediatric wing, but he did not serve as her primary physician. She was now in middle school, but still comfortable and happy in the children's wing. From what Joy reported, Dr. Parry came by one day and abruptly told her that she was too old to be in the pediatric wing. She should move to the adult pulmonary wing of the hospital, then he would take over as her primary physician.

Joy bristled. This was her territory. She knew the nurses, the therapists, the custodians, the children's play therapist. She felt secure there.

I had suspected this would be on the horizon. I knew that it would be a hard sell for Joy and a difficult adjustment. Although hospitalizations were frequent, they were never easy. Factor in this change and one is asking for trouble. Joy flat out refused. Dr. Parry was very patient in dealing with Joy. After a period of time (I do not know how long), the move was inevitable. Joy finally realized that she was out of place on the pediatric wing. She took the move gracefully.

Over the space of a few years, Joy and Dr. Parry both had worked on their relationship which became amiable with mutual respect and agreement. Now an adult and in college, Dr. Parry approached Joy about speaking to his medical school residents. Joy agreed. She faced those students with confidence, experience, and words of wisdom. As she spoke, it became apparent those students were under her spell. They hung on her every word. She knew more about her disease, lab tests and results, drugs, therapies, breathing tests and, most importantly, patient care and treatment, than most medical professionals. They were about to embark upon an unchallenged career in medicine. By the time she finished, the students were speechless. Dr. Parry was proud of her.

The role of medicine takes into consideration the person's thoughts, feelings, personal needs, spiritual life, family, life's goals, and future dreams. Proper care respects the whole person – their past, present, and future. Medicine cannot and should not function solely from the physical. Medical treatment may begin with lab work and results, but the entire life of that person rules from start to finish. Primary above all, the physicians and medical staff would do well to learn and practice the art of listening.

Over the years, Joy developed a wide network of friends within the medical profession. They would joke. They shared about their families, their lives, their activities. They respected Joy as a peer and learned to work with her as one who was knowledgeable and informed. Joy in return became their friend. She was not intimidated by the status of anyone, nor was she too good for those who were less fortunate.

The Top Ten

With more truth than humor in her words and backed by experience, Joy wrote an article in the "Sem Times," March, 1996.

A Patient's Top Ten
By Joy Harris

If you think your first two weeks of the semester were tough, try studying from a hospital study carrel. Reflecting on my nine, long, and extremely boring days there, I have decided to use my experiences to sensitize students to the plight of the patient. These will be some very helpful suggestions whether you are counseling someone in the hospital or find yourself a patient.

Top ten ways to survive a hospital stay:

10. *Watch out for nursing students or new people. You can identify them by phrases such as "Wow, I've never done this procedure before. Can I try?" or "What drug is this and how fast is it supposed to go?"*

9. *One of the benefits of going to a Catholic hospital is that you have the chance to play BINGO two times a week. If you're lucky, you could win a coupon for a hamburger at McDonalds (a popular prize I'm sure on the cardiac floor).*

8. *Know that lab is synonymous with torture. Their favorite times to draw are between 1:00 a.m. and 6:30 a.m. And realize, when they come in they are very cheerful people and love to flip on lights – bright lights.*

7. *Realize that when you move your bed up or down it could get stuck that way. You can do breakfast at an elevation of five feet, but if you have to go to the bathroom . . .*

6. *People always walk fast in a hospital so the trick is to get that person to transport you in a wheelchair. These are some of the most exciting times you'll have.*

5. *A shower in the hospital just isn't the same as at home. But, if you're under three feet tall and have an aversion to water, you'll probably be okay.*

4. *If your friends ever ask if you need anything or if they can bring you anything, always say, "FOOD!" Any meals you can get that don't involve hospital preparation are valuable. There is more than one way to fix chicken but the hospital hasn't discovered it yet.*

3. *You can tell your doctor really cares for you when he says something like: "You're looking much better today. Your hair isn't flying in every direction."*

2. *Musical interludes will soothe you to sleep. When three IV beepers go off in a row, they create a musical masterpiece with rhythm and tones approximately a third apart. "BEEP   BEEP... Beep...beep   beep."*

1. *Being in a hospital is not a pleasant experience for anyone. Try to have a sense of humor because a positive and feisty attitude can carry you a long way toward recovery. Most of all, lean on your family and friends, their prayers, their calls and visits, and your faith. The LORD knows your trials and His grace is sufficient for you.*

Dr. Parry wrote this note to us after reading this section of the book:

Thank you for sharing this chapter. It was a privilege to be allowed to participate in Joy's health care and to know Joy as a person. Her expectations were remarkable as was her courage. Your ability to share shows the same strengths. Again thanks for this deeper insight of a very special person.

Rod Parry

Joy and Mike

XIII. A Love Story

Mike and Joy's Theme Scripture:

I John 4:16 – We know how much God loves us, and we have put our trust in him. God is love, and all who live in love live in God, and God lives in them. (New Living Translation)

September 26, 1995

I had an offer for coffee the other day from Mike, but I haven't called to take him up on it yet – confusion.

Mike: "How Joy and I met. Michelle Martin invited me to visit Trinity Baptist Church. After the service, a group went to Nick's (a restaurant) for lunch and I accompanied them. I did not remember meeting Joy, but she was also a part of the group. I learned later that her friends had gathered to bid Joy an informal farewell. She was leaving Trinity to work at New Hope Church."

October 17, 1995:

I am enjoying working with G, but don't have him quite figured out yet. He asked the other day how I felt about being single. I have been thinking about my answer ever since. I said, "Sometimes being single is hard because I get lonely. But other times it is very freeing when I don't have to get permission from anyone to go or do anything." I still feel that way, but I sure don't like thinking about it so much. I wish I didn't worry about it. "Oh well, whatever," was my conclusion. I struggle so much to accept myself and my limitations. I don't see how anyone else could accept them or me.

October 25, 1995

I'm feeling very weird tonight. I've had this feeling for a couple days now. I feel like there's something wrong with me, but I don't know what. It's not like a guilt thing, but more like an odd or "out of it," thing.

I have decided I'll call Mike and see what happens. This is my year to risk, right? But boy it is scary, scary, scary! Grandpa is here and not appearing to be doing very well. Mom is very sad and worried. No one really knows what to do. Well, better get to bed. Bye, Joy

Mike: "Back in September at Nick's Restaurant, Joy was evidently listening when I was asked about my vocation as a social worker. I received a phone call from Joy asking about my work in Child Protective Services. She was working with a Native American family and had some general questions. We went out for lunch and everything blossomed from there."

December 10, 1995

Mike and I had treats last night. We had a great time. Mike dumped water in his lap and we laughed. We talked about school, ministry and fun stuff. He is so easy to talk to, and I feel so comfortable with him. I'm not sure yet in what ways I'll continue to get to know him, but I'm comfortable with the way things are going.

I feel lonely sometimes but am not willing to take the risk of hurt or failure (an inappropriate risk) to either push or push away Mike right now. I'm not going to say yes or no, but I do enjoy talking and doing things with him. LORD, you are leading me.

Mike: "I actually don't recall if this was a first date or just the real first evening together. Joy invited me to the performance of the *Messiah*. Of course I said, "Yes." What I didn't know was that she turned pages for the organist. I sat by myself. I had no clue what this was. After the event, we went out for dessert. It was a very cold December night. At the restaurant, I must have been a little nervous. I spilled a whole glass of water all over my clothes. I remember Joy's big burst of laughter from the gut that permanently made a lasting impact."

January 8, 1996

Mike and I seem to have struck up a good friendship and have been out a couple times. But I am so unsure of this – not necessarily of Mike, but me. I am so scared of hurt and rejection. In fact, I have such fears that I am almost prepared to just say forget it. The potential for pain overwhelms the positives of a relationship. I know that is a bad and unhealthy attitude, but some days I feel so worthless that I question why anyone would love me or want me. It is a struggle I will have to work through. I am just feeling bad about myself and questioning the extent of my relationship with Mike. I am feeling now that maybe he isn't interested. I go back and forth.

LORD, I leave this up to you. I am scared and already fearing rejection. My future is in God's hands, and I have to be willing to trust His leading and will for my life.

January 17, 1996

It seems that the more time I spend with Mike, the more comfortable, yet uncomfortable, I get. He really has a true heart and spirit. He has a care-givers (kind of a pastoral) heart. He so understands and is sensitive toward people. The more I get to know him, the more I am impressed. Again, though, I have to go back to the faith walk. I have so much going on in my life – this relationship is going to have to fit in with my life and in God's will for my life. Time will tell (though things are getting tense).

LORD, continue to inspire and move in me.

The subject of a lung transplant came up again. Eight years had passed since it had first been introduced to Joy by Dr. LaFaire in Israel. There was no denying that Joy's health had continued to deteriorate. We did not bring up the topic of lung transplant because Joy was well aware of her health options. She made her own decisions, and we respected her knowledge and wisdom. In her own time she would explore the lung transplant option. It would be a gut wrenching decision.

January 23, 1996:

I set the appointment for January 29, 9:00 a.m. at University of Minnesota Medical Center. I talked to Pat and Chuck Asche today about a transplant so they know the entire story. From here on out it gets messy. I don't know how I'll explain to Mike this facet of my life. I think Mike actually likes me, but I find that an intimidating thought. Last weekend went very well so I'll see how this weekend goes.

February 5, 1996

Saturday, Mike took me out to dinner and a movie, and it was great fun. I think I'm starting to let down my guard and that's scaring me. I haven't told him yet about CF, but I plan to soon. I think I like him, really like him, but I'm afraid to let myself feel so, too.

Talking about taking risks is sure easier than actually doing it. Valentine's Day is coming up and who knows what will happen. I always assume <u>nothing</u>. I don't know to expect anything anyway because we haven't really talked about it. I just am really at ease with Mike and enjoy his company. I think Mom and Dad are holding their breath too – waiting for a cue from me.

LORD, give me patience and strength, the wisdom to be me and to know how to handle each incident, person, and day that I meet.

February 13, 1996

Well, it's Valentine's Eve. I am not sure if anything is in store for me tomorrow, but that's okay. On Sunday evening, Mike told me finally about his dream – he was dialoguing with God while this evil was being wrapped up and contained. Then he told me the clincher, he has been married before. Whack right in the head. I wonder what my face and expression looked like.

All the possible difficulties this brings up. But he was accepting of my CF. He deserves the same back. She was having affairs. He has been divorced 1 1/2 years and they were married for three, no kids. Wow! Only by being honest, though, can we talk about it and work through those issues. I thought about saying, well, maybe this isn't the right thing to do. But I can't seem to imagine not having Mike around and seeing him. I also need to leave some of the control of this to God. He has brought us to this point and I have faith in His leading. I think this relationship, no, I know, it has changed to the point of going further. I can only go where God leads me.

I loved the statement from this week end. "God has not called you where He will not enable you to go."

Mike: "Doubt – there were many times when I questioned if I could continue to go further in the relationship with Joy. I could not ignore the prognosis – knowing her health. I have always been a very active person. Yet knowing Joy, I was inspired to slow down to a pace in order to walk with a very special person who saw life in an entirely different spectrum. It was her zeal and spirit that touched the core of who I was. Her entire life was moved by the Holy Spirit.

"When Joy and I first met and began talking, I was not that far into my life as a Christian. When I accepted Christ as Lord and Savior, everything was new to me. My life had been completely different than that of Joy's. I really had only a simple basic understanding of faith. You see, I grew up in a family that really did not have anything to do with church, faith, and God. This carried into my adult life. I struggled with the addiction of alcohol, a broken marriage, and financial bankruptcy.

"Coming from where I had been in my walk, I would have never thought it possible to be involved with a woman whose life was so completely different. Yet she took a leap of faith trusting me on my journey and struggle. She simply touched my life as a person who cared. Truly God's hands were at work in both of us from the first that we met."

March 4, 1996

I feel really comfortable with Mike. I really enjoy his company. We talked this weekend. It's so scary, the amount and depth that I will tell him. I scare myself being that open. We talked about us, about the difficulties of risking, trusting, and dating. He said, "Do you want to just be friends? What do you think we are? What do you want us to be?"

Great, I get to go first. I said we were dating, not seriously, but dating and I like it that way. I am comfortable with that. Mike agreed. He said he's not ready for "engagement" or a fast relationship. I said, "I'm not either." Both of us agreed that we need to do things for ourselves too/still. But the stage seems to be set and good communication along with it. I really like Mike and don't want to screw this up. But there will also come a time when I should tell him about transplant, and I don't look forward to that time. I'm really going to need him with me. But if he can't be, I'll understand that too.

March 13, 1996

My over-analysis of Mike and I and my fears did not pay off. Mike and I are fine. But talking to Terri did raise and highlight some issues I needed to talk through. Do I like where Mike and I are and the informalness and slowness of the relationship? Yes and no. No, because I know I am wanting more. But yes, because moving slow allows me to enjoy the relationship without having to face my fears of intimacy and rejection. So where am I? I don't know. I can wait and, in actuality, am probably not ready for anything serious. I also know that it's not fair and I don't want to pressure Mike if that's not where he is.

Joy, are you trying to control again? You need to leave this relationship in God's hands. Relax, enjoy, and take things as they come.

March 18, 1996

This was an interesting weekend, and a great one, at that. We watched movies. I think I'm falling for him (Mike). It is so easy to be with him and talk to him. We are getting quite close. This scares me. I know he would kiss me because we've been close, but I usually either freeze or back away. I just freak. I have a hard time looking into his eyes because I feel like he can see right through me. He tells me more and more about himself each week.

March 28, 1996

Romans 7:18-20 – . . . I have the desire to do what is good, but I cannot carry it out. For what I do is not the good I want to do; no, the evil I do not want to do – this I keep on doing. Now if I do what I do not want to do, it is no longer I who did it, but it is sin living in me that does it.

What do I do that I do not want to do? How does that fleshly desire interfere with what I know to be right? Answer: Argument, words, fear, truth, doubt.

I miss Mike, being able to curl up next to him and watch a movie. I miss the sweet smell of his shirts. I miss our time together. I worry our lives may part, but my goal is to enjoy the time and memories we have now.

Good night, LORD. Continue to hold me in your care. Heal my body and soul to restore me to your work. I have missed my time with you too, Lord. Restore me.

April 2, 1996

Mike and I talked again just so that all is understood. He is in no way ready for or interested in a "serious" relationship, that being "marriagish." I agreed. That is not where I am, either. I wouldn't say that we've gone down to the "friend" level, but are at a very "just casually dating" level. I'm not sure why I worry about it so much except that maybe Mike is such a neat man. I would hate and fear losing him. We'll see. I asked if he prays about it. He said he prays for me. Neat. Time for my quiet time.

May 13, 1996

Mike and I are doing fine, but still I sometimes wish for more. I need action or something more I can rely on. Is it that I am insecure? Yes, it may be. There are days when I just want to be held. Today is one of them.

May 19, 1996

Well, I spent the evening at Terrace Park again, but this time I was not alone. Mike and I spent about an hour there just talking and watching the sun, ducks, people, pets, sky, and the water. We talked about the casualness of our relationship. Mike is still at that point. I am, too, though, at times, I feel like I need or want more. To keep this a more casual relationship is a discipline for me, but one that I think is healthy right now. I still fear getting too close, and I don't think I'm ready yet for what being close would mean.

May 28, 1996

I'm not sure I should write this or not. Mike and I are spending more time together and, though neither one of us would probably admit it, it is a "closer" time. We are seen together at church. He is inviting me to family events and I him to my friends and family events. We just are so comfortable, so close when we're together. It is scary. Last night I dreamt he kissed me (though I don't think this was the first time I've dreamed about that). But it seemed so real, so reasonable. I wonder if it will come true. I leave all this in the LORD'S hands and grace. It won't be worth having without that blessing.

June 4, 1996

God is so good. He is so good to me. I don't remember ever being this happy, well maybe, just not in a long time.

Mike kissed me for the first time on June 2 at approximately 11:15 pm when he brought me home. He would have kissed me back at the apartment, but I kind of avoided it there. Sometimes I am still so afraid to feel too much, afraid to lose, too. But we are kissing and he is holding my hand now. We are very close, and I miss the days and nights I don't see him. I am afraid of what I want and what I know I can't have and what I am committed to not having. I really, really like Mike but what is next and coming? I am scared of my feelings and, at the same time, not feeling.

Oh, LORD, I am so thankful for your providence in my life and for Mike. I leave the future in your hands to lead and guide me in what needs to be done. You come first; your will be done in my life.

June 8, 1996

I vented quite a bit last night. I almost feel like the fool today, but I can't keep the walls up forever. I need to break them down and, if Mike can't handle it, I need to know that now. We have to set clear boundaries now, too. We won't go physically where we can't go emotionally or commitment-wise. I live in confusion, but I live in faith.

June, 12, 1996

Well, I am afraid I am losing Mike, but I'm also afraid of having him. If we both know this isn't going to be serious, how do we keep it going day to day? We went to the opera yesterday and had a great time. Are we still okay or have things changed and are we splitting up now? I hate this!

The feeding tube discussion is going to come up again tomorrow, and I'm not looking forward to it. But, I know I have to take care of Joy first without regard to how it affects Mike. Mike may stay or he may go, but I need to get on top of this weight thing and get healthy, as healthy as that can be.

June 16, 1996

Wow! So much has happened since my last entry. I don't know what to do or write about first. I have scheduled the feeding tube surgery for Friday and know this is the right thing to do. I also told Mike on Thursday. He is the most incredible man I have ever met. He supports and accepts me, cares about me even when I don't care about myself. All this week, I have been concentrating on the Matthew 5 "do not worry" passage, and the week has fit so tightly together that it is incredible how God works through Scripture and through people.

Mike and I also talked about where we're headed. I like being independent, but I don't want to be alone. This phrase summed up totally the way both of us are feeling: it is understood that we will take one day at a time, and, if either one of us comes to the point where we can't handle what is happening, we will talk about it, then. The fact that Mike's and my thoughts run so close is almost scary. He means an awful lot to me. He is sharing with me his faith goals and prayer requests and struggles. We are at a new level in this relationship. We are sharing heartfelt and honest feelings about where we've been, what we struggle with, and what we dream about.

Thank you, Father, for blessing me in ways I could not even imagine. Great is thy faithfulness!

June 20, 1996

Mike is off to Promise Keepers tonight, and I will pray for him this weekend. I have such a respect for this man I can hardly express it. He did see tonight that I was on oxygen. I wonder if he will ask about it later. I have to keep in mind that, if Mike can't handle where I am, then I need to know that. Now Mike knows. We'll see from here.

Mike seems very committed now to moving toward seminary and growing in God. I am very proud of him. It takes a lot to do what he is doing especially knowing from where he has come. He has just rented out an apartment; little, but cute, and it will be a cozy home, a place of rest for him. Plans are in the works for his birthday, and I am thoroughly looking forward to it.

June 25, 1996

Mike is back from PK, and it was a very good experience for him. He is beginning now to put confidence in his abilities and gifts, not just putting himself down because he doesn't have the knowledge his friends have. Mike could really go places. His heart is the largest and most tender I have ever known. For as difficult as his experiences have been, it is a miracle he has overcome and even succeeded far beyond what he has known. I know I love him. I'm not sure in what way, yet, but I love him as much as any other human being I know. When he came home, we talked quite a while about his experience and we stayed close, cuddled and enjoyed each other's company. Sunday night was the first time he put his arm around me.

LORD, I thank you every day for the gift you have brought into my life with Michael's friendship. He has blessed and encouraged me in more ways than he'll ever know. Thank you, LORD for such a precious gift.

June 30, 1996

I am having a down day and doubting myself and my value again. I'm not sure why. Maybe I've been cooped up too long and need to begin getting out again; but my strength seems to be waning. I get tired so easily and this heat is a killer. I am doubting my relationship with Mike, too. The idea of surgery and this feeding tube is also bothering me. I just seem to be worry-focused tonight. I think I need some retreat time. Maybe this weekend.

LORD, hold me tonight.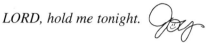

July 18, 1996

Mike is and has been wonderful. He has been such a gift to me that I can't express enough my appreciation for him. His birthday went so well. He was <u>totally</u> *thrown. I'm glad I was able to demonstrate, at least in a small way, how much he has done for me – a thank you. He still amazes me – his care, openness, sensitivity, and giftedness.*

August 10, 1996

I never really finished my last entry because pain and TPN (Total Parental Nutrition) *interrupted it. Sorry, Father, it's been so long since I picked it up again.*

August 18, 1996

Mike and I are doing wonderfully. I think I am falling in love with him. What would be scarier is if he felt the same way. He is searching out the possibilities for ministry, and I am so proud of him. He will do wonderfully, so wonderfully well. I still question where my life is going and what the future holds, but the most I can do is take it one day at a time. My life and future is and always will be God's to lead and direct.

LORD, you have given me so much. I thank you for all that you have given me and led me to become. My birthday is a testament to your power and grace.

August 25, 1996

Here I go, ready or not, on my 27th year of life. I have a feeling that this year will be a telling one. My birthday this year was <u>the most special birthday</u> *I have ever had. Mike made the evening so special. His mom and sister even bought me gifts. I was in awe. Mike took me to supper at Red Lobster and then to the show, "The Cardigans." It was an excellent evening and the show was so cute. We went back to Mike's apartment afterward, and he gave me the rest of my gifts. His mom had made a chocolate chip cake/bars and Mike frosted it with caramel pecan frosting. It had 26 candles and a 27th on it, all lit up. It was beautiful. He gave me a Celine Dion CD and then the shocker. He gave me a pair of gold hoop earrings which had two little gold balls and a pearl on them. They were and are so beautiful. My hands were shaking I was so nervous. Mike truly went above and beyond anything I ever expected or dreamed.*

The card was the last thing I read which made my day. It was a card that said how I have touched his life . . . (words could never express the love that's in my heart for you.) Mike signed it "Love, Michael." This was the first time he has ever signed it that way. When I asked him what love Michael meant, he said it was about a special friend and a special day. I don't know that he meant it in a serious way. But I know what I am feeling and it is beginning to feel more like the "L" word. I do love Mike and I think I know that. What will happen from here, I don't know. Michael Allen Sauers is one special man, and every day that he is in my life is a day I am thankful for.

LORD, you have sustained, encouraged, and uplifted me for 26 years. Here we go on 27.

September 24, 1996

Mike and I are doing well. I feel things getting a little deeper each time we see each other, something I find desirable yet uncomfortable at the same time. I need to be the best I can be and not take Mike for granted – his patience, care and sensitivity. I hope to learn even just a percent of his sensitivity and caring spirit.

LORD, keep me in your care and love. May I learn each day how to become more like Christ.

October 28, 1996

Mike is so wonderful. I know now that I love him and that is scary and exciting as well. I want to tell him so, but am afraid. Will that love be returned? Does it matter? I need to express my feelings – for myself and for him. Whatever happens after that I'll handle. I am so thankful for Mike. My heart is so full. How can I ever fully express all that is in it?

January 20, 1997

Michael is so wonderful. He uplifts me and encourages me so. The big day, Valentine's Day, is coming up and it will be a special one. I hope I can find the courage to tell Mike, "I love you." They seem like such simple words, yet they are so compacted with meaning they are intimidating. But they are words I need to say before I no longer have the chance to say them.

February 3, 1997

How can a page contain all that are in my thoughts? And in what order do you place life, love, and faith? Questions without answers. On February 1, Mike and I verbally expressed our love for one another. It may make life exciting yet scary at the same time. It is going to be difficult to maintain sense and perspective because love adds so many new emotions and feelings to our relationship. I know I love Mike. I have for quite a while now. To know he feels the same is powerful.

Thank you, LORD, for the gift of love and your love toward me. You are first. You are my LORD. I John 4:16.

March 21, 1997

Mike never ceases to amaze me. He shows care in so many ways. On Valentine's Day, he sent me a bear holding a sucker in my NABS mail box. Each day before Valentine's he sent me a Muppet Valentine. Each one was so cute and special. We went to a Baroque dinner theater concert, and the evening was beautiful. The poem I wrote to him was neat. I think he was quite blown away by it. He also gave me a dozen red roses, truly beautiful roses as was he.

I love Michael for all he is and all he does for me and so many others. When I was in the hospital this last time, he brought me a dozen pink sweetheart roses along with a St. Patrick's Day bouquet. I have to say, these hospital stays are getting more difficult each time. I feel myself sad, and I am struggling to maintain a positive outlook. I am tiring quickly of being ill and without energy. Still, the LORD is healing me and restoring my spirit a little more each day.

May 5, 1997

On April 23, Mike gave me a special gift. He gave me words of encouragement – that all I do is having graduated in life, further than most people ever get. He declared this could be our anniversary, as we've not had one up to now. He gave me pearl earrings. They were beautiful, as is he. I am in love with this man, more than I've ever loved any other. He completes me. We are not on the same page yet, but our hearts are speaking the same language. Only time and the leading of the Lord will tell the completion of this story and our lives.

June 4, 1997

My best friend
The man who accepts me as I am
Encourages me in all I do
Challenges me to grow, to risk
Comforts me in struggles and pain
Prays with me, "Thy will be done."
Him I will honor.
Him I will trust.
In his hands I place my heart, my love.

Respectfully lead one another,
       Support one another,
             Hold accountable one another.

May nothing on earth come between the love and commitment to one another.
       Until death brings parting.
           Forever blessed.

Why I am thinking upon these things is ironic. With one best friend I stand on the brink of marital separation – divorce. With another, I stand on a peak at the pinnacle of joy – her wedding day. How do I bridge the two opposites and where do I fall in between? How can the institution of marriage and love span such great extremes; both on a crest, yet such different meanings and outcomes; both will mean new life but in such different significant ways. How and where do I go? I fear. I question. I am sad, confused.

LORD, help me to show grace to these women.

June 18, 1997

I struggle as Mike and I are close. I ask myself if this is right – if he is right for me. I pray about it. I pray for him and for me. I know I love him. I wouldn't ever want to hurt him. I just can't help but think how much more he could do, more he could be if he loved someone other than me. But, the LORD has brought us together for a purpose and for that I will see this through. The LORD'S plan is perfect and he holds my life in his palm.

LORD, I release to you my love, my friends, my family, my life. LORD, your will alone is perfect and holy. May I but try to live according to your will and word. Guide me in this life endeavor.

July 4, 1997

Mike's birthday was a smashing success. He was totally surprised and loved the grill. He deserves so many great gifts. I wrote him a note, as well, which he appreciated, too. Minneapolis went well. I love spending time with Mike. It's so easy, so comfortable. He makes me laugh, makes me feel cared for. He sat in the car with me when I needed to do my treatments. He is such a blessing. Our trip to Omaha didn't go quite as well since we waited so long for a play that would go too late. But it was a good trip, still.

I had so hoped to have had surgery by now. My semester is pretty much gone if I'm called from here on out. But I just long to be healthy, to breathe, run, live as I could. I long to be healthy for Mike, to be able to do things fully, independently, with strength.

August 26, 1997

I am now 27, beginning my 28th year of life. I always wonder what each year will hold. That, only you, O LORD, know.

I am writing with my fun pen and what a birthday I had. Michael outdid himself on this one. I sometimes wonder if he really knows how much this birthday meant to me. I will have to tell him. The "Chicago" concert was great as was my birthday party at Gigglebees.

LORD, you have blessed me so. I can hardly fathom it. I am certainly not deserving of the love, the gifts, the care that you and all your servants have given me. Our grace is abundant in many ways. I just heard the song, "It Is Well with My Soul," and it is so true. My soul rests in your hands. I worry about the future, about my relationship with Mike. I know you hold it all in your hands, and it is well in my soul. Amen

I love Michael and he says he loves me, as well. LORD, I thank you for him. I pray we would follow in your will and grace. He is my strength and the love of my life right now. My greatest fear would be to lose him, but I am obedient to you as my LORD and Father, first and foremost.

LORD, hear my prayers, give me peace. Search me, know me, and lead me in the way everlasting. I love you LORD.

August 28, 1997

Michael is an amazing man. We talk about my life and future, how undetermined it is. I live with uncertainty. I have no choice. Mike does, yet he chooses to come beside me, to enter into that uncertain world. What an amazing man to choose such a thing when so many opportunities and possibilities are available to him to do otherwise. I'm not sure I could ever bear to make the choice of a life or career without him. He means so much to me. I love him so. LORD, lead and guide both of us in the choices we'll make each tomorrow.

September 22, 1997

I miss Michael. I am also getting more tired and about ready for the hospital. So much has happened since last writing. It's incredible. Diana was killed. Rich Mullins was killed, both in car accidents not wearing seat belts. What a tragedy. At the same time, Franklin Graham came to SF and had a total crowd of 62,000. What a joy and answer to prayer! Amazing the dichotomy of the world and its events.

LORD, you are the great comforter and caretaker. Hold us tonight in your strength and grace.

September 28, 1997

Mike and I have had some close talks this week and these talks seem to add more confusion than resolve it. Michael had three resolutions he wanted to accomplish:

> *1) Establishing friendships*
> *2) Financial control*
> *3) No alcohol for 6-12 months*

All these before dating or becoming involved with anyone again. He has accomplished all but the last one. It is this one he struggles with the most both behaviorally and spiritually. He said he does well, then falls back and it makes him so angry and defeated. But he has come so far to this place. He has an in-depth knowledge of himself – who he is and what he wants. He just can't seem to follow through with the discipline needed to break the bad habits and begin to establish new ones.

I am beginning to understand a bit more about myself and my needs in this relationship. I'm not sure what it will all end up being, but I know I need to pray about it. I can be patient and supportive right now. Mike needs to be encouraged and to know he is valuable even though he may not feel worthy of it himself.

There will come a time though if Mike chooses not to grow or can't grow, that I will need to make a choice to stay or to go. I am not prepared to make that choice right now. I am prepared to make a commitment to try to help Mike and support Mike toward growing. It may be too much to hope that we would eventually begin to grow together but for now, my faith rests in the LORD and his work both in my and Mike's life.

LORD, prompt me to be one who is growing, learning, and following you. I can only be responsible for myself.

This was Joy's last journal entry until June 6, 1998. The 1997 fall semester was a difficult one. She was in the hospital in September and again in November. She was using oxygen twenty-four/seven. It was quite evident that her health was rapidly deteriorating. The students at the seminary recognized it. She finally succumbed to using a handicapped sticker for her car. Just walking down the stairs at church was exhausting for Joy. Upon reaching the bottom, she would go into an office, lie on the floor, and lay prone until she could get air.

It was amazing what she could accomplish under those health limitations. She worked with the children's Sunday school and puppet ministry at Trinity. She continued to take semester classes toward the Master of Divinity degree. Joy had the ability to conserve and expend her energy to fit the need of the moment. At home, I listened to her as she took medications and treatments. I was concerned. Silently, I wondered why she was discharged from the hospital in November. She obviously was still very ill. Elaine Schaeffer, a dear friend and book buyer at Crossroads where I worked, asked one day early in December how Joy was doing. I told Elaine that Joy needed lungs and soon. She could not survive many months beyond Christmas. Yet Joy plodded on, silently, trusting her LORD.

2-3- A different kind of entry

Prayer   healing   Love   o   Worship

Salvation   Faith   glory   to God

grace

Hebrew   Scripture   Prayer   Petition

Love   יהוה   YHWH   Why? I need?

I adore? I praise

awesome my   God   God

Abba

He's mine

Love   unconditional   1 John 4   no fear

I am His

Prayer

Commitment   Hope   Prayer

XIV. THE CRISIS OF LIFE

From Risk to Trust – A Faith Journey

September 26, 1995

I have dedicated this year to "risking" my comfort zone. I need to take the time and patience to hear God. I also need to be willing to submit to His voice. I need to take hold of God's power and follow through in these things. LORD, give me the hope, the patience, and the strength to do so.

Today in chapel Tom Johnson presented a message on allowing God and praising God for turning our weaknesses into His glory. Paul had afflictions and pain and asked that it be removed, but God gave Paul what he needed, not wanted. Paul rejoiced that God could use his weakness for God. "For in weakness my strength is made perfect."

I am also working through my issues with CF this year. Where does it fit into my life, my story, and my ministry? This message spoke directly to me. Through me and my illness <u>God</u> is glorified, and I must discover how that reality plays itself out.

Since 1988, Joy had lived with the knowledge and a potential need of a lung transplant. Joy had suffered a pneumothorax (collapsed lung) in Israel. For three weeks, she lay critically ill in the Jerusalem Hadassah Hospital and an additional two more weeks in the Sioux Falls hospital. Recovery had been difficult and, at one point, was questionable. Dr. LaFaire introduced the double lung transplant option to Joy. Joy wisely and flatly turned it down.

Fast forward seven years to 1995. The subject of a lung transplant surfaced as a current reality. Joy could no longer ignore the inevitable. The deterioration of her health during the last few years urged its consideration. It was risky elective surgery. Of all transplant surgeries, the lung transplant is the most serious and difficult. It is a last ditch effort over-shadowing all other treatment options. Joy knew this better even than her parents. One evening, as I was helping her with the percussion of the respiratory therapy, I told her she could have lungs from my body. Little did I know.

Joy interrupted, "Mom!"

"Yes?"

"I have to have a total lung transplant. They're all infected. New lungs from a partial transplant would receive infections from my present lungs."

"Oh!" Now I am sad.

The seven years following 1988, Joy had put forth her best efforts to reclaim health or at least to stop the progression of the disease. But it was a losing battle. Typical of cystic fibrosis, improvement of health is a misnomer. It doesn't get any better, period! Amazingly, during those years of declining health, Joy had completed five years of college, taught two semesters of supervised education – one in history and another in math, and worked four years in part time employment to pay college tuition. Presently, Joy was enrolled at North American Baptist Seminary to complete the MDiv (Master of Divinity) degree.

October 26, 1995

> *I am still thinking about lung transplant, but question whether that is a road I want to travel down. I know my Father is here and listening, but I need a human touch, too. I feel lonely though I'm not alone. I could really use a best friend; someone who I could tell everything and he/she would still accept me, hold me, and help me decide what to do.*
>
> *LORD, hold me tightly. Give me peace and patience to await your will.*

Joy was totally cognizant of lung transplant risks, but her options were dwindling. She had experienced four hospitalizations within the last year with further loss of lung function. The oxygen tank now accompanied her everywhere. Each breath she took was a reminder that her time was shrinking. She was battling an unknown factor which she described as a "faith journey." It was the fear of losing total control. During and after lung surgery, she would basically surrender her life and body to medical professionals. Joy had always been involved in medical decisions. She had managed her care in cooperation with doctors and nurses. This surgery implied total submission as life and death decisions would be made by others, many of whom would not know her. In reality, that trust was one she would give to God. He would be in control.

January 14, 1996

> *Transplant – this is going to be purely a faith journey. I can't deny the fact that a full life is something I long for, but God, you know that. I am confident about this journey. LORD, you have brought me to this point and only you now can and will receive the glory in this weakness of mine.*

Other hurdles were facing Joy. She had to seek approval from state and federal insurance. In addition, the hospital financial offices required $10,000 reserve cash for back-up to insurance. Trinity Baptist Church, students and faculty at the seminary, the Downtown Lions Club, as well as individuals, began a fund for contributions toward the needed cash. Joy would have to go through extensive medical tests as a prelude to acceptance on the waiting list. All these steps took months to achieve. Joy learned that she had a rare blood type. By virtue of Joy's physique, her lung cavity was very small. The donor lungs would have to match Joy's size and blood type.

In December 1996, Joy was approved for placement on the waiting list. The long list of requirements was finally met. She was given a beeper to carry with her at all times for notification if and when donor lungs became available.

It was a stressful time for our family. But we continued our normal schedule – Joy, her seminary classes, I with my full time work at Crossroads, also directing the sanctuary and children's choirs at Trinity, and Gordon with his teaching. Jami had graduated from college and was living and working in Nashville, Tennessee.

<u>January 23, 1996</u>

I set the appointment for January 29, 9:00 am at University of Minnesota Medical Center. I talked to Chuck Asche and his wife, Pat, today about the transplant. I work with them at New Hope Church where he is pastor, so now they know the entire story. From here on out it gets messy. I don't know how I'll explain to Mike this facet of my life.

<u>January 29, 1996</u>

Well, the process is underway for meeting the criteria for transplant approval. I can't decide if I'm excited, worried, or just scared spitless. But, I need to do this because of all that I have been given and been blessed with. It's time I act on those gifts and trust in God's grace and will for the outcome.

Now, how do I tell people, the seminary, church, Mike? Oh boy, the difficult part is yet to come. The testing process and anticipation, too, is almost just as difficult. Pray, pray, pray. Joy

<u>February 26, 1996</u>

I found out more about transplant. I have type B blood, a more difficult one. There is only one other person on that list. This is getting so close, so fast. It's almost overwhelming. The major testing is done now. It's just a matter of gathering and submitting all the data.

Am I ready for this? I don't know. I do know I'm tired of meds, allergies, wheezing, weakness. I'm tired of being sick and tired. My list of plans and desires is so long, yet my strength and energies are so short. I don't know how to tell folks. This will change and I know that. I'm just not sure how and at what time it is appropriate to do so. I'm going to need everyone and all the prayers and support to get through this struggle.

Father, hold and embrace me in your healing care.

<u>March 4, 1996</u>

I really like Mike. There will come a time when I should tell him about transplant, and I don't look forward to that time. I'm really going to need him with me. But if he can't be, I'll understand that too.

I am so scared. Some days I am overwhelmed. Other times I feel totally carefree. I need a Psalm tonight. I need to be held too. LORD, embrace me in your love and care. Gently guide me where you would have me be.

Joy

<u>June 8, 1996</u>

I talked to Mike about my fears and frustration involved in surgery. I take everyone with me, and I hate it. It is so unfair. I vented quite a bit last night. I almost feel like the fool today, but I can't keep the walls up forever. I need to break them down and if Mike can't handle it, I need to know that now. I live in confusion, but I live in faith.

LORD, I've missed my time with you. I need to recover my devotional and spiritual life. I need renewal and your love and comfort to restore me when I am confused and struggling.

Thank you, LORD for presence in my life now and in many different ways. LORD, you need to be first. *Joy*

I was not aware that Joy regretted that loved ones would have to accompany her on this difficult medical journey. I not only would accompany her, but willingly take her place. It was, indeed, not fair that she was suffering and living a journey of pain.

<u>May 13, 1996</u>

I have a long road ahead, a long medical road. Is it fair to take everyone with me? Do I have a choice? What is fair? I seem to have more questions than answers tonight. I am confident of a few things however. I love my LORD and my life. I have been very blessed and gifted. One day at a time, and I'll move ahead in faith. *Joy*

<u>May 19, 1996</u>

It isn't fair that I have to take those who I love and care about with me through this medical nightmare. It is so unfair.

This week I will go again to Minneapolis/St. Paul to meet more doctors and get more information on what is going on. LORD, I'm taking you with me, and I'm really gonna need you.

Mike, I feel like I have known you forever, like I could be with you forever, but forever may be too long for me.

I put my life and my future in your hands, in your outstretched arm, LORD.

Joy was seriously underweight. She had attempted various means to put on weight but had been unsuccessful. The transplant team added another requirement – an implanted feeding tube. It would necessitate surgery not anticipated by Joy. The surgeons would not okay Joy for the lung transplant until this final step was met. It was a difficult time as Joy wrote in her journal.

May 28, 1996

LORD, I need you in these next few weeks and months. I need weight and sustained health, something I know you can provide. I believe I am making the correct decision with transplant, but I take one day at a time.

The earth is filled with your love, O LORD. Teach me thy ways.

June 10, 1996

Well, I got a kick in the butt today that knocked me out of my pity party attitude, and I totally deserved it, too. I was at the surgeon's office, (Dr. K), being kind of a know-it-all and defiant. When he had finished explaining things, he talked about the girl next door. He said her situation makes my life look like a piece of cake. I arrogantly said, "I don't know about that," and he got very quiet. I said, "Well, there are worse." He said, "Just trust me on this. If this little girl even lives to be twenty five years old, it will be a miracle."

Then it hit me – what an idiot I have been. To think that I know anything or have the market cornered on pain and difficulties is a completely selfish, vain idea. I don't ever remember being so ashamed of myself. I have been crying for the rest of the day.

God has so so blessed me, yet I worry about now and about tomorrow. I am so vain to worry without truly appreciating what I have been given, the experiences I've had, the gifts, all that God has blessed me with. What right do I have to complain or to wallow in self-pity?

As I drove home, I listened to Bruce Carroll's new disc. The 9th song ("I Want to Trust You") about allowing and trusting God with your life hit me. I know I have a faithful and loving God who has blessed me beyond anything I have deserved. It is my job to be thankful and faithful with those gifts.

Dr. K. may have said the words, but the conviction is of the Holy Spirit. Do something about it, Joy.

June 12, 1996

LORD, I need to be in your will and do what is important to you and for me. Let me not forget that there are others who are as sick, live as difficult lives, or struggle as much; many struggle more. Give me a sense of peace. I need your love and comfort, LORD.

June 20, 1996

Feeding tube is scheduled for July 1. Just want to be done with it! LORD, I love you <u>so</u> much.

II Corinthians 12:9 ". . .My grace is sufficient for you, for my power is made perfect in weakness."

June 25, 1996

When I spoke with Beth on Friday (University of Minnesota Medical Center), she told me the gal ahead of me on the list just received new lungs on Thursday morning. I am the only one left now on that list which utterly scares me. There was always an element of safety when she was ahead of me. Now I'm next. I'm not sure I'm ready for this.

Am I ready to give up my disease on the hope that I will survive getting new lungs? Am I ready to die? Yes and no. Father, I need your peace and assurance.

July 18, 1996

It has been a while since I have written because of a combination of absences due to surgery (feeding tube) and neglect. Surgery took more than I thought it would out of me. It was a success and failure at the same time. My lungs sailed through with flying colors. My stomach, though, shut down. It has been almost three weeks since surgery, and am still trying to recover. My weight is up and down, but hardly <u>up</u> where it should be. Patience in illness is not my strong point. I want to be better, stronger, weigh more yesterday. I just need to be patient and consistent and it will come.

<u>August 18, 1996</u>

Well, I seem to have a habit of not finishing things lately. My life is going very well though a little slow at times. I am ready for school. The stomach tube is now working at a rate of 85 ml/hr., something that truly is a miracle. No one thought it would work at all.

Time with God

Joy used her journal to visit and converse with God. She could share with Him her deepest thoughts, loves and devotion. She trusted Him with her fears, her questions, concerns, and fears. She knew He would understand. The journal became her friend. She could be honest with this friend and work through the realities of her life and her future. We, as readers of her intimate heart musings, have been granted insight into Joy's life, a life that had incredible meaning, despite pain and suffering. With God's help, her amazing life accomplished more during her thirty years than most of us will accomplish in a lifetime of seventy to eighty. God surely must have taken pleasure in making her an example of His power. We have been blessed and challenged by her voice and her witness. We also can identify with her feelings and loves.

We have had access to Joy's relationship with God through her prayer life recorded in her journal entries. But there is another prayer journal that I have chosen not to print. It is prayer lists in the back pages of her journal. Her conversations with God went beyond the daily entries. Joy noted dates when prayers were asked, when answered. She wrote two-three word comments on many of the requests. You would probably be surprised to know who was on that list. Those requests and loves were between her and God. Just believe you were prayed for and that she loved you deeply.

<u>January 20, 1997</u>

Life is complex, yet it isn't. It's about who you are and in whom you are. I am just a servant, a vessel and I reside. My heart and will reside in Him. In class today we talked of the power of Christ – his humanness and what that means. It hit me. We so often try to define and theologize Christ's divinity, we forget what he taught and modeled for us just in his humanness.

Christ, minister to me through your humanness and example.
Come beside me as I struggle.
Hold my hand in my fear and impatience.
Love always,
Abba's child.

1996 Resolutions

* *Develop prayer and devotional life.*
* *Trust and take comfort in God's leading in my life.*
* *Envision big – dream God's dreams and prepare to be moved!*
* *Action – you have the faith. Now go, do something about it. Share your faith story.*
* *Pray, Pray, Pray!*
* *Evangelize, don't just talk about. Build relationships and share Christ.*
* *Encourage, empower, and model. Mentor, don't dictate.*
* *Do not worry. Trust in God's leading, timing, and providence.*
* *God be glorified, for it is by His power only that I survive and succeed.*

January 14, 1996

At my levels, I should be dead, disabled, or at least on a ventilator, but LORD, you carry me each day. You have cared for me, healed me, and blessed me far beyond anything I could ever ask. This is why I can feel confident in your hands, LORD.

Joy could depend on God to enter into her life, to walk beside her whether through dark valleys or beside still waters. She would know His peace into that uncertain future she faced and where no one could go with her but God. He would deliver her either to Himself or to a ministry within His created world.

October 18, 1996

As I reflect on past journal entries God's faithfulness is written boldly across every page. I will struggle and I will be successful. God's hand in my life is a constant. Today I defined my intimacy with God as "a struggle yet a life-sustaining relationship; a journey with fear but a journey of faith."

Thank you, LORD, for being faithful to me. I will never outgrow my need for you nor will I ever know enough to need to stop learning about you.

Abba, Daddy, I love you.

March 20, 1996

PRAYER *– Six independently lonesome letters which together form a powerful word. This community has had a lot to pray about this year: births, deaths, surgeries, illness, accidents, accomplishments, cancer, praises, and problems.*

There is a peace that comes through prayer alone. Personally I want to thank the community for its commitment to pray together and alone. Not that we may honor each other or the body, but that <u>God is honored and works for good for those who love Him</u>.

April 25, 1996

It has been far too long since I have journaled and been deliberate about it. I've had quiet time but not necessarily quality time.

ACTS

<u>A</u>cknowledge – Father, you are so great and your love and presence is so steadfast. You are always there to hold me and comfort me as I need you. Thank you.

<u>C</u>onfession – I have not been faithful in my prayer time or devotions. I've missed my time with you. I have had a bad attitude about some things and apathy about others.

<u>T</u>hanks – LORD, I thank you for your healing touch and for the blessings you have given me. I thank you for great friends and family. There are many things I am thankful for, yet why do I feel like crying?

<u>S</u>upplication – Daddy, I am going to need your guidance this year – transplant, president, scheduling, church, Mike. It all seems overwhelming at times. Abba, give me the wisdom and strength I'm going to need each day and throughout the year to survive, thrive, and stay healthy. Give me patience and a sense of contentment with doing my best.

All glory be to you, for without your spirit and presence, I would be nothing. Father, I do not lack for materials, but I do, so need, your presence and strength in my life, something you have been faithful to give me.

Overwhelmed tonight: Father, give me peace and rest. Touch me ever so gently with your grace and healing presence.

May 13, 1996

I am at Terrace Park. It's been too long since I have written and taken quality time for quiet time. Things are going well, maybe that's the problem. Yet, there is something missing. Your touch is what I need today. Already I have seen it: children playing, ducks gliding side by side across the lake, sparrows chirping and flittering in the trees, and a squirrel gathering food then returning to his tree home.

Some days I feel very lonely and unworthy, others energized and ready to take on the world. Right now I am of the former.

<u>August 18, 1996</u>

LORD, you have given me so much. I thank you for all that you have given me and led me to become. My birthday is a testament to your power and grace.

<u>Prayer of Examination:</u>

+ *I am God's child and my life rests in His caring, sheltering hands.*
+ *God has gifted me for ministry. I trust His leading in my life.*
+ *I have been blessed far beyond what I could ever deserve.*
+ *Grace alone has redeemed me, made me His child.*
− *I need to uphold others. I can be critical.*
− *I need to learn humility. Be still, take time to know God.*
− *Concentrate on simple joys. I can be arrogant and overbearing.*
− *I am a sinner like all humanity.*

The truth − I am a sinner. God has saved me and blessed me. What an almighty God I serve.

\<u>November 28, 1996</u>

Thanksgiving and WOW! There is so much to write, to tell, to be thankful for. I am <u>so</u> thankful for Mike. I am thankful too to a seminary community who supports, prays, and visits me when I need it most. My heart is so full, how can I ever fully express all that is in it. It is the holiday season now. How beautiful it is!

I love you LORD.
  I worship you.
    My soul rejoices.
      LORD, You are great and worthy of glory.

I spoke in chapel one week ago and it went <u>so</u> well. I can't say I remember everything, but I know the Spirit of the LORD was in that place. After this weekend I will be on call for new lungs and a new life − exciting yet scary.

<u>March 21, 1997</u>

Sadness struck me again. Three people have died in this last month. One, his father writes journal entries about his grief and feelings. These bring my own grief to the surface, and I cry with those who are mourning.

Where do I fit in this scheme called life, this world created by a God who knows and loves everything in it? I don't know. I pray for those who suffer, mourn, and struggle. LORD, uphold us all.

<u>March 28, 1997</u> – *Easter – Happy Resurrection Day!*

What a holiday! To celebrate the grace that Christ's triumph over death has brought is incredible. Mom got me the book <u>Grace Awakening</u> for Easter, and I think I will like it. I am seeing so much grace around me; it is beautiful, so precious and delicate: two newborn babies, friends, the love of Michael, smiles that twinkle and gleam of care I have seen in so many people's faces.

LORD, I cannot even begin to describe the awe and gratitude I feel for you, for my family, friends, and community. Your grace covers me, and the people of your grace inspire and encourage me.

<u>May 25, 1997</u>

I'm reading <u>Pursuit of Holiness.</u> I have been re-awakened to my need to be holy. I need to strive more consciously for that process of transformation and obedience in my daily life.

<u>September 22, 1997</u>

<u>Gratitude Journal</u>: *It will be a must, and I'll put it on the computer as I use it every day. How often am I thankful and how often do I pray with joy and in praise? I need to do more!*

<u>Gratitude</u>: *I grew up in a family where unconditional love was practiced.*
                I am mentally healthy and gifted intellectually.
                I have a best friend, Michael, who listens and affirms my human worth.

What don't you hear?

to those you around you
- voices of wisdom

Listen
ature

Prayer Prayer
Prayer, Prayer, Prayer
Prayer, Prayer,
Never ceasing

Intercessory thoughts

S i l e n c e

To God's
Still small voice

Be still
not busy!

To the
Sights

S o u n d S

God points
out to you.

To Scripture that
it may fill you up
teach you, comfort you.

TRANSPLANT
12-22-97

XV. GOD'S TIMING

July 4, 1997

My Strength and My Redeemer

I wait, LORD, in your time
For the right lungs,
Right donor,
Right time.
LORD, you alone hold the future.
You hold me safely,
Securely in your hand.
I rely on you,
Gain strength from you
Live my life for you.

Joy

December 22, 1997

The phone range about 1:50 a.m. Gordon reached to pick it up. I interrupted, "Let Joy get it." She had been up past 1:00 writing a paper for one of her seminary classes and had just lain down. Joy's voice echoed upstairs as we lay quietly in anticipation. We heard animated conversation peppered with laughter and humor to whomever it was. We did not know.

In a little while, Joy called upstairs, "They have lungs for me."

I jumped spontaneously out of bed and started running in abandon with no clear thought as to what to do first. Gordon just lay quietly in bed. I grabbed a suitcase and randomly threw clothes. In a panic, I insisted that Gordon start packing. Joy said to stay off the phone because they would call back in a few minutes to give specific instructions. The wheels were in motion.

After the second phone call, Joy got on the computer, wrote a quick sentence or two, then punched the address file she had previously compiled. She called our pastor. We were in the car at 3:00 a.m., on the way to Business Aviation which would fly us by hospital ambulance to St. Paul, Minnesota. It was a cold, but mild winter, unlike the previous bitter winter of '96. The air ambulance flight to St. Paul was only forty minutes. Joy chatted nonstop until we landed. She was excited. She had waited a year and seventeen days for donor lungs.

We walked directly from the plane to an ambulance that was waiting for us. We drove from the twin city of St. Paul to the University Medical Center in

Minneapolis with lights flashing and rolling, the siren blaring. (The hospital currently is known as Fairview University Hospital.) By 4:00 a.m., we were in the emergency room. The medical staff started prepping Joy for surgery, but seemed in no particular hurry. By this time, we were apprehensive. Finally at 6:30, the nurses arrived to rush Joy away into the surgical room. We quickly said our good byes, then *swoosh*, she was gone. I wanted to have a prayer, but was near tears and could not speak. We were led to the waiting room.

We began to receive phone calls, one from Chuck Hiatt, president of the seminary. I appreciated that he prayed for Joy over the phone. Visitors began to arrive. LaRae and Jeff Mills appeared with a dozen beautiful red roses. Others arrived: Harvey and Carol Mehlhaff, Peter Fehr. Mike Lerud came with chocolate candy. Don and Robin Voigt and Andy Owzarek were with us. Mike Sauers, Joy's special friend, drove up early in the day.

Between 10:00 and 11:00, the social worker and nurse came to the surgical waiting room to reassure us that the surgery was going well. They mentioned that Dr. B, the transplant surgeon and head of the team, had quick and gifted hands. Later in the afternoon, they returned to let us know that all was proceeding on schedule. They cautioned that Joy would not be responsive when we saw her after surgery, due to residual anesthesia.

Randy Stewart drove from Sioux Falls. Joy and Randy had been friendly rivals in Old Testament and Hebrew classes, always competing to make the best grades. He would tease Joy that she could use lungs of a sheep as a substitute donor. He brought her a stuffed lamb that presently stays on a bed in our home. When he approached us about 6:00 p.m., he announced that Joy was already in her room. He had been there first and saw her! We quickly made our way upstairs.

Amazingly, Joy was alert for a brief time after the operation. Mike joined us beside her bed. Mike and Joy repeatedly told each other of their love. She asked for a pad and pencil. She wanted to communicate, but her hands shook. We saw scribbles for words and sentences up and down the pad. The surgery certainly did not slow her mind.

The nurses in the surgical ICU were amazing. During that first night, I sat quietly alone with Joy for a period of time. I could not help but observe the nurse who was assigned specifically to Joy. She carefully and continuously monitored and adjusted the numerous machines and tubes that surrounded Joy. There was not an orifice left that did not feed Joy, breathe for her, remove fluid from the lungs, pump drugs into her body, excrete waste matter, replace blood, etc. All this flurry of technology was replacing life functions and keeping Joy alive. I took from my wallet a picture of Joy and attached it to the bulletin board. I wanted the medical staff to know that this was not just a body controlled by machines –

it was a life, a sweetheart, a daughter, a sister, a friend to so many, and most certainly, a child of God – gifted and committed to serving Him.

Late in the evening, Gordon, Mike and I found the family waiting room and claimed sleeping space for ourselves. We had no idea that we would be there for days. Joy had originally assured us that recovery after surgery would be two to three weeks, with another month of follow up as an outpatient. We had no reason to believe otherwise.

Dr. Peter Fehr, a former missionary with the NAB conference and a practicing physician in the Twin Cities, arrived the next day. He and his wife, Doris, offered us a place to stay. After several days of sleeping on vinyl couches at the hospital, we took them up on their offer. We were treated like family, we felt at home without interfering with their schedule, and we had wonderful visits. Evenings in their home became our place of rest and recovery. We were very thankful for their generous hospitality.

New Lungs – New Hope

God's timing is impeccable. In the fall of 1997, Joy worked with the Sunday school children at our church. I served as director of the Sanctuary Choir during Mark Landry's sabbatical absence. I also worked with the children's music preparing both choirs for the Christmas program which was scheduled for December 21.

On that Sunday morning in December, Joy had a Christmas craft prepared for the children. She distributed it among the classes and coordinated their activities prior to the program. This is our most anticipated event of the year as the entire worship service was dedicated to the celebration of Jesus' birthday. It had occurred to me during the fall and up to the time of the program, that if we got that most important phone call, all plans for this special presentation would be off. But God came through in perfect timing. The celebration of His Son's birthday is important to Him also. As I have written, that call came during the early Monday morning hours, December 22. Yes, LORD! Our hopes soared.

The more than twelve-hour surgery occurred on Monday morning. Tuesday, the 23rd, was rather uneventful, but for one conversation with Dr. R. She was a fellow at the university hospital and had been a participant in the surgery. This evening she was in Joy's room.

Joy asked for her clipboard. She scribbled a question for Dr. R. "Lungs?"
Dr. R asked, "New lungs?"
Joy shook her head "No."
"Old lungs?"
Joy nodded "Yes."

Dr. R hesitated, then approached the bed as Joy anticipated her answer. "They were terrible, just terrible! You basically had only small balloons from which to breathe." She demonstrated by holding her thumb and index finger together.

The brief conversation with Dr. R was a hint of what was to come. Even though I knew that Joy's lungs had deteriorated and she was failing fast, I believed that new lungs would be a promise of new life and a promising future. I lived with that hope and belief knowing that God had perfectly designed the course of events. He had taken care of Joy in past crises. It never occurred to me that Joy could suffer incredible reversals in the days to follow.

Jami was scheduled to fly home from Nashville on Wednesday, December 24. Since Joy seemed to be recovering without complications and we were without a car, I arranged to return to Sioux Falls with Mike Sauers, to check on our dog, Yent'l, meet Jami at her scheduled arrival, and drive back to the hospital in time for Christmas day. On the 24th Jami and I attended the traditional Christmas Eve service at Trinity which was very meaningful to both of us. I packed additional clothes, gifts, and also my CD player with several of Joy's favorite CDs. Joy loved her music. As a last minute thought, I went by Crossroads and checked out Billy Graham's new book, *Just As I Am*. Although this book, seemingly, had no relevance to our present circumstances, it became uniquely meaningful to me during the uncertain days that followed.

XVI. God Is In Control

The Crash

Thursday, December 25

Jami slept during the entire trip to Minneapolis. When we arrived at the hospital, Gordon informed me that, on Wednesday, Joy had gagged and coughed up blood from the surgical site. He was glad I was not there to witness it. All seemed to be better today. The nurses had Joy sitting in a special chair the afternoon of Christmas Day. I was a little nervous that they had her out of the bed so soon. We opened some of her gifts, but Joy seemed listless with hardly a response, watching with little expression. That was not like Joy. She suddenly gagged. The nurse and assistants rushed in and moved her back into the bed.

The doctor told us that they would sedate Joy heavily which would completely immobilize her – a drug coma. The spiraling down began.

Friday, December 26

Joy continued to decline. Gordon, Jami, and I stayed all night at the hospital. Dr. B arrived to tell us that Joy was experiencing rejection. Large doses of Prednisone would be administered. He assured us that within twenty-four to forty-eight hours, we would see a dramatic turnaround. Gordon, Jami, and I stayed another night at the hospital.

Saturday, December 27

Mike recalls that week: "Joy and I had spent several years dating, hanging out in the hospital, talking about our lives and God's grace. After the transplant surgery, I returned to Sioux Falls with the confidence that Joy was healing. The life-changing moment shocked me to my knees when Gordon called. 'Joy is not doing well. The doctor does not think she is going to make it.' I fell to my knees in my living room bursting into tears. I returned to Minneapolis.

"I had a couple of rough days and nights and was emotionally wiped out. I was sitting in the patient waiting area. I saw Gordon walk through the door after he and Joyce had a meeting with the doctor. He shared that Joy was not going to make it because of the infection. I remember the embrace from Gordon and the tears flowing from both of us.

"I prepared myself to go to her and say good bye. I don't recall everything I said or prayed during the time I had alone with Joy in her ICU room. I expressed to God my heartfelt love for Joy. 'If there is any way I can show my love for her, I will do it with all my heart and soul.' I knew, for me, it was to ask Joy to marry me, if God would allow. Sometimes one is amazed how God works in our lives.

We are surprised when the miracle does happen. I truly believe it was through the work of God's hand that day that Joy and I were able to share our time together as husband and wife."

<u>Sunday, December 28</u>

On Sunday morning, I called our pastor, Daryl Dachtler, and requested they pray for Joy during the worship service. Jill Callison, from the Argus Leader newspaper, quoted Daryl in an article published December 25, 1998: "We had prayer chains. We had small groups, home Bible studies. We utilized Sunday mornings. We had some very pointed prayer times, praying through the evening, and some occasions where people would just say, 'We're going to do this.' It wasn't organized as much as people saying, 'This is what we're going to do.'"

Joy's SATS continued to decline. (SATS is the abbreviation for "oxygen saturation" – the measurement of how much hemoglobin has oxygen attached. It should be above ninety-two percent. In most healthy people, it measures above ninety-five percent.) I watched apprehensively all day looking at the monitors for a sign that Joy was responding. I did not like what I saw. And we waited.

Where was Dr. B?

Jami flew back to Nashville on Sunday afternoon as scheduled in her itinerary. She had just arrived home when I called and urged her to fly back to Minneapolis. She booked a return flight and got to the hospital at 3:00 a.m. Jami's friend, Ann Lawrence Werth, was gracious enough to meet her flight and bring her to the hospital. The three of us, Mike, Gordon and I, were in the ICU hospital waiting room spread out among the couches, sleeping in our coats and clothes with thin cotton blankets when Jami and Ann walked in.

Monday night Joy was not responding as the doctor had promised. What could be happening? In the evening, Dr. B reported to us that Joy's condition was critical. He stated very directly that nothing more could be done and dropped it at that. Silence fell among the group of doctors and nurses surrounding us. Dr. R broke the silence and suggested an angiogram be performed. Dr. B agreed. Preparations got underway. It took about thirty minutes for the medical technicians and nurses to unhook all the machines and tubes. I timed them. The SATS continued to slowly slide as 100 percent oxygen was administered.

Karen, the hospital chaplain, introduced herself to us. We followed the gurney as the technicians wheeled Joy into the elevator to go downstairs to x-ray. As we turned the corner near x-ray, unexpectedly Robin and Don Voigt, close friends of Joy's, appeared. We all gathered in the small waiting room. There were seven of us – Karen, Mike Sauers, Jami, the Voigts, and Gordon and I. We were quiet as we sat together. Karen began the conversation and asked if there was a specific

Bible passage that was especially meaningful at this time. I answered that the Lazarus event had been in my thoughts. Jesus wept and wept bitterly when he witnessed the grief of his dear friends. I knew that Jesus identified with our pain. Even though Lazarus had been dead for three days and buried, Jesus command-ed him to get up and walk. After that dramatic miracle, the Bible did not tell the rest of Lazarus' story.

God also was not finished with Joy's life. He had called her into ministry, she responded, and was equipping herself for ministry. She was devoted in her pur-suit of a ministry and in fact had already proven herself. Her life would bring honor to His name. How could He not raise her up? We then held hands, the seven of us, and we prayed. It was a moment of assurance, and we knew and experienced the presence of God. God will have the last word, not Dr. B.

Joy was wheeled from x-ray and the doctors reported to us that they found only one small clot in her lungs. She was returned to her room. Tubes and mon-itors were reattached. Then we saw it. Joy's SATS were up ninety-eight – nine-ty-nine percent. Amazing!! Dr. R commented, "I don't know what happened. Maybe she just likes to travel. We should take her on more road trips." Well, not exactly. There was no medical explanation, but we had an answer. God showed His hand, and Joy was His child. He grieved with us, and He would raise her up in His own time.

The doctors changed their tune. The 750 mg. of Prednisone was cancelled. The battle was now with infections. Gordon was in Joy's room when the physi-cians, along with nurses and pharmacists, gathered to discuss options for her medications. They were standing in a half circle. Gordon recalls vividly their conversation. Their discussion was not in total agreement. The doctors wanted to aggressively fight the infection with five powerful drugs. The pharmacists argued that was not possible. Those medications in combination would destroy Joy's kidneys. Finally after pros and cons were laid out, Dr. T stated, "We have no choice. We have to push the envelope." It was decided.

Dr. B explained to us that during surgery Joy's cavities had been washed with antibiotics to kill organisms from previous infections. It achieved results. However, the bugs retreated, colonized, and then reorganized. They returned with a vengeance and were resistant to all antibiotics, but two. The bugs were eating new tissue surrounding the anastomosis (the surgical site where the new lungs were attached to Joy's body). This weakened the sutures so that the new lungs were unattached. The first bronchoscopy confirmed that fact. As the camera at the end of the scope projected on the screen, the sutures hung down loosely within the airway. Joy's new lungs were literally hanging by a thread. A war was being waged within that small body, and it appeared to be a losing battle. But God would not allow Satan to claim the body of His child.

A Parent's Voice

I often spoke some comment or information regarding Joy's care or her needs. One day, I mentioned to the nurse that during Joy's hospitalization in Jerusalem (1988), an open pressure sore developed on her tail bone. The nurse took note of that information and within a day, a new bed was brought into the room. This was no ordinary bed. It was operated totally by computer. The mattress was supported by air baffles. It constantly hummed as it moved continuously up and down and around appearing like waves with Joy's body floating as a ship upon the sea. The foot, head, and sides could be raised, lowered, or tilted by computer technology located at the foot of the bed. All of this technology was especially useful when the respiratory therapists regularly performed treatments. With the push of various buttons, the bed would roar up its engines, begin to vibrate and tilt Joy into up, down, and side positions as she breathed an aerosol mist through a mask.

Dr. B had given strong instructions about an instrument used during respiratory treatments. The therapist was not to go beyond a specific area of Joy's trachea. It was used as a precursor to trigger a cough since Joy was in an induced drug coma and could not cough on her own. I observed one particular therapist several times forcing the use of this instrument and meeting resistance from Joy. I was not happy with his actions. I mentioned it to Gordon and he also had noticed how rough this man was. I reported this to Dr. B as sensitively as possible. The next day, a big and bold-lettered sign in black ink stuck to the wall above Joy's bed instructing the therapist <u>not</u> to force that tool beyond a certain point of Joy's trachea. The message was received.

On another occasion, a new male nurse was assigned to Joy. He appeared nervous and unsure of himself. He would scratch his arm, then his head – a no, no! I observed other questionable actions. Immaculate practices were absolutely imperative. Even as parents, we were instructed in hand washing techniques. Face masks were a part of our required attire. The next day, I mentioned to one of the staff what I had observed from this male nurse. He did not return to care for Joy.

I guess that Dr. B learned I was *observing* too much. One day, we met him as he was leaving the hospital. Gordon asked about Joy. Dr. B was not at all hopeful. He told us in very matter of fact words it was unlikely that she would pull through – not what we wanted to hear. Then, as an off-hand remark, he said he would hate to bar us from her room. Oh, yeah! I thought. Just try to keep me out of my daughter's room. I was not one to interfere with her care, but I was not going to sit silently when questionable actions occurred. I will be more cautious, but I will not close my eyes. Joy had always been very vocal and decisive in her medical care. All of her doctors had learned, at one time or another (usually the hard way), to respect her voice. She could not speak for herself now. I will speak for her. At any rate, I became more discreet in voicing my concerns.

We Wait

Isaiah 40:31 – . . . they that wait upon the LORD shall renew their strength; they shall mount up with wings as eagles; they shall run, and not be weary; and they shall walk, and not faint. (KJV)

This scripture again grabbed our attention. It is the one we adopted as our family "life line" years ago when we faced insurmountable challenges caring for the health needs of Joy. Forgetting all of those routines of past years, we were now at the mercy of a different scenario. Our high control, legalistic schedule, and teamwork would make no difference at this point. We were no longer in control. We were in a *waiting* mode. We had to release Joy as she lay balanced between life and death – only machines keeping her body functioning. The end result of the controversial drug combinations was yet to be revealed. All the while, Joy lay on the bed of constantly moving air baffles, surrounded by machines that monitored her oxygen, vital signs, drugs, and pumped fluids in and out of her fragile body.

God Is in Control

One evening I went into Joy's hospital room to sit with her. I was frustrated and losing hope. All of the machines surrounding her bed, under her bed, beside her bed, over her bed were humming, gurgling, and beeping. The music from the CD player placed on the window sill competed with the sounds coming from the machines. The lights were low. The green glare of lighted monitors and computer screens cast a shadow over Joy's lifeless body. I stood up, stepped to her bedside, and watched her body as it moved rhythmically under the air baffles. Joy looked ghastly. Her entire body was swollen; so swollen her eye lids could not close. The nurse put blinders over her eyes so that dust would not settle on her corneas. Her arms were puffy with skin stretched by the edema. I was alarmed that we could abuse my precious daughter in the name of health and medicine.

I had a few questions for God. In desperation I asked, "What are we doing here? Are we really prolonging life or simply postponing death?" It was not a rhetorical question. I wanted an answer! I hovered at her bedside, just me, the machines, and my Joy. At that very moment from the distant CD blared the chorus of Twila Paris' song, "God Is in Control." I was stunned. "Okay, God. I hear You. You have spoken. You are in control; not these machines, not the medical professionals; not me. I will trust in You. Yes! You are God and I trust You. Thank you."

<u>Wednesday, December 31</u>:

Joy was basically unchanged – no better, no worse. I interpreted that as progress, knowing that God was in control. I was also reading through Billy Graham's book, *Just As I Am*. I was greatly comforted by the story of his evangelistic team and how God provided for their needs. Answered prayer was amazingly evident beyond all their expectations. I thought, if God can do that for Billy Graham and his team, He can surely answer our prayers for Joy. Joy was not a "Billy Graham" but she had been called by God. She was gifted. She was totally committed to using all of her gifts and energy for God's purposes. I was convinced that God would use her as He had specifically called her. He would not allow her life to be wasted.

On that Wednesday, Gordon and I were in the waiting room of the surgical ICU wing. The nurse came to get us, saying that Dr. L wanted to speak with us. Dr. L was the cardiovascular surgeon who had repaired Joy's ventricular septal defect (abnormal opening in the heart). He was standing outside the door of Joy's room accompanied by two other doctors. Dr. L, a wonderful Christian, said that Joy is seriously ill. We know that, so what's this all about? He repeated that statement several times with no further comments. The two behind Dr. L refused to make eye contact. They stared totally at the floor the entire time. Finally I got it. He's trying to tell me that Joy is going to die. No! No! No! I wanted to scream. I cannot accept that. My whole body rebelled. I looked at Dr. L and shook my head "no" in defiant body language. I turned and walked away refusing to listen to him any more. Doesn't he realize that God is in control?

I returned to the waiting room in tears. Pretty soon, Marget, the social worker, came into the room. No one else was present. We talked. I told her about Joy, her life, her personality, her gifts. I wish she could know Joy, then she would realize how special Joy was. She was no ordinary person. She had every reason to live. She would make this world a better place. She would spend her life reaching out to all who needed care, hope, love, Jesus. We cannot deny the world this beautiful person.

I saw Dr. L later in the afternoon. He stopped me. He reached out and took my hands and spoke gently to me. He explained how difficult it is to speak to families. Just last week he had to inform a family of eight with small children that their father would not live. Such a sad time for all. I completely understood his dilemma. I thanked him for his sensitivity. I truly appreciated his words. I held no grievances against him.

It was hard for everyone involved. It was interesting that one of the men who helped to transport Joy to various areas of tests and surgeries commented to me that this young lady, Joy, was special. He said she was different than others he transported. I feel that most of the medical staff who worked with Joy also picked up on her spirit. God was in her being even as she lay in that coma. Angels were hovering above and around Joy. It reminds me of Joy's journal entry a year earlier.

January 2, 1997

> *I am about to embark on a year of a lifetime to put it mildly. It could be the last year of my life or the beginning of a completely new one. I am scared, excited, apprehensive and impatient all at once. I know I don't take on this year alone or weak, for I am taking on this year with my LORD walking beside me, sometimes even carrying me. I take, too, in my heart the passages of Scripture that mean so much to me,* **Isaiah 30:18-21.** *Looking again at my theme passage I know and feel God's graciousness and grace. He will say to the left or to the right. I need to be listening and obedient. LORD, guide me that I may see and feel your touch, your grace in my life this year.*
> – Donna Joy Harris

18 Yet the LORD longs to be gracious to you; He rises to show you compassion. For the LORD is a God of justice. Blessed are all who wait for him!

19 O people of Zion, who live in Jerusalem, you will weep no more. How gracious he will be when you cry for help! As soon as he hears, he will answer you.

20 Although the Lord gives you the bread of adversity and the water of affliction, your teachers will be hidden no more; with your own eyes you will see them.

21 Whether you turn to the right or to the left, your ears will hear a voice behind you, saying, "This is the way; walk in it"

That night I called Barbara Hagan. I knew they would be celebrating the beginning of a new year with their annual Bunko party. I asked Barbie to have a time of prayer at their New Year's party, an odd request for such a happy social occasion. We were desperate. We called everyone we could think of – our missionary friends, family, churches. Pray, pray, pray.

We decided to spend the night at the hospital. At 2:00 a.m. I walked down to Joy's room. Her SATS had jumped to ninety eight percent – God's reassurance to us. He knows, He cares, He loves, He answers. Thank you!

The next day, January 1, Joy's temperature spiked at 103+. During the days of January 2-5, her temperature slowly came down, a little each day – no changes, some progress, no declines. The war being waged within her tiny body was fierce. The bad bugs were in retreat and we waited.

A week later, a bronchial scope assessment indicated that healing was evident, and we were encouraged. On January 8, oxygen from the ventilator was reduced to fifty percent and Joy's SATS remained in the mid-nineties. For the first time, Dr. B said Joy had a chance. This was the first significant progress, and God gets the credit. Thank you.

On January 14, the nurses informed me they will reduce the drugs that have kept Joy in a coma and allow her to wake up. I told the nurses I will sleep in the hospital waiting room. Please come get me when Joy awakes. At about 2:00 a.m. the nurse came to the room and said Joy was awake. I quickly made my way down the hall. Joy was indeed awake. I talked to her. Tears rolled down from the corners of her eyes, onto her cheeks, into her hair. I rubbed her arms and blotted her tears. My precious daughter was awake and alive.

During the previous five days, adjustments had been made with the Nitrous Oxide reducing it in small increments. By January 15, the Nitrous Oxide was turned off and Joy's SATS stayed up. However, Joy began to exhibit extreme agitation. She felt she was suffocating. I stayed the night again at the hospital.

On Friday, January 16, a CT scan was performed and two air pockets were found in the upper lungs. (A CT scan is the abbreviation for computerized tomography – a visual picture of tissue density to determine if there is the presence of abnormal density.) On Saturday, two chest tubes were reinserted in the right and left upper lungs. Joy told me when she came back that she could feel when they inserted the tubes. I was not sure she actually felt the pain or just the pressure. At any rate, she was more comfortable with the release of pressure from the air pockets. But she still exhibited anxiety.

On Sunday, January 18, Mike Sauers arrived. I was so glad to see him for Joy's sake. She was in and out of alertness. They placed her in a chair for an hour. One memory will forever be etched in my mind. The hospital allowed trained dogs to come on the floor of the hospital with their owners as a means of social therapy for patients. Joy had always had a dog and was thrilled to see one come along-side her as she was sitting up. I wish I'd had a camera. Joy stretched herself as far as possible from the chair, stuck out her neck and puckered her lips as the dog stretched his neck to meet her. The dog and Joy did not actually kiss, but came really close – one of the most precious moments I can remember during a time of such anxiety and stress.

Mike was with Joy until 2:30 Monday afternoon. Joy had been in a chair for an hour and fifteen minutes. After Mike left, she became very agitated. Finally, in the evening she calmed down and slept. The ventilator was turned down to four breaths with volume support.

Joy was still adjusting even though it had been a week since awakened from the drug coma. On January 20, she remained calm, but not alert. She was probably recovering from exhaustion, anxiety, and efforts to breathe. She sat in the chair for more than an hour. The doctors reported that they will put in a trach, probably Friday. With a trach Joy would have more independence of movement. By evening, Joy again exhibited restlessness, so the staff increased the breaths from the ventilator. It was a constant two steps forward, one step back, inching up little by little.

During the following two days, January 21-22, we encountered an issue for which I was unprepared. Joy experienced what the nurses referred to as ICU psychosis. When one has been medicated for so long, they become disoriented and cannot distinguish between day and night. Reality becomes distorted, and they experience episodes of fear and delusions. Joy had no eye contact and exhibited a wild look in her eyes. She flailed her arms and legs and constantly thrashed from side to side. I continually spoke to her calmly while gently rubbing her arms and face. She would calm down for a minute or two then start all over again. I stood at Joy's bed side all day throughout these cycles of rest and agitation. It was difficult, very difficult. Thankfully, Joy was more alert the second day with brief eye contact and diminished agitation. The doctors reported that Joy will be transferred from surgical ICU to pulmonary ICU next week and her care taken over by the pulmonologists.

By January 23, the doctors were able to perform the tracheotomy, and it went well. Joy awoke from the anesthesia with a smile! It was beautiful. She smiled for the first time since the transplant. The 24th was Joy's best day ever. Joy smiled, and smiled, and continued to smile. She was alert all day. She talked constantly but no sound. I can't lip read. It was really cute. The next day was Sunday. How I wished to worship. Oh, Heavenly Father – You are so good, so wonderful. How can I express my love and gratitude? I will worship You here in my own little sanctuary.

The Waiting Room by Gordon

"I became the student in the waiting room at Fairview University Hospital. Joyce was an inspiration to me throughout the month. I stayed beside her all but one night in the month. That evening, I traveled to Sioux Falls to teach all day for a doctoral seminar. Hugh Litchfield finished the week-long seminar for me. We were blessed by friends at North American Baptist Seminary and all around the world.

"We lived in the waiting room of the hospital with wonderful families that waited also while their loved ones struggled between life and death. When we spent the night, we would forage for pillows and blankets, then claim couch space. As in Israel, an ICU waiting room knows no strangers, religious differences, or cultural distinctions. We loved the families that lived there and learned much from that community. We rejoiced with them when their loved ones showed some recovery. We shared their pain when hope was exhausted."

Jill Callison from the Argus Leader interviewed Dr. Jordan Dunitz, Joy's primary pulmonologist in Minneapolis. She quoted Dr. Dunitz in an article about Joy on December 25, 1998, one year after the transplant surgery. He said:

> *Joy's in a very exclusive club. A transplant that goes perfectly is out of the hospital in seven days. Ten to fourteen days I would say is typical. Joy is on the very, very end of the spectrum. She had as rough a recovery as anyone I've seen who's survived. It's a tremendous endeavor for the patient to undergo transplantation. Even though it's potentially life-saving surgery, it is elective. The patient chooses to do it and takes a significant risk.*

XVII. New Challenges

An Agenda of Adjustments

Now, with the successful tracheotomy, Dr. B explained that it was time for Joy to move to the pulmonary ICU wing. The pulmonologists would take over as primary physicians. The doctors visited Joy to introduce themselves. They reassured her that the care would be excellent. Joy accepted their reassurances, but still realized that the changes would be formidable – new nurses, different room, changes in routine. I shared Joy's feelings, but made no comments. It was an inevitable move and an indication of Joy's improvement.

The move was made, and we met the nurse assigned to Joy. She was very friendly and professional. We did not have to wait long before the first of many trials. Joy needed a new porta cath, a direct line into a major vein into which medications are administered. Her present porta cath was about two years old and had been her second one on the right side of her shoulder. It required a surgical procedure, but routine. During the operation, I waited for Joy in her room. The wait grew longer than anticipated. I nervously paced the floor. And still I waited. Finally, the rumble of the bed coming down the hall announced that Joy was back. The doctors were beside the bed as it was pushed into position. All the tubes were attached. Dr. R reported that they were unable to access the artery on the right side due to a sharp turn in its course. Repeated attempts were made with no success. They decided to abort the procedure and continue on the left side. This attempt was successful. The doctor explained that Joy would have a large bruised area over her right shoulder and chest.

There was more to follow. This new porta cath needed to be accessed that night for administration of medications. I watched as the nurse explained how she would access the cath. She said she had done many of these in the past, especially for kidney patients. When finished, she hooked up the IV tubing for the meds to be pumped into the artery. The nurse returned to the computer to chart. Immediately, Joy was in pain. The expression on her face indicated that she was, indeed, hurting. I told the nurse. The nurse checked the porta cath, then returned to the computer. Joy still complained of pain. It was quite obvious. I again mentioned it to the nurse. Nothing. I spoke to the nurse again. Finally Joy settled down and seemed comfortable. As I think back, pain medicine was probably combined with the IV drug, which would account for Joy's rest. At the time, I thought the porta cath was now working properly and the problem, whatever it was, had resolved itself. The IV drug was eventually finished with no further pain indicators.

The following night, twenty-four hours later, the porta cath was accessed for Joy to receive a blood transfusion. We had a different nurse this evening. When the blood started moving into the porta cath, Joy made facial contortions indicating acute pain, more severe than the previous evening. I spoke to the nurse. She did not seem to think there was a problem. Joy was writhing in pain. I walked out of the room. Dr. R was in the hall with other staff in conversation. I interrupted her, "Joy is in pain." She said there was medication to numb that pain. I went back into the room. No relief for Joy. In a stern voice I said to the nurse, "Please get the doctor in here, immediately. Joy is in a lot of pain." This time, she was out of her chair, left the room, and brought the doctor back with her. Dr. R checked the porta cath. The drug from the previous night had never been completed. The needle had not penetrated the porta cath, and the drug had collected in Joy's chest tissue. Joy's chest was swollen and, when pushed, bounced like jello. The doctor took a syringe and began extracting excess fluid.

Joy and I were not happy, to say the least. Joy asked if that nurse would receive supervisory action. The doctor said, "Absolutely." This whole episode reinforces the necessity of someone to be available to follow a patient's care and needs, especially if the patient cannot speak for him/herself. I recently perused the physician reports from the hospital and saw no mention of this incident. Maybe it was reported in the nurse's notes.

Joy experienced a continuous series of good days followed by hard days. Joy's care was quite complex and progress was slow. I was with Joy from morning to night; only leaving occasionally for a bite to eat. In the evening, I would leave between 9:00-10:00 p.m. and drive to the home of Marge and Harold Lang, pastor in St. Paul.

When Doris and Peter Fehr left for an extended vacation in January, the Langs opened their home to us. The Fehr's were very apologetic, but their plans had been set for months. We were just thankful for their hospitality. The Langs gave us a key to their home. We could come and go at any time of the day or night. We had access to the washer and dryer, which was truly a blessing. Many nights, I slept on a cot beside Joy. I absolutely loved taking care of Joy. I did not miss my employment at Crossroads Book and Music. Russ and Cheryl Borchardt, owners, were amazingly generous to give me extended leave not knowing when I would return.

Desperate for Air

On a Sunday morning in February, Mike and I arrived earlier than usual – before 8:00 a.m. I walked into Joy's room and saw Joy lying prone; her entire body jerking as she gasped for air. I looked at her SATS, and they were dropping dangerously low. The nurse sat at the computer with her back to Joy. I urgently spoke to her. "Joy's SATS are down and she can't breathe."

The nurse said "I know" while continuing to chart. "The doctor has been called. I told her to relax and take deep breaths."

I began to rub Joy's feet, hoping she could relax. All the while, her SATS continued to slide. I stepped out of Joy's room and, in desperation, asked Mike to call Trinity. "Ask the church to start praying." I stepped back into Joy's room and spoke to the nurse again, all the more frantic. Joy was fighting for air, and the SATS continued their downward slide. "This has never happened before, I said." Not a word from the nurse as she charted.

At that point, Joy lifted her index finger. "This has happened before?" I asked. She nodded, yes. I could not stand it any longer. I walked into the hall again and anxiously looked up and down. Still there was no sign of x-ray. Then Dr. T turned the corner at the end of the hallway, walking casually with a slow gait. "Doctor, please come," I called. Immediately he picked up his pace. When he walked into the room, he burst out loudly to the nurse, "Get pulmonary, STAT. Call x-ray STAT. Call Dr. R. Call etc., etc. STAT, STAT, STAT.

Suddenly, we saw action from this nurse. In no time at all, the room was full of people. The x-ray technicians pushed the lumbering machine into the room to administer the bronc. When I last looked at the SATS, they were fifty-seven! (The doctors never wanted SATS to drop below 90.) The machine was plugged in, the trachea opened, the tubing inserted, and Joy's lungs washed. Plugs of mucus loosened and were suctioned. Joy immediately began to breathe without effort. I walked out to tell Mike, who had waited anxiously outside the curtained door. "Joy is breathing easy now. I suppose we should call Trinity."

This same scenario occurred two more times that week. It so happened that Dr. T was there each time. He finally commented to the other pulmonologists, "Do I have to sit outside Joy's room and wait for more of these episodes?" The doctors came back to inform Joy that they needed to perform a bronc, consider laser surgery, and possibly put stents into Joy's lungs. The bronchoscopy confirmed that scar tissue was growing, inhibiting air flow, and closing the airways. They would first go into the lungs and laser the scar tissue. A stent would then be implanted. There were three stent procedures – one at a time, not all at once, and of course performed under anesthesia. Photographs were taken of each lung. Dr. Dunitz showed me the photos. Her lungs were clean. He was proud of those pictures. I am sure that Joy's entire medical history will be one for the records.

The bronchoscopy results were critical in Joy's care. They were numerous and fascinating to watch. Tubing was inserted through the trachea and gently guided into the lungs. A very small camera at the tip of the tubing projected the entire procedure on a monitor. It not only allowed the doctors to view the process, but also assess the situation and determine follow-up procedure. Joy watched while lying very still. Video and still photos kept permanent records.

Hope Beyond Medicine

Joy had grown up with pet dogs – in the Philippines, in Texas, and, of course, Sioux Falls. They were her love and constant companions. Our policy was, no more than one pet at a time. At the present, we had a Pomeranian dog, Yent'l. For the past several years, Joy had asked for her own dog. Her request was for a specific breed – a toy Yorkshire terrier, like Randy and Susan Reese's dogs. My response was always "No. We have one dog in our house and that's all we can handle." There was no negotiation regarding this issue.

During the month of January, when Joy was still in the drug induced coma, I was ready to concede. A new puppy would be the miracle medicine to inspire Joy on her road to recovery. I mentioned my plan to Gordon. He was not too excited, but I was determined to try anything. At the appropriate time, when needed, I would tell her we will get her puppy when she comes home.

It was mid-January during which time Joy was adjusting to pulmonary ICU. She had endured several challenges and there was more yet to come. Joy was discouraged and having a particularly rough day. Now is the time. "Joy, when you get home I will get you your Yorkie, but we have to get home. They won't let us keep a dog here." That was all Joy needed. Her spirit and attitude were immediately reversed. Her thoughts became fixated on the puppy that would be hers. She asked me to call Susan Reese and get the name of the breeder, which I did. Then call the breeder, which I did.

"What shall I name the puppy?" This became her focus. She studied and thought. As soon as I arrived each morning – "What shall I name my puppy?"

One morning as I popped in, Joy commented before a good morning greeting, "I know what I'm going to name my puppy."

"What?"

"Picaboo!" Joy had been watching the winter Olympics, and Picaboo Street had just won the gold medal for down hill skiing. This was January. It would be the end of June before Joy got her Picaboo. But she never lost hope.

R and R for Mom and Joy

On weekends, Gordon and Mike drove north to Minneapolis. Mike would stay with Joy on Saturday, and Gordon and I would take in a movie or go out to eat. Sunday afternoon, Mike would have to return to Sioux Falls where he was employed as a social worker for the SD Department of Social Services. It was hard for Joy to see Mike leave without her. She loved this man, and every week-end she had to say good-bye. She invariably went into a depression. It was hard to watch. I understood her feelings, but by Monday morning, she was ready to get back to the hospital routine. She had to get home for that puppy and her "man."

The physical therapist had been working with Joy since the second day after the transplant surgery. By March, the therapist introduced walking. First it was hanging her legs off the bed, then standing. Next Joy walked with assistance from her room to the nurses' station. The distance was gradually increased until she could walk to the end of the hall. It was slow progress, but Joy gained in strength and eventually began to walk independently. This took place later in her rehabilitation as the therapist carefully charted her progress.

I could tell that Joy was feeling better because she began to complain about her hair. It was long and straggly. Joy mentioned her frustration with her hair when Randy and Sara Stewart came to the hospital to visit. Randy said he could take care of that. He whipped out his scissors, put a sheet around her, and hair started to fly, literally. The nurses didn't know what to think. We had fun and Joy was okay.

After being in ICU for four months, Joy was finally moved to a private room. As she began to gain strength and the weather warmed, I would push her in the wheelchair down the hall, into the elevator, to the first floor, and outside to the patio. She enjoyed the fresh air and sunshine. After so many weeks and months confined to a small room in the hospital, Joy felt closed in. She loved the out-door spaces with the fresh breezes, the warm sunshine, the return of the birds, and colorful greenery. She also got to greet people as I wheeled her down the hallways. Joy was a people person. She loved the parks in Sioux Falls and often used her journal, as we have shared, to write thoughtful meditations inspired by the peaceful surroundings.

Do you remember the story of Joy and the dog almost kissing soon after she awoke from the drug coma? Now in a private room, trained dogs would come to the hospital once a week for patient visits. One evening, unexpectedly, Joy exclaimed, "Mom, I just saw a dog go by!" I went out to the hall and sure enough there were three dogs walking the halls. One was a miniature pinscher. I invited them into our room, and we had a great time. Joy also got acquainted with some of the other patients and their friends through this social therapy.

I did not realize how closed-in a hospital could feel until the weekend of Easter. Now that Joy was in a private room, I felt I could leave her for a day or two. She begged me not to go home, but I so wanted to worship. As I drove along the interstate and saw the beautiful world of open fields and sky, I felt alive and refreshed. It was a renewal of faith and thankfulness. That evening, I received a phone call from Joy's nurse. She said that Joy was crying and emotionally down. She would have to undergo another very sensitive operative procedure. She asked if I could return. Of course I would. The next morning, I was in my car moving down the road. Perhaps Joy was aware that all was not well with her body when she asked me to stay.

A fourth stent was needed, this time in the lower right lobe. Dr. Dunitz cautioned that it was a small area and that the procedure would be difficult, but he needed to attempt it. After surgery, Dr. Dunitz reported that the surgery was not entirely successful. That specific lung was very congested and the airway tight. The stent could not fully enter the airway. That lung would continue to be troublesome for the remainder of Joy's life.

Joy's next challenge was to wean herself from the ventilator. This would be tricky. The longer one is dependent on a ventilator, the more difficult it is to breathe independently. A ventilator not only pumps oxygen, but keeps the lungs rising and falling. After so long, the brain does not speak to those muscles and the muscles atrophy. Joy was determined. In no time at all, she was off that ventilator. She accomplished this on her own. She was after that puppy. She also had a young man whom she loved very much. Mike stood by her during the surgery and entire hospitalization. He faithfully drove from Sioux Falls to Minneapolis every weekend except one to be with her.

Comic Relief

Joy was still in pulmonary ICU when doctor's realized that scar tissue from the lung transplant was growing and inhibiting her breathing. The doctors informed her that they would need to remove that scar tissue by laser surgery. Dr. Dunitz came to Joy's room along with some nurses who would give assistance and technicians who would transport. Dr. D explained to Joy that she would have to sign a permission form for this procedure releasing any litigation should there be complications. He also said that the surgery had to be performed under anesthesia because it was a very delicate operation. He did not want her to move. He said that if she moved ever so slightly, he might miss, the laser could shift and damage her lungs – perhaps even blow a hole in her lungs, and that would not be good (his exact words).

Joy listened and then asked for her clipboard. (She was still on the ventilator and could not speak audibly.) She wrote on her clipboard and handed it to Dr. D He studied her hand writing, but could not decipher the words. She wrote again. Dr. D stared at it for a few moments, then looked at Joy. "How many times have I screwed up?" Joy nodded vigorously. The entire room burst into laughter. Dr. D was stumped. He finally stammered, "Personally or professionally?" Boisterous laughter again. This is one of my favorite memories of that auspicious time in the hospital.

A different incident – Marget, the social worker, came to Joy's room to inquire about her insurance. I had visited previously with the financial office. It was very confusing, and I was not informed regarding all the legal implications of her coverage. Joy had always been directly involved in the mountains of red tape. Marget and I were standing at the end of Joy's bed with our backs to Joy. Marget began questioning me about the details of Joy's insurance. I was answering as best I could, but actually with little knowledge. All of a sudden, we jumped in shock as our ears were plummeted with loud metal banging upon metal. Joy got our immediate attention. She had picked up an eating utensil and whammed it against the bed railing several times. We looked as her mouth was moving furiously with no sounds. Neither of us were lip readers, but we soon became aware that Joy was communicating. From then on Joy was in charge!

Discharge

In May, Maria came to Joy's room to introduce herself to us as the outpatient nurse who would be working with Joy in the future to prepare her for discharge. There was now an end in sight, but Joy was still in the recovery stage. We longed for home but would be patient until that day arrived. On Thursday, May 21, 1998, exactly five months to the day of Joy's transplant surgery, I wheeled Joy to the CF clinic which was located in a different wing of the hospital. Joy met with Dr. Dunitz and Maria. I also was present in the examining room. As the appointment drew to a close, the subject of discharge was not discussed. That was fine with me because I did not want to rush it. We prepared to leave, and then Maria announced that Joy needed to be discharged. It was time. Dunitz did not protest. Perhaps he thought Joy was getting close for a discharge date but was acting on the side of caution because her health was still precarious and risky. Or perhaps the financial office was putting pressure on Maria to initiate a discharge. At any rate the decision was made, and Maria began the myriad details for discharge.

Swiftly, arrangements were made for us to stay at the Kidney House, a home away from home for transplant patients and their families. Cost was minimal. Maria hurriedly got pharmacy involved. Also the Hennepin County Home Health Co-op was contacted to meet us at the Kidney House to instruct us in all of the drug therapy. It was a rushed up affair. We took with us twenty-seven prescriptive medicines.

Friday morning before our discharge, Dr. B, Joy's transplant surgeon, came into Joy's hospital room. Joy had just walked into the bathroom to take her shower. I asked her to come out. Dr. B, who is more than six feet tall (Joy is less than five feet), put his arm around Joy and gave her a hug. He said, "You are an amazing woman." Those kind words do not often come out of that man with the gifted hands. He is all business but also has a big heart. Yes, she is amazing, I totally agreed. But we have an even more amazing, yes, **awesome** God.

We moved to the Kidney House that afternoon only a short distance from the hospital. Joy and I were glad to be "free." I planned a good breakfast for Joy. On

Saturday morning, I made my way down the hall to the large community kitchen and got involved with the preparation. I was frying the bacon when I suddenly became aware that I had left Joy alone for too long. I had a very disturbed feeling. I ran down to the room. Joy was sitting on the bed with the trach in her hand, blood coming from the opening. Joy looked at me with fear in her eyes. "Joy, should I call the ambulance?" She nodded. I ran back to the kitchen where the phone hung on the wall and dialed 911. Joy was soon on her way to the emergency room of the hospital. I jumped into the car, drove to the hospital emergency room, and joined Joy.

For all that rush and panic, we sat in the emergency room for several hours. Dr. Dunitz was in the middle of his clinic appointments and could not interrupt the schedule. Eventually, Joy was moved to a room – back to the same old routine for another week. Maria realized the discharge was premature and said that will be the last weekend discharge she will ever attempt again. Our next discharge went much smoother.

And One More Time

June, 1998

Joy's first request, upon her second discharge, was to go to church. We got up early enough, but, after completing all of our medical routines and therapy, we were going to be late. Never mind, we still would go. We arrived twenty minutes late and sat in one of the back pews. The choir sang. I looked at Joy and tears were running down her cheeks. It had been almost six months since she had been to church.

During the month of June, we lived at the Kidney House so that Joy could keep follow-up appointments with the physical therapist and the CF Clinic. Once those daily appointments were out of the way, Joy and I *did* the town. She could not wait to explore Minneapolis. Every day, I lifted the wheelchair into the trunk of the car. Joy sat in the front seat with the map in her lap. As navigator, she charted our course for her chosen exciting adventure. When we arrived at our destination, I opened the trunk, took out the wheelchair, plopped Joy into the chair, and off we went. We had such fun. Joy thrived outside the walls of the hospital. After being confined to a hospital room and bed for so long, Joy was not going to let any opportunity pass. It was the best medicine possible.

I prepared chicken and sausage gumbo over rice for our first full meal. Wow! Joy ate with gusto. She could not get enough. Her favorite meal request from then on was gumbo. Oh, how I took joy in her feast.

While Joy received outpatient care during June, she requested we drive home on the weekend of Michelle and Aaron Kilbourn's wedding. Randy Stewart drove his big RV to Minneapolis and escorted us the 4 1/2 hours to Sioux Falls. When we walked into our house, Gordon had the table beautifully set and supper waiting. We sat down to a family meal. Joy was home. She slept in her own bed. We were family. Jami was living in Nashville and we missed her. After the wedding, we returned to Minneapolis for the completion of Joy's medical follow-up. Joy spoke from her heart.

June 7, 1998

> *Mike and I attended Aaron and Michelle's wedding tonight. It brings up so many wishes and dreams I have. I don't know what the future holds, but I know I love Michael. He has stood by me, loved me, encouraged and supported me these last five months in a way that I could have never imagined or asked of anyone. He is so special and we have both grown from this.*
>
> *LORD, I again leave this in your hands. You know my heart and you know all my days written in the Book of Life. I trust you, love you, and only want to serve you. Bless this servant. May I bring only glory to Your Name.*

December 1997

June 1998

XVIII. GOING HOME

<u>May, 1998</u>
For the "Sem Times"

Count It All Joy

*On the eve of leaving the hospital here in Minneapolis, I am packing up many
cards, thoughts, prayers and memories. It has been a long road. Many days
the road has been unpaved, rocky, and quite painful. But, as I move out and
on, the impact you have made on both me and my family's lives these last few
months is unmistakable. Your prayers, thoughts, cards and visits have carried me and nudged me along, healing me in ways beyond physical medicine.
God has so graciously and humbly healed me.*

*It is hard to find the exact words and expressions that capture the gratitude
I feel for all of you at NABS and for your churches who have prayed for me.
Know that you and your prayers made a difference. I look forward to telling
you more when I return. I love you all and look forward to seeing you back
in Sioux Falls the weekend of graduation. Joy Harris*

<u>June 27, 1998: Going home!!</u>

The car packed to the hilt! Joy asked if we could stop by the training camp of
the Vikings and just watch. We had a nice afternoon. As it started to cool down,
we continued our journey. Approaching our home in Sioux Falls, we pulled into
our driveway, and there stood the sign Dan Leininger had painted back in
December. It had been updated from "JOY we love you, to the Harris family" to
"Joy we love you. **Welcome Home!**" It had stood there in the yard the entire six
months waiting for the healing daughter to come home, touched by God to bless
our lives.

Joy could now walk free unburdened by the oxygen tank she once carried over
her shoulder. Her face was no longer crisscrossed by canula tubes that wrapped
over her chest, up her neck, around her ears, across her face, and into her nose.
She brought home with her a state of the art vest attached to a machine that would
do the work of percussion therapy as Joy breathed the aerosol medicine from a
nebulizer. This machine had three different vibration settings – low, medium, and
high. It was less labor intensive, took less time, with greater effectiveness. The
trach was still a part of her life, but she was able to conceal it so that one would
hardly notice. It was removed about six months after her discharge. Joy spent the
summer regaining her strength through an exercise regime in rehab. And of
course, she could now spend time with her best friend and love of her life, Mike.

June 6, 1998
A New Beatitude: Blessed are those who have needs, for I will fulfill them.

The Gift of Dependence

God gave me a gift – that gift, for most of my life, has been dependence. In a nation and culture that applauds and promotes independence, this may seem like an odd concept – that dependence could be a blessing. Now, I wouldn't have it any other way.

I used to think I was independent and accomplished life on my own. I was missing God's hand. Independence is an illusion because none of us is fully in control in this world. God is. Once I acknowledged this, I saw God's blessings all around me.

Dependence showed me how strong a family can be. It has unveiled love that is unconditional. Through dependence on God, I have been moved by prayer – both my own and the prayers of others – some of whom I have never met. Dependence has brought me peace and joy in situations that would have otherwise taken me over the edge. God fills and has fulfilled me so graciously.

My life is not my own, but God's. I am but a vessel or an instrument through which God will reveal himself to others. My task is to reflect His message of grace and love to all.

Thank You

August 31, 1998

Every day I want to say thank you to a family who graciously gave the gift of life to another in the midst of watching their small child die in a hospital bed.

I just finished one of the most difficult pieces of text I have ever had to write. It didn't have any big words, deep theological concepts, or exegetical arguments. It was a thank you note, a note of thanks for a special gift. How do you address a grieving family thanking them for their gift of life? What words are adequate enough to both express feelings of joy in new life and yet sorrow over the loss of such a precious young life?

Then I thought about grace. How does one truly describe it? None of us is worthy of it – the physical death of one man exchanged for the eternal death of mankind? Do I remember to thank God daily for His graciousness or maybe I take that for granted. So tonight, I write a thank you, in the best words humanly possible, to my LORD, my salvation. Even more important, I will choose to live out and share the gift of grace with all who will listen.

Thank you YHWH.

The Gift of Life

June 6, 1998

A little boy, a healthy eight year old child, died and gave life to a very sick woman, a woman who would have died without that precious gift of life. How like salvation and Christ is this? A pure, whole man willingly gave the gift of life when he hung on the cross for all humanity, as ill and sinful as we are.

Just as the LORD would want everyone to know, acknowledge and receive this gift of life, so I wish all unhealthy could experience this new life. In the same way, I will work to ensure that people understand Christ's gift of life – that it is eternal, that it offers hope, that it is an ultimate love gift and unconditional!

Grace / Graciousness
What a Theme and What a Blessing

Though I haven't always been responsive or alert to God's presence in times of trouble, I have, in the last few years, become more fully aware of God's work in my life. In times of struggle, which has been a constant in my life, I have found God teaching me, blessing me, and supporting me through His community, the church.

What have God and others whom God has brought into my life taught me? I have learned what humility really means. There is no reason on this earth why I should still be alive. I would be fooling myself to believe anything I have done or not done has led to my survival, success, or abundant life. Humility, I believe, means taking the focus off myself. Focus belongs on God. He is the one in whom I will boast, not in myself because nothing I do is of myself alone. I alone am weak but in my weakness, His strength is perfect. I can only do what I do and be who I am through Christ and His power. So I have learned to fully depend on Him, on His strength. I put all my faith, my life, and my future in His hands. God truly deserves all honor for who and where I am today. What grace!

Because of my own struggles and the struggles of others, I have a unique understanding of human frailty and pain. Through all the difficulties I have seen and experienced, God has revealed to me many blessings. I watched many people come and go throughout my hospital stay. Some of those who I met in the hospital left whole. Some did not. So, though I have struggled greatly with chronic illness, I recognize I have been richly blessed. I can walk. I have my hearing. I am alive. God has truly blessed me. What graciousness!

Finally, even in difficulties, I have not been alone. God has comforted me, cared for me, and loved me personally and through His people – through my family and the family of God. God's love has been so powerful in my life. He has given me a loving, caring family and the loving support of brothers and sisters in Christ. The world longs for that kind of love. I know. I wouldn't trade it for anything because love and care play such a crucial role in healing – physically, spiritually, and emotionally. I continue to heal because of it.

Problems and difficulties – what do we do with them? How do we respond when problems come into our lives? I believe we can learn from them, recognize blessings in spite of them, and support one another through them.

OR

We can refuse to take anything from them, become angry or embittered by them and be uncaring or negative because of them.

What we do with the circumstances we are given will be up to us. God will never give you more than you can handle. His grace is sufficient.

Problems are certainly not about to end. In good times you may find it quite easy to spot God's goodness and work in your life. But in the tough times will you be open to receiving God's instruction, recognizing God's blessings and leading in your life? Will you give and accept support from those God puts in your life?

Grace and Graciousness
God Coming to Us in Times of Difficulty
What a Theme and What a Blessing!

The Angel Motif

We can never underestimate the work and value of angels in God's world. God's angels are active, they are protectors, they are messengers, and they are obedient to God. The scriptures are full of references to the work of angels. The gorgeous double chorus from the oratorio, *Elijah*, by Mendelssohn, "For He Shall Give His Angels," was a constant refrain in my heart and mind that gave me great comfort when Joy was teetering on the brink of death after the double lung surgery. The scriptural reference comes from **Psalm 91:9-12**.

> **If you make the Most High your dwelling . . . then no harm will befall you. No disaster will come near your tent. For he will command his angels concerning you to guard you in all your ways; they will lift you up in their hands, so that you will not strike your foot against a stone.**

As a clarification, I would never make assumptions about the work of angels in Joy's life without first giving credit to God. Angels are subject to God, and we cannot trump God. We, Gordon and I, never spoke of or paraded the angel theme. But it cannot be denied that God had something to do with Joy's survival. Could it have been angels? I cannot claim that special intervention. I only know that God was in control. It began at birth when Joy was confined to the neonatal ICU for healing from surgery when more than half her intestine had to be removed. (Explained in Section II, "The Miracle Baby.") Gordon and I would sit and watch her. We could not hold her, so we put our hands into the holes of the isolette to touch her and stroke her. I had this image of God's angels surrounding her little body, cradling her in the palm of His hands.

In high school, Joy suffered a massive lung hemorrhage. It was only by God's prompting at 1:00 a.m. that I awakened to find her in a pool of blood on her pillow. Jeanette Kostboth sent a beautiful card and plaque. The plaque read: "God is watching you because He loves you so much He can't keep His eyes off you." Joy hung this on the door to her bedroom where it stayed for years. It now hangs above her dresser. Jeanette wrote in the card:

> *. . . Being ill can be tough, and it takes a lot of energy to learn how to cope with it. Aren't we fortunate to know we can use Christ's strength! I've sure found in my life that I can't go it alone. When I told Jesus He would have to pick up the pieces because I was at the end of my resources, He did! I'm sure you've found that to be true, too.*

> *Joy, although you must get very discouraged, remember adversity builds character and patience and compassion for others. You already know what takes nearly a lifetime for some to learn. Hope this little picture reminds you of how much God loves you – and we do too!*

A collapsed lung in Israel left Joy in a weakened debilitated state confined to a hospital with no improvement day after day. The doctor finally resorted to an old drug that years past had lost its usefulness. By God's grace, she immediately began to show improvement and was finally allowed to fly home for another two weeks of extended hospitalization.

The lung transplant in 1997 was the ultimate test of God's healing hand. For three weeks, Joy lay in a drug induced coma during which time, on separate occasions, doctors tried to prepare us for Joy's death. It became clear to us, in one dramatic moment, that God was in control. Joy was on the ventilator for four months, in ICU for four months, in the hospital for five months, not including one month of outpatient follow-up, and finally home six months to the day of surgery.

It appeared that God acted only in times of crisis, but not so. He prepared Joy for service early in her childhood in unspoken ways. At two years of age, she demonstrated sensitivity to others. Gordon told me of this incident: I was still in Manila with Jami for follow-up care after Jami's birth. Gordon was with Joy in Baguio, and they had been invited to dinner by a missionary family. On the walk to their home, and with no prompting, Joy picked flowers to present to the family. How many two-year-olds would consider such an act of hospitality?

Joy always emanated a serenity, an aura of peace. She never complained, although she always struggled. My brother, Don Behm, commented, when he first met Joy, when she was just four, that she always had a smile on her face. Her walk was very smooth and without effort, perhaps to conserve energy and oxygen. Her Uncle John Harris sent a Christmas card with his art work and composed verse:

What is Christmas?
A little JOY of gentleness and grace
Whose lovely petite countenance
Puts angels in their place.

Many of Joy's friends picked up on the angel theme. A little plaque given to Joy by Robyn and Don Voigt at the time of her lung transplant, hung from the door knob of her room. It read: "Angels are with you every step of the way and help you soar with amazing grace!" An angel figurine was given to Joy by a best friend when she graduated from high school. At Joy's memorial service, Mike Sauers' five-year-old niece, Kelsey, approached me with a beautiful figurine of an angel. She wanted me to have it in memory of Joy. She cautioned me to be careful because it was fragile and would break. I assured her that I would take very good care of it. It will always be on a special shelf to remind me of Joy.

Joy's friends remembered her in other ways. The characteristics that her friends discovered in Joy can only be explained by God's special touch upon Joy's life. In the margin of **Psalm 139:1-12**, Joy noted in her Bible:

Awareness of God in My Life

You hem me in – behind and before;
You have laid your hand upon me.
Such knowledge is too wonderful for me
Too lofty for me to attain.

A friend wrote this verse to Joy. I do not know who. It was unsigned.

Joy

When I think of you
I picture a delicate ballerina
Dancing on top of a music box.
You were something I had
But I never really used.
I just sat you on my dresser
And forgot you were there.
But then one day
Someone walked in and wound you up.
You began to dance and the melody was soft.
I then looked at you dancing.
I began to realize how special you were.
But now I wind you up everyday.
I like to listen to you and watch.
I now appreciate the ballerina dancing
In you.

Five Years Old, Christmas 1975

7-4-97

Listening to God
Terrace Park

Life - blooming, dying
     - children, activity
   trees, grass, flowers, cotton
   tadpoles, water, birds
   moms, dads, brothers, sisters
Rock ants, fly, squirrel

   Firm, mark the way, offer rest
   create structures, landscape, shelter
   home to, animals, hiding place

Relationships - all colors, races
   friends   hide and seek
                        communication
   parent/child   song - Mother
   people/pets   daughter
   environment - circle of life
   laughter, anger, needs, fulfillment
   hurt, caring, nurturing

XIX.   A SPIRITUAL CONNECTION

Michael wrote me the most beautiful love letter I think I've ever seen. I shook as I read it. Our love is so deep. It's a spiritual connection and an understanding of each other that's hard to describe. I love him so much!

A Love Letter to Joy, by Mike Sauers

<u>August 24, 1998</u>

I have been thinking about your birthday and what it means to me. When I think of your special day, I think about the Love it has brought me. I also think of the many times these past few years that I have tested this Love. Sometimes it has been for selfish reasons, sometimes for the fear of the unknown, or maybe just that I'm afraid – afraid to really share the Love I have for you.

I Corinthians 13:3 – If I have the gift of prophecy and can fathom mysteries and all knowledge, and a faith that can move mountains, but have not love, I am nothing.

Joy, know on this day that I'm thankful for the Love you share with me.

I Corinthians 13:4-5, 7 – Love is patient, love is kind, it does not envy, and it does not boast, it is not proud, it is not rude, it is not self-seeking, and it is not easily angered. It keeps no record of wrongs, it always protects, always trusts, always hopes, and always perseveres.

I ask myself what would it have been like not knowing Joy? My answer, "Empty." Joy, you have, in a sense, taken me in. You know my background, you have shared my hurts, you have trusted in me when I have not trusted myself.

Joy, in you I see compassion that touches others in a way that only your Love for our LORD shines from you. You have struggled with health all your life, yet remain a beacon of hope and inspiration to many. You reach out with the tender touch of care to those in need enriching them in faith, love, and understanding.

Joy, know on this day that you have inspired me to be more than just being. It may not always show on the outside, but within, the spirit is on fire. Know that I have felt the tender reach of your hand, the kindness of your heart, the patience of your care, but even more is the trust and hope you have in me. Know that I Love you for sharing this with me.

I Corinthians 13:8 – Love never fails.

Joy, when you were called for transplant at Christmas, I was excited, afraid, alone, and questioning life. During the course of your hospital stay, I found myself growing more with you. I ask myself why would this be? I believe God has the answer to this question. Through you I have realized Love is beyond the physical beauty of a person, beyond one's health, beyond our own desires of what Love should be. It's a spiritual connection between people. It's the glow of one's own inner strength, faith, and beliefs that God shows through a person. It's withstanding tests, trials, fears, and knowing that someone special is still there for you. Know on this day that within my person, my Love for you never fails.

I Corinthians 13:13 – Now these three remain,
                              Faith, hope, and Love,
                              But the greatest of these is Love.

Joy, I'm so very thankful that God has blessed me with the Love I share for you. I had a hardened heart which now has been opened by your Love for life, the life Christ has created in you. No matter what road the journey takes in our lives, know that on this day of your 28th birthday, I feel even more blessed with the life you have shared with me. I'm grateful and thankful to our LORD and Savior to share this special day with you.

LOVE ALWAYS,
Michael

Gratitude for Life

Joy continued to list yearly goals in her journal:

> Goals for 1998:
> - *Be reflective, not reactive*
> - *Patience, patience, patience*
> - *Organize, prioritize, systematize, get going from there*
> - *Listen to God in silence, in worship, in others, in the world*
> - *Share, show, send grace out*

August 31, 1998

> *I am now 28 and one week into my 29th year. Amazing! What an important Day – a true gift from God. How does one express such joy and gratitude for life, for every day, for every blessing? I struggle to find a word(s) that captures that feeling. It's too profound for words.*
>
> *LORD, you alone know the future and for that I am thankful. I will attempt to live each day, making decisions within your will, knowing you will guide my actions and open the doors for opportunities where Your purposes may be served and Your name be glorified.*
>
> *School is about to start and ministry is underway. I am so thankful for the opportunities I have been given, and the blessings You have bestowed on*

Your work. Guide me, keep me safe and strong. Prompt me when I need it, teach me where I am weak. Love me. Hold me. Walk with me – whatever the year may hold.

Engagement

November 1, 1998

*Well, it's been two weeks engaged now and does it feel great or what?! On Friday night, October 16, Mike gave me a ring and asked me to marry him. I was totally scummed out in stretch pants (cream) and my Minnesota (UMN) sweatshirt, no contacts or make-up. We were just going to watch a movie – our usual Friday night venue. Mike picked me up and we went to his place. He rented "An American President," our first movie, first date on December 28, 1995. After the movie, Mike turned off the TV and put on the CD (Utmost) song "The Covenant." Then he brought out two candles and a vase of one dozen red roses and another vase of two single red roses. He turned out the lights then read me the piece he had written. I was completely floored. It was the most special I have ever felt. Mike even started to choke as he finished. He then pulled out the ring and asked if I would marry him. NO QUESTION ABOUT IT! **YES!** All I could do was grin. I was so happy. We stayed there for awhile and talked and cuddled, then came home and showed Mom and Dad. They are very pleased!*

Things are truly in motion now. We have reserved the Worship Center and talked to Daryl so all seems a go. It is overwhelming sometimes to think about it – exciting, yet scary. Mike feels the same way. All this time Mike had been teasing me. On September 14, Mike slipped. When we were talking about Vike's season tickets he said, "Remember now, you're married to a social worker." He pulled off quite the surprise.

Wow! It seems unreal to hear myself talking about marriage and a wedding, something I never thought I'd have the privilege of experiencing.

I love Mike so much. I can't imagine life without him. Come beside me, LORD. I'm gonna need you.

Goals for 1999:
- *What is the Good News – preach it*
- *Wisdom is knowing God*
- *Share your feelings, be honest*
- *Let go!*

Wedding Plans

January 14, 1999

Wedding plans are fully underway now. I still can't believe it – so amazing. My dress should be in soon. It's very pretty. It's an A-line empire waist dress in white. The bodice is beaded with capped sleeves, a sweetheart neckline, and a v-back. The skirt is full with a sheer white chiffon with a small train, a very lightweight dress. The veil goes down just to the V on my back and has a small headband piece. Beautiful!

The bridesmaid's fabric is bought and now just needs to get here since it was ordered in Minneapolis. Soon, hopefully soon.

This wedding seems so far away yet coming fast. I wouldn't mind being married tomorrow if that was possible. I love Michael so and long to begin our new life together.

Since my Christmas article in the Argus Leader, I have been overwhelmed by those who have been moved by it, people I've never met. So many people were praying. I can't imagine or even fathom how many prayers were spoken on my behalf. LORD, you overwhelm me and have surrounded me in your grace and love.

I am feeling well right now - I almost feel guilty about it. Why is Joslin dying? Why can't she continue to live? Why does an entire nation have to starve? Why do human beings slaughter one another?

Graduation – God's Little Ovation

May 22, 1999

Well, God – we did it – though you played a greater part. Your hand has guided me, your arms have sheltered me. It is to your glory that this accomplishment stands. I am on my way toward fulfilling my greatest dream. My dream job of working at NABS is just around the corner. My dream husband and marriage is only days away. How much more could anybody ask for? You give and you giveth grace so freely. I am in awe of such an awesome God.

When my name was called, people began to clap, then LeAnn Gerber stood, and the whole audience and faculty stood for a standing ovation. I was awestruck. You deserve that credit and I will spend my life giving back to you – serving you, loving others through and to you. What else could bring more joy?

Chuck then brought me to the podium and talked about my struggle and my spirit, my future and my ministry to which God has called me. It was an enlightened Spirit moment. I feel only thanks and blessings both by God and those who have prayed, cared for, and encouraged me. I then went on to hug

Dad, shake Mike's (Hagan) hand and went to sit down. My tissue had been gone about ten minutes into the service. It was such a meaningful time. I could have used a dozen tissues. What a day! At our open house many came and we had a great time of chatting and sharing.

I cannot possibly express all the depth and breadth of my gratitude. LORD, you know. My only request has to do with my body. LORD, heal me, this wound in my right lower lung. Protect my kidneys. Hold me close to you that I may hear your heart beat. Joy

Questions and Worries

Joy could not ignore the realities of life. She was struggling. She felt beaten down between the "highs and lows." Joy wrote of them but did not speak of them. She was determined to be patient and look on the bright side.

June 10, 1999

High, low. High, low. It's enough to drive a person crazy.
High = wedding, feeling well, strong
Low = kidneys not working

I am worn out by the constant flux and emotional roller coaster. I need renewal time or a wise word somehow from somewhere.

I have worked so hard and come so far. Kidneys, don't fail me now. But they do worry me. Creatine, 2.8; BUN, 62 = not good. I will try patience and try to focus on what is going well, but I worry.

Then there are the other questions I have. Will I be a good wife? Can I handle this, how will I do? I think I just need to find a good devotional, some quiet space, and soak. LORD, I need to soak in you – to take in your Spirit and grace. Restore me, my body and spirit that I might serve that much more my God, my LORD. Joy

Marriage – A Covenant Love

<u>June 26, 1999</u>

Joy was never more beautiful. She and Mike planned the wedding ceremony almost entirely. The theme: "A Covenant Relationship," the promise of love. Scripture and music were a primary part of the ceremony.

<u>Scripture</u>: Exodus 9:3-9

Jeremiah 31:3, 31-35

1 John 4:7-11, 15-16, 19

<u>Music:</u> "Joyful, Joyful We Adore Thee," Beethoven, trumpets and organ processional

"My Lips Will Praise You," Twila Paris, solo by Melissa Hiatt with a youth ensemble

"I Will Be Here," solo by Natalie West

"The Covenant," duet by Robin and Don Voigt

"All Creatures of Our God and King/Doxology," medley sung acappella by a trio

<u>The vows, written by Joy and Mike, were particularly applicable and beautiful:</u>

Joy/Mike, today I covenant with you before God, our family and friends.

I promise to love you as God has called me to do.

To encourage you and pray for you,

To care for you when you are sick or well.

I will cherish you in times of joy and difficulty.

I promise to protect you and not harm you,

To honor and respect you for all that you are,

To laugh with you and learn with you today and each tomorrow.

I will remain faithful to my God and faithful only unto you.

* With no prompting – spoken together after their individual vows:

I promise to love you with all my being, for love bears all things, believes all things, hopes all things, and endures all things. I will love you now and forever more.

Exchange of rings:

With this ring I seal my covenant with you. Wear it as a symbol of our ever-lasting love and faithfulness.

What a gift, God, you have given me. What joy. You have opened the doors, led us through the crazy maze of life and brought us to this point. For this I thank you, I praise you, for you are the LORD, my LORD and our LORD as we embark on a new journey not as one, two, but three.

Let go, Let God!

Let go, Let God Let

Father go.   Let God!

Let God

Son   and   Spirit

Let go, Let God, Let go.

Expect Great things from God
Attempt great things for God
Wllm. Carey
1792

Let go, Let go. Let go. Let God

God Let go.

Your heart's
desires and fears.
Your worries and
cares. Take
your life,
your will

Let go, Let God Let go, Let go God

He will provide!

5-13

XX. The Good and Faithful Servant Reward

The Prelude by Mike Sauers

It has been difficult for me to reflect upon those days prior to Joy's death. I knew for some time that Joy was not doing well. Joy became ill in the fall of 1999 with the flu, then pneumonia. The annual flu shot immunization had been eliminated from her drug regime in 1995 due to an egg allergy. This current virus infection triggered a series of medical emergencies. The physicians were attacking each complication as it flared up. It was necessary to suppress the immune system so that the body did not reject the lungs. Yet in order to treat infections, antibiotics had to be administered. It was a constant see-saw balancing act between the two dynamics of treatment.

During the 2000 New Year, Joy experienced two of her greatest disappointments – the January wedding of her sister in Memphis and the February funeral of her grandfather in Louisiana, both long distance trips. Joy was to serve as matron of honor and considered Jami's wedding a priority. She was determined to make the trips even though acutely ill. The physicians strongly discouraged her as her health was critically compromised. It was hard on Joy. She was frustrated that her health prevented these trips. Actually, the week of Jami's wedding, Joy was sent from Sioux Falls via ambulance to Minneapolis to the hospital. The doctors even considered transporting Joy by air ambulance because she was so sick. Joy would not allow me to inform Gordon and Joyce.

During the spring and summer months of 2000, when Joy was admitted to the hospital or there for clinic appointments, the cultures of her lungs revealed the infections were becoming more resistant to medications. Living at home with her, I could see the slow decline in her overall health, her breathing, and the physical ability to do things she used to enjoy.

Joy had been on many IV medications at home, which few people knew or realized. In July, when we went to the Triennial Conference in Sacramento, one of the suitcases we packed was entirely filled with IV medications. This was the accepted practice for Joy after a hospitalization.

There are decisions that, in hindsight, I regret. Joy was admitted to the Minneapolis hospital late in October, 2000. After several days at the hospital with Joy, I traveled to Sioux Falls, feeling that Joy would be on the mend by the time I returned. She always had been in the past. I've had to ask myself why I did that. Joyce came to stay with Joy and kept me informed. I did return to the hospital twice. The first time, Joy had regained some health, and I felt it was safe to return to Sioux Falls. The last time, Joy could not recover. I never left Joy's side once I was in her room. I learned to give this regret to God who gave me peace.

I still think of Joy often and what she meant to me and my life. Now I simply have the gentle tears of the wonderful time we shared together. I remember her jubilance for life, the laughter, the tender heart, but mostly the incredible faith and trust she had in Jesus our LORD and God. I truly loved her with all my heart.

Evening Shadows Fade into Darkness, Joyce Speaking

In October of 2000, Gordon and I were in Rapid City to celebrate his retirement as a Colonel in the Army National Guard having served twenty-two years as chaplain. Jami flew from Nashville for the event. It was a stretch for Joy to travel from Sioux Falls. On Wednesday, she had a bronchoscopy and experienced a difficult recovery from the procedure. She called on Thursday evening not sure that she could physically manage the trip. We told her it was her decision. On Friday, she called again to say that they were on the road. She said she would try to make the trip. Gordon assured her that, if it was too much, just turn back. We were pleased that she would make the effort. In hindsight, we realize how providential and important that weekend was for us. It would be our last time together as a family.

Joy arrived at Camp Rapid carrying her oxygen compressor. She did not look well. Her face, hands, and feet were extremely bloated. When Jami saw her sister attached to the oxygen, she reacted in surprise, "Why are you breathing oxygen?" That equipment had been abandoned after Joy's transplant. Now to witness it again shocked Jami. Jami later expressed guilt that she had greeted her sister so abruptly.

Putting that aside, the weekend was a wonderful event for us as a family. We felt pride in Gordon's achievements and the tributes to his ministry in the Guard. I have often thought of the sacrifices he made in time and effort to serve in the Guard. Initially, in 1976, when Gordon was approached about the chaplaincy, I protested. I needed him at home, but Gordon agreed even though, at the age of 36, he would not be eligible for retirement pay. After a number of years, the Guard made an exception in Gordon's case and reinstated retirement benefits allowing chaplains up to sixty years old to remain active. Gordon faithfully served and even committed seven years of his time to be schooled in the Basic Officer Course, Advanced Officer Course, and the Command General Staff Course. He did all of this for his family, and I am truly grateful.

On Sunday, Jami returned to Nashville and we to Sioux Falls. On Wednesday of the next week, we invited Mike and Joy for supper. We enjoyed our time, and I remember laughing hilariously with Joy and Mike about a movie they had just seen. Joy was animated as she talked to us. I felt secure that she felt well and her lungs were healing. The next day, Thursday, October 26, Joy called me at work.

She had undergone another bronchoscopy. The results were not encouraging. She said the doctors told her they could do no more for her. Her lungs were highly inflamed. She needed to go back to the hospital in Minneapolis. Joy was a master at disguising illness. In this case, she fooled even her parents. Mike and Joy drove to Minneapolis on Friday. They brought their dogs, Picaboo and Doozy, by the house on their way out of town. On the phone, I told Joy, "Call me if you need me. I will drop everything and drive up."

I did not hear from Joy on Saturday and assumed that all was going well. On Sunday, before we left for church, I needed to put the dogs outside. Unfortunately it was raining. Picaboo is afraid of the rain. This dog is what psychologists call neurotic. She thinks the sky is falling and will not go outside to potty. Doozy, of course, is compliant. Picaboo just hangs close to the door refusing to walk on wet grass with millions of water droplets raining from the heavens. I decided to just put both of them in the utility room and try again after church when, hopefully, the rain had stopped.

After church, we went out for lunch with friends. I had planned to go back to the church to prepare for children's choir, which was my regular routine. But I told Gordon that I wanted to go home first and call Joy. When I arrived home, the first thing I did was put the dogs out. Unfortunately, it was still raining. Picaboo would not budge, not even to step outside the door. She hid under the table trembling and crouching in fear. Doozy came back in, ran to Picaboo under the table, and just gave her "thunder" (barking and growling). I had never seen Doozy do that. She was exasperated with Picaboo. They were a team and Picaboo was not cooperating. Finally, I took a large umbrella, picked up Picaboo, walked outside, put her down on the wet grass, and held the umbrella over her as she squatted. At last! The entire incident aggravated me. We had always thought Doozy was a little dense, but she proved us wrong. I praised her for taking the initiative in confronting Picaboo. We were proud of her.

I called Joy. I told her I would be leaving early Monday morning to drive to Minneapolis to be with her. Her voice was rather soft and flat. She said that Mike needed to drive back to Sioux Falls today (Sunday) to go to work on Monday. I asked Joy if she needed me. She would not say. I asked her again. Typical of Joy, she said, "Only if you want to." I asked her a third time. Finally Joy admitted that she could "use me." I said, "Okay. I will pack a few things, go by the church, make arrangements for the children's choir, and be on my way." I told her it was still raining, and it will be evening before I get there, hopefully between 9:00-10:00 p.m. Gordon mentioned that Lewis had their phone cards on special, and I should buy at least two before I left, which I did. (We did not have cell phones at that time.) Betty Buchholz, our church administrator, was still at the church. She assisted me in children's choir and was very capable and efficient in all the activities of church. As I was leaving, she gave me a hug. She must have sensed the seriousness of the moment.

I cannot remember the exact time I left. It was probably about 4:00 p.m. I drove in pouring rain the entire trip. I think I got there a little past 9:00. Joy was pleased to see me when I walked in. The staff mentioned to me that she told them I was coming. I realized, then, that it was very important to Joy that I be there. I told Joy about the incident with Picaboo and Doozy. She did not seem amused; she said that had happened before. Joy let me know that she had been scheduled to have a bronc on Saturday, but it was never done. This concerned me because Joy cannot have anything to eat until after the bronc is administered. She had gone all day Saturday without food. She probably had a supper, but that was entirely too long for her to be without nourishment. I got the disturbed feeling that Joy was not getting the medical attention she needed. Of course, it was the weekend when everything slows down.

The respiratory therapist arrived to give Joy her treatment, which included a mask aerosol followed by percussion on her lungs in various positions. The treatment was rather vigorous, but not very productive. Joy commented that she knew the congestion was in her lungs, but just couldn't bring it up. By that time, it was after 10:00. I prepared myself for bed. Joy was not quite ready for bed. I laid down on the cot beside Joy's bed. In only a few minutes, Joy suddenly gave a horrendous, gut wrenching cough. I sat up. In her hand was a blood saturated tissue. I jumped out of bed as Joy continued to cough.

I literally ran down the hall to get a nurse. At the nurses' station I desperately said Joy needed a nurse/doctor (I'm not sure who I requested). The nurse paid little attention to me and continued about her business. I ran back to Joy's room, picked up the nurses call cord, pushed the button, and screamed for a nurse. They could hear me all the way down the hall. Joy continued to cough bringing up more blood with each cough. Soon, not only were there nurses in her room, but a doctor, a respiratory therapist, and several staff members. I heard the doctor say, "Oh, God." Joy spoke in a high pitched, squeaky voice, "Help me. Help me." I looked back at the doctor and nurses and they just stood frozen in their tracks. Joy was hemorrhaging and the professional medical staff did not know what to do. I heard the doctor say, "Get X-ray." One of the staff picked up a dish-pan and rushed it over to Joy as she continued to cough. Thank you for that. The tissues that Joy had coughed into were swimming in the blood.

I was praying, "Oh, dear God." I went to the other side of the bed and wrapped my arms around her head, and audibly prayed, "Oh, Dear God." She finally stopped coughing. The bottom of the dish pan was covered in blood and what appeared to be spongy matter. I thought she had coughed up tissue from her lungs. When I questioned the respiratory therapist, she said it was not lung tissue.

I guess it was coagulated blood. I do not know. I was traumatized and shaking. Joy told me later, "I know what's going to happen."

"We'll talk about it in the morning," was all I could say. Please, don't ask me to go there.

I pulled out the phone card and called Gordon. I also called Mike. He said a similar coughing episode had happened on Saturday, but not as severe. Gordon and Mike made arrangements to drive up on Monday morning. Mike had just gotten home.

The doctor ordered a C-Pap, which the respiratory therapist argued had not been effective in past situations. She actually said that it did not improve long-term health or life. But still we tried. The C-Pap forces oxygen into the lungs. The mask has to fit tightly around the face and head so that air does not escape. It was very frustrating because the apparatus was too large for Joy's small face. We were constantly adjusting it. I talked to the nurses more than once and insisted that the pulmonary physician see Joy first thing in the morning. I was beginning to feel that Joy was put on cruise control and not considered a priority. She had been at the hospital since Friday. I could see no positive results. Things were going down hill.

Dr. H was there in the morning. He asked Joy how much she had coughed up. She answered a "half cup," her pat answer to that question. I can tell you for a fact that it was much more than a half cup. I would not dare correct Joy's answer. First of all, she would be angry with me, and second, I felt sure that the evening doctor and nurse would have charted it correctly. I was surprised when I read the transcript of the doctor's notes – he actually wrote a "half cup." I wondered, did the nurse not chart an approximate amount? How could such inaccuracy occur?

The doctor indicated that a bronchoscopy would be scheduled for Tuesday. Joy's lungs needed to settle down. Also a biopsy of the lung tissue would determine if there was rejection. The medications to fight the infection were not entirely effective and another culture would need to be done.

Gordon and Mike arrived on Monday morning..

The doctors scheduled the postponed bronchoscopy for Tuesday. As usual, Joy would be on a restricted food diet. They would need to administer an anesthesia. The procedure involved a washing of the lungs, a biopsy to determine if there was rejection, and a culture, since medications had not been effective in fighting the infection. We waited all day. Again!!

On Tuesday afternoon, a new patient was admitted to Joy's room. As early evening approached, it became evident that the bronc would again be postponed. A dinner tray was served to the new patient. A respiratory therapist, who had taken care of Joy in the past, popped her head in the door and asked if all was going well. I said, "No. Joy has been without food all day. The bronc has been cancelled and she needs to eat. A dinner tray has been served to the lady in our room. Joy has not gotten her food." The therapist said she will take care of it immediately. I am sure she did. She was a good therapist. Then we waited and continued to wait. I finally approached the nurses' station and asked that Joy have a dinner tray. All other patients had been served and their trays picked up. I was more than a little perturbed.

The head nurse came down to our room. I was not in a social mood. I explained to him the situation. "Joy has to eat. This is the second time this weekend that she has gone without food all day. It is extremely important that she have nourishment. It is vital to her recovery. You and I can walk to the dining room, get food, eat, and walk back. Joy is stuck in this bed. What kind of hospital is this that one cannot get the very essentials of life?" He was very defensive, but I was in no mood for excuses. Joy finally got her tray.

Wednesday morning the bronchoscopy finally was administered. Fentanol was the choice of anesthesia; doctor's order. Joy always commented that she liked Fentanol. It made her feel good. The bad news – she would hit bottom when it wore off. Sure enough, Joy came back from the procedure breathing free and feeling on top of the world. Since Joy was on the mend and feeling chipper, Gordon, I, and Mike decided to rent two rooms at the Kidney House and sleep there. Mike and Gordon would drive back to Sioux Falls on Thursday.

I was encouraged by Joy's *feel good* on Wednesday and decided Thursday morning to wear the blue denim bib overalls with a red white striped shirt I had brought along for an occasion such as this. On Thursday morning, we drove to the hospital, parked, walked into Joy's room in ICU and were greeted with a very sick Joy. Gordon had a class Thursday night, and Mike needed to get back to work. They decided to drive back to Sioux Falls anyway, and I would keep them updated by phone.

The hospital personnel anticipated Joy moving back to the regular floor on Thursday. As the day wore on, it became very apparent that Joy was going nowhere. The medical staff decided to keep her in ICU. I called Gordon. I told him that Joy was not well, her decline was evident throughout the day. He asked if he should come. I said, "No. Teach your class and let's talk again in the evening." I called him later in the evening. Gordon said the class had a very meaningful prayer time for Joy. He will call Mike and they could travel together on Friday morning. I suggested that he call Randy Stewart who had been so attentive during Joy's transplant.

The nurse who attended the desk in ICU came by several times to check on Joy. During the five month hospitalization back in 1998, she had been very friendly to Joy. Before her shift ended, she stopped in to encourage Joy. She told Joy that she would be back on Monday and wanted to see a big smile on her face.

By Thursday evening, Joy was so weak that she could not pick up utensils to feed herself. I picked up the fork and started to feed her. She did not resist. She would point to her next bite. She was served a very tender pork loin with a well-seasoned gravy. She really liked that. Mashed potatoes were on the side, but Joy skipped those. She was a rice eater, having lived her first four years in the Philippines. I think the vegetable was green beans. She ate maybe one bite. What she really liked was the peach cobbler. Joy ate all of the cobbler. I considered it a rare privilege and honor to feed my daughter. Oh, how I loved her.

We struggled with that contrary C-Pap all night. I wish now that I had tossed it out. It simply was no good and just a nuisance. We had to call the respiratory therapist several times to help adjust it. The last time, he complained, so we didn't bother him again. The nurse assigned to Joy was also taking care of another man next door. She apologized the next morning that she could not attend to Joy. I asked her to give Joy a bath, which she was more than willing to do. I went upstairs to the dining room and brought down a breakfast tray to eat with Joy.

A Sacred Time and Place

I ate only a few bites of breakfast and set the tray on the window sill. Already there was a flurry of activity in ICU. A young man from lab came to take blood gases from Joy's artery. I told him that Joy hated those blood gases, they were so painful. Without another word, he gathered up his equipment and left. Thank you! A kidney doctor came to inform Joy of the risks and benefits that long-term drug therapy would have on her kidneys. Joy already knew that, but said nothing. The heavy drugs during the critical transplant had damaged her kidneys. Her kidneys would never survive another drug combination. The drugs could possibly save her lungs, but would shut down her kidneys.

I saw doctors huddled with Dr. N outside Joy's room. Mike and Gordon arrived just in time to hear his report. Randy Stewart was with them. Soon Dr. N came into the room and sat down in a chair beside Joy's bed. He reported that the biopsy from yesterday's bronchoscopy was inconclusive because the tissue they were able to extract from Joy's lungs was too small. I cannot remember much of his report on the lab cultures. He then told her that they could put her on the ventilator and push strong drugs to fight the infection. Joy had always said that she would never go back on the ventilator. I asked Dr. N if there were other options. He said the only other option would be to hook Joy to an IV that would allow her to rest comfortably and peacefully and gradually . . . . I did not hear the rest of his words. Without hesitation, Joy said that's what she wanted. I jumped from my chair and walked to the window and back. The group of doctors who had politely stood outside the walled curtains, suddenly appeared and moved silently into the room. I guess that was part of their education. How do you tell a patient she is going to die? Maybe they wanted to see my reaction. I was not about to give them the satisfaction.

Joy then told Dr. N that she wanted to go home. He said he would see what could be arranged and left with the other doctors. He returned shortly to report that Joy would have to be transported by helicopter air ambulance. They would try to make arrangements. Dr. N left again.

I pulled my chair to the other side of Joy's bed. So many thoughts were going through my head. Should I share them? Yes, yes. "Joy, I should be there on that bed, not you." She shook her head vigorously. I continued, "I've lived my life. You are young and so gifted, so much to live for and to offer." She continued to shake her head. I realized this was not debatable.

And then I changed my focus. I said, "Just think, you will have a new body. No more treatments. No more pain, suffering. You will see Jesus and live with Him." There was so much more I could have said, but I was still in shock. I think I told her that I wanted to go with her. I wanted to say "I loved taking care of you especially during those six months after transplant surgery." During the last month of June, we had so much fun exploring Minneapolis and the surrounding area. Then I made a stupid comment, "You had almost three years of life after the transplant." Joy said, "But I wanted to live to 40." Of course she did! Her love for Mike was complete.

August 31, 1998

Michael and I share a spiritual connection and an understanding of each other. I struggle to find a word or words that capture that feeling. Our love is so deep. It's too profound for words. I want to be able to share all my life and leisure with him. I love him so much!

Joy's call and commitment to ministry was everlasting.

January 14, 1999

LORD, you overwhelm me and have surrounded me in your grace and love. I am so thankful for all you have given and blessed me with. I so want the rest of the world to know, feel, and experience your all encompassing love and providence. LORD, equip and strengthen me for that task. Mold me into the servant you would have me to be.

Joy absolutely loved life and was willing to go the length and breadth to be used by God. But God knew better. He said, "Come to me. You are weary. I will give you rest." Joy repeated the statement, "I'm tired." I'm tired, as if to apologize for giving up her body. She had fought hard and vigorously all her life. But it was time. I understood. She knew it and acted upon it. As I have reflected on those moments, Joy seemed to relax. The expression on her face lacked that struggled, pained look. She was at peace. Joy knew her Father. She was not afraid. He would be there to welcome her. She was willing to let go and let God.

May 13, 1997

LET GO! LET GOD!

So many things are lying heavy on my heart tonight, heaviness both for myself and others. I alone cannot bear the anxiety, pain, or worry. And so I let it go.

Let go of it all.
Let go of your heart's desires, its fears.
Let go of your worries and cares.
Let God take your love and your will.
Let God provide.
Let God hold you, calm you.
Let your heart find rest in His strength, ease in the struggles of life.

Submit to the Father, Son and Spirit.
God, take these burdens upon you.
Let my heart find rest in your strength,
Ease in the struggle of life,
"For your yoke is easy and your burden is light."

For this and these concerns I pray.

Dr. N returned again and said that it would be too risky to take Joy to Sioux Falls by helicopter or ambulance. The medical staff worked all the angles, but could not justify it for Joy's sake. Joy accepted that. Looking back, it was the best decision.

I saw Dr. Dunitz in the hall. He was Joy's primary pulmonologist during and after her transplant. I knew he would be in to see Joy. I sat Joy in a chair and pulled up a second chair. Dr. Dunitz soon came in and sat beside Joy. They talked. I realized his personal feelings for Joy. He was truly touched by her life. A few weeks later, Dr. Dunitz wrote in a letter to us:

. . . I would like to express to you what a terrible loss we all feel with Joy's death. Her spirit was an example for all of us. She did more with her ailing lungs than most of us manage to accomplish in perfect health. I enjoyed helping to take care of her and I will miss her. Clearly she touched many people.

As the day progressed into early afternoon, Joy asked Gordon to get the Bible. He found one in the room set aside for families of ICU patients. Joy asked him to read that scripture. Gordon asked "What scripture?"

"You know, that scripture."

After fishing for more information, Gordon finally figured it out.

Lamentations 3:21-26

21 Yet this I call to mind and therefore I have hope:

22 Because of the LORD'S great love we are not consumed, for his compassions never fail.

23 They are new every morning; great is your faithfulness.

24 I say to myself, "The LORD is my portion; therefore I will wait for him."

25 The LORD is good to those whose hope is in him to the one who seeks him;

26 It is good to wait quietly for the salvation of the LORD.

Joy gave us the theme for her funeral. She asked that Hugh Litchfield deliver the message. Hugh was a dear friend of the family and Joy's homiletics professor. When Joy prepared sermons for churches that needed a supply preacher, she would call Hugh to get his feedback.

Joy then wanted to talk to me and Mike about her dress to be worn. "I want the blue dress that I wear to church. Do you know which one it is?" I said "Yes." "It's in the closet of the wardrobe, toward the back." I asked Mike, "Do you know where it is?" He said, "Yes." "Mom, my make up is in . . . ." "Okay, Joy."

A hospital chaplain arrived. We talked briefly, then she asked if she could sing a song. Being a musician, I did not know what we would be in for. We consented. She pulled out some cards on which words were written. In a gorgeous contralto voice with no accompaniment she began to sing the music of Marty Haugen.

Shepherd Me, O God

(Refrain between each verse)
Shepherd me, O God,
Beyond my wants, beyond my fears, from death into life.

God is my shepherd, so nothing shall I want,
I rest in the meadows of faithfulness and love,
I walk by the quiet waters of peace.

Gently you raise me and heal my weary soul,
You lead me by pathways of righteousness and truth,
My spirit shall sing the music of your name.

Though I should wander the valley of death,
I will fear no evil, for you are at my side,
Your rod and your staff, my comfort and my hope.

You have set me a banquet of love
In the face of hatred,
Crowning me with love beyond my pow'r to hold.

Surely your kindness and mercy follow me
All the days of my life;
I will dwell in the house of my God forevermore.

Final Refrain

("Shepherd Me, O God," by Marty Haugen. Copyright 1986 by GIA Publications, Inc. Used by permission.)

Our time in that room and hospital became a sacred place. I sat close beside Joy's bed, Mike on the other side. Joy turned toward Mike and stayed facing him. Joy kept repeating, "I'm tired," as if to apologize.

Mike, time and again said, "It's okay."

I wanted to scream, "It's <u>not</u> okay." It was all I could do to hold my tongue. Thankfully, I said nothing.

Giving Permission to Die

One of the greatest gifts we can offer our family and friends is helping them to die well. Sometimes they are ready to go to God but we have a hard time letting them go. But there is a moment in which we need to give those we love the permission to return to God, from whom they came. We have to sit quietly with them and say, "Do not be afraid . . . I love you, God loves you . . . it's time for you to go in peace. . . . I won't cling to you any longer . . . I set you free to go home. . . . Go gently, go with my love." Saying this from the heart is a true gift. It is the greatest gift love can give.

(BREAD FOR THE JOURNEY: A DAYBOOK OF WISDOM AND FAITH by Henri J.M. Nouwen. Copyright ©1997 by Henri J.M. Nouwen. Reprinted by permission of HarperCollins Publishers.)

I have been comforted by those thoughts and words. Mike was the wise one.

Early in the afternoon, people started arriving. I still do not know how they could be there so soon after Joy's decision to stop all medical intervention. News does travel fast. Gordon talked to our pastor by phone, Daryl Dachtler.

Harvey Mehlhaff, pastor from Faith Baptist Church, arrived. He hugged me and said repeatedly, "Oh, Mother, oh Mother, oh Mother." I was too stunned to take it all in. I had no tears.

The phone was ringing constantly, one call after another. Jami called and I talked to her as Gordon read scripture to Joy. Randy Stewart used his cell phone to bring Sioux Falls to the room. Staff members at NABS in Sioux Falls closed their office doors and joined with faculty, students, and administration to pray through the afternoon. They praised Joy for her courageous decision and told how much they enjoyed working with her.

Maria, Joy's discharge and clinic nurse, and Marget, her social worker, came to Joy's side. Maria hugged me for a long time. Pastor Andy and his wife arrived. She sang the hymn, "Great is Thy Faithfulness." How could she know this would be the theme of Joy's funeral?

Randy Reese walked in. I was surprised to see him. He later commented that God's presence and His Spirit were overwhelmingly real and heavy in that room.

Peter Fehr sat in the room with us sharing not in words but thoughts and feelings. Aaron and Michelle Kilbourn, close friends of Joy and Mike, drove from Sioux Falls to be with Joy. They had participated in Joy's small group Bible study.

Tami MacDonald called from Sioux Falls. Joy responded to one of Tami's comments, "I will miss you, too."

Jami called again. Joy could not hold the phone by this time so I held it to her ear. They talked for a long time. I do not know what was said. Joy listened, Jami talked. After Jami's phone call, Joy said she could not take any more calls.

Later in the afternoon, the head nurse came in and said very abruptly, "We have to move Joy to another floor. It's hospital policy." The staff began rushing around. I could not understand and thought it disrespectful. But we complied with her instructions. We were escorted to another room one floor above. The nursing staff brought Joy into the room on a wheeled gurney.

I left the room and went into the hall where Mike, Gordon, Randy, Aaron and Michelle waited. I said that I just could not bear to watch them move Joy from the gurney to the bed. When the nursing staff left, we all gathered in the room, much smaller than the previous ICU. Tears were trickling down Joy's cheeks. She probably was confused by the quick transport through the halls on the gurney. She may have thought we had left her, abandoned her. No way. We all found places to sit. We sang hymns as Joy lay quietly.

At 10:00 p.m., Aaron and Michelle indicated that they had to depart. We understood. The nurses brought in cots for the four of us to sleep. All of this time, Joy was half sitting up, propped by pillows with eyes closed. The only medical equipment was the very slow drip from the IV. I never once saw the medication drip. It kept Joy comfortable, not struggling. I was thankful for that. But then I thought, let's stop this whole thing. Joy can come back. It's not too late. Then I realized it <u>was</u> too late. They're killing my baby. I knew it was, indeed, too late. Weeks later, I shared those thoughts with Gordon. He said it was not the drug that killed Joy. It was the massive infection in her lungs. I could live with that.

We decided to take shifts. Gordon would take the first two hours. I would take the next two hours, and Mike the last hours. We each gave Joy a kiss and told her we loved her then settled down. When it was my turn, Joy lay still, so quiet and peaceful. After about two hours, Mike stirred and said he would take the next watch. I said, "It's okay. I am fine. I can sit with Joy." He repeated his request and I finally relented. I laid on the cot where he had slept. As I rested, I heard voices. In a sleep daze I thought Joy and Mike were talking with each other. I lifted up from the cot. I did not want to disturb them and laid back down. In a flash, I suddenly realized Joy could not speak.

In a few minutes, Mike spoke to us and said that Joy had taken her last breath. I quickly was up, but Gordon was beside her bed first. Gordon said a prayer as we held hands around Joy's bed. We lingered there quietly. The nurses came into the room to check her vital signs. They clocked the time, 3:30 a.m., then left.

I looked at Joy. I was shocked. She changed so suddenly. She was gone. She had left us. So matter of fact! Mike told us what he said to Joy. "During the last moments I had with Joy, I took her hands, kissed her, and told her of my love for her. I shared that we would be okay. 'Your friends love you, your mom and dad love you. Jami loves you. I love you . . . its okay. It's okay.'"

Joy had been waiting for her lover. It was their last good-bye and she knew it was okay. She gave up her body and moved into the very presence of God and into the loving arms of her Savior.

<u>July 4, 1997</u>

> *A woman was sitting at the base of the tree with her young daughter in her lap. She was singing beautifully, a song about how meaningful and special her daughter was to her. I don't remember the words of the song, but I remember its warmth. It was a simple, beautiful song sung with love. . . The mother-daughter image and song stuck with me. God was speaking through these people. I realized how like that mother God is. He longs to hold us, sing to us, and love us in his lap if we will slow down long enough to listen. This little girl was so content and at peace in her mother's arms. So God holds us.*
> *Joy Harris Sauers*

Returning her earthly body to the world, Joy entered the presence of God and received the promised reward of eternal life.

Thirty years and two months of life in a body.

One year and four months of marriage to her best friend and lover.

An <u>eternity</u> with Jesus her LORD and Savior, God her Father, Abba, Daddy, as she affectionately called him.

We had to gather our things, and I continued to wait for some sign of life from Joy. Gordon covered her face with the sheet. Oh, please don't do that. I went back and uncovered her face. She had not returned to us. I was in disbelief. I covered her face. Then I went back again to look for Joy, this one whom I had carried in my womb, to whom I had given life. She was no longer with us. She was in the arms of her Savior who had given her eternal life. I had no tears. I was numb.

Psalm 116:15 – Precious in the sight of the LORD is the death of His saints.

XXI. THE BLESSING

Then Comes the Morning

Gordon, Mike, Randy, and I started our drive back to Sioux Falls at about 4:00 a.m. Gordon and I were in the car I had driven to Minneapolis six days previous Mike drove with Randy in our other car. We started the trip in silence, each to our own thoughts. After traveling about an hour, I began to think about Joy's funeral. I voiced a few thoughts, and Gordon suggested I write them down. I hesitated and sat frozen. No. There was too much finality to that action. I kept my thoughts to myself. Then, as if in a stupor, I reached for a pen from my purse and some paper from where I do not know.

I thought of Joy. What would she want? She would want her funeral to be a witness. Joy had a wide network of friends – within the health industry, the seminary, churches, the community – not all were Christians, so many we did not know. We already had her scripture text. She had told us that just yesterday. I began to jot down a plan. Hugh Litchfield will deliver the message. I want the seminary/community choir to sing the anthem, "Here I Am, Lord" (Take and Use Me). It has such a stirring and challenging message. The melody is beautiful and harmonies simple but lush. Joy would like that. I'll talk to Ted Faszer.

Our family scripture all these years has come from Isaiah 40:28-31. Michael Joncas' music, "On Eagles' Wings," will be perfect as a solo by Pastor Daryl Dachtler with congregational singing on the refrain. I will get permission from the publisher to print the words in the bulletin. I will include two of my favorite hymns, "Like a River Glorious," and "There Is a Redeemer," concluding with the third verse:

> *When I stand in glory, I will see His face,*
> *There I'll serve my King forever in that holy place.*
>
> *Refrain:*
> *Thank You, O my Father, for giving us Your Son,*
> *And leaving Your Spirit till the work on earth is done.*

(THERE IS A REDEEMER, MELODY GREEN. © 1982 BIRDWING MUSIC / BMG SONGS / EARS TO HEAR MUSIC (admin. By MUSIC SERVICES). ALL RIGHTS RESERVED. USED BY PERMISSION.)

I will ask Dan Leininger to sing "There Is a Redeemer," in his beautiful lyric tenor voice. It will be nice if Janice Houts and Darline Bill can play piano and organ duets. Janice was Joy's piano teacher. For several years Joy had been the page turner for Janice at the piano and then for Darline on the organ for the Christmas concert of *The Messiah*.

Of course I want the hymn "Great Is Thy Faithfulness" as a prelude, then a congregational hymn for the recessional. Gordon wants the hymn, "God of Our Fathers." That would be excellent as a trumpet trio with congregational singing. I'll ask my brother, Don Behm, from New Jersey to put that together. Chuck Hiatt, president of the seminary, will give the closing prayer. I want to speak at my daughter's funeral. I have something to say. Mike, Joy's husband, may also desire to speak. I want this funeral to first be a witness to unbelievers. That was what Joy's life was about. It will give tribute to a life that God honored and one that honored God.

Gordon chose the scriptures: I Corinthians 15:50-58, Philippians 1:19-21, Revelation 21:1-4, and finally Isaiah 40:28-31, and Lamentations 3:21-26. Del Donaldson and Mike Hagan will read the scriptures alternately.

When we asked Mike Hagan to speak the final words at Joy's internment, he asked to recite a Hebrew prayer. "Of course." Joy loved Hebrew, and Mike had been her teacher. She took one year of class Hebrew followed by another semester of reading Hebrew from Mike.

HEBREW BLESSING

Baruk atah adonai elohenu	*Blessed are you, O LORD our God*
bore hashemaim vahaaretz	*Creator of the heavens and the earth*
'osheh col ha' olam	*Maker of the whole world*
Qach na' 'achotnu 'ad hayom hahu'	*Receive, please, our sister until that day*
Lehithraot simcha, Joy. Amen	*See you later, Simcha, Joy. Amen*

For the close of the internment, I will ask Don, my brother, to play on the trumpet, "Savior Like a Shepherd Lead Us." This was the hymn at Joy's wedding and also ours. It seemed a fitting conclusion.

We practically had the entire service planned by the time we got home. It was about 8:30 a.m. I still had on that atrocious blue denim bib overalls and red and white striped shirt. I vowed I would not wear it again. I quickly cleaned up and changed.

People started arriving early Saturday morning. First, Chuck and Janelle Hiatt, president of the seminary, then Ted and Marietta Faszer. Marietta asked if there was anything she could do. Since we were expecting a lot of family, I immediately said my house needs to be cleaned. She showed up later with bucket in hand, rags, cleaning utensils, and spray bottles. When she was finished, she said my house had already been basically clean. (However, I knew the bathrooms needed attention along with dusting and some clutter removed.) I was so thankful for her time and work. People started bringing food. Tom Renner raked the yard in very cold rain and wind. It was a busy place – bustling with so many wonderful, supportive friends and family.

On Sunday morning, we showed up for worship at Trinity Baptist Church. Pastor Daryl had assured us that we did not need be there. We walked in the back and already the choir was in place. Gordon and I looked at each other and made our way into the choir. I imagined that some people thought that strange – we should be cloistered away in deep mourning. I could not think of a better place to be. Actually, most people did not realize we had lived with grief all the years of Joy's life. It was now a strange mixture of grief with rejoicing. Joy was free, in the loving arms of her Savior. What I did not realize was the excruciating grief that was yet to engulf me – body and soul.

Our families were present for the funeral. Jami arrived from Memphis on Saturday night; my brother, Don Behm from New Jersey; my sister Jeannie and her husband Ken West from Mississippi with their daughter, Trish; Gordon's sister Jane and her husband Phil Smith with their daughter Emily from Texas. Their older daughter, Jennifer, was extremely disappointed when her flight was cancelled because of snow. Jennifer and Joy were born the same year only a month apart. Gordon's mother could not attend, but managed to make the trip a year later with her daughter, Jane, to visit Joy's grave. Mike's family lived in the area and all were present.

In the "Angel Motif" section I wrote about Mike's five year old niece, Kelsey. who approached me before the service with a porcelain figurine angel. She said, "This angel is for Joy." I thanked her and told her it will always have a special place in our home. She reminded me that it was fragile and could break. "I will be very careful. Thank you so much."

As we greeted people and watched them arrive, I was amazed that so many community leaders attended – Crossroads personnel, Lions Club members, medical professionals, The Assistant Adjutant General and Sergeant Major from the South Dakota Army National Guard. The place was packed. It was an overflow crowd with some watching by way of video camera in the family life center. As a surprise to us, Janice and Darline closed the service with a piano-organ duet arrangement of the "Hallelujah Chorus" from Handel's oratorio, *The Messiah*. My prayer was that God would be glorified in the life of his servant, Joy. So many people in the following weeks approached us, "This may seem strange, but that was the best funeral I have ever attended." Thank you, LORD.

Grief Is Everybody's Business

July 23, 1996

I have a heartache. Some days it hurts more than others. My heartache is my health and this last week it has hurt quite a bit. I believe each of our lives are touched by heartaches and they make us who we are. I have not experienced the same heartaches as you.

I have not experienced the heartache of death of a parent, sibling or child.

I have not experienced the heartache of addiction, violence, an accident or injury.

I have not experienced the heartache a natural disaster leaves behind.

I have experienced the heartache of physical suffering and the limitations that come with that.

Each of us has had a unique experience and for each whose heart aches, there is pain.

The Psalmist asked the question in **Psalm 42:5** .
Why are you downcast, O my soul? Why so disturbed within me?

And answers it in the affirmative:
Put your hope in God, for I will yet praise him, my Savior and my God.

God is present in my history, present in my thoughts, and present in my soul.

Good News and Bad News

Grief knows no stranger. It comes in many forms; it strikes with severe accuracy; it stays for a lifetime. There is no medical cure for grief. Yet there is hope. Not a hope that allows one to escape its piercing pain. Pain it will be, no matter all efforts to deny or refuse its residence in our lives. The hope of which I speak can be found only in the body and blood of the Savior, Jesus Christ, God's Son.

Joy gave up her body at 3:30 a.m., Saturday, November 4, 2000. We said a corporate good bye at her funeral on Wednesday, November 8. We talked of her life, her witness, her inspiration to all of us. Since November 1974, when Joy was diagnosed with cystic fibrosis, I have lived with an uninvited companion – that of chronic grief. But the reality of the final separation from my daughter was the ultimate grief experience. I was swimming in tears. My heart screamed silently. My lungs yelled in protest. I had never known such excruciating pain and sadness.

One month later, on Sunday, December 3, I faced the truth about grief and its place in my life. It was communion Sunday at Trinity Baptist Church, and we were given instructions regarding the bread and the cup. We would not be served. Individually, we would stand, walk to the altar, take the elements in our hands, and return to our seats. Silently, we were to meditate upon the meaning of this sacrament in our lives and consider our response to Christ's sacrifice. Then we were to accept the bread and the cup identifying ourselves with Christ.

I sat in the pew and looked at the bread. Christ's body was broken. I looked at the juice. Blood flowed from His wounds. In my heart, I witnessed the crucifixion. I thought of Mary, His mother, as she helplessly mourned the suffering of her firstborn. I wept. Only one month previous, we had witnessed the death of our daughter. I experienced Jesus' death on multiple levels, personally identifying with the grieving mother, but also as a child of God whose own child was saved by His sacrifice. Christ's resurrection three days later claimed victory over that death.

I can now move on, knowing that Joy is alive, living eternally with God, the omnipotent, one and only holy God. She received forgiveness of sin when she accepted Jesus into her life. He, Jesus, paid the penalty for her sins, and she was declared clean. Joy became the adopted child of God. Her inheritance as His child was life eternal. The heavens were opened for Joy to enter into the Holy of Holies. That is the hope. The grave holds no victory. I can say with assurance, "I understand the hope." It is the same hope spoken so eloquently by Paul as recorded in the scriptures.

See the Hope! I Corinthians 15:55-57

55 Where, O death, is your victory? Where, O death, is your sting?
56 The sting of death is sin, and the power of sin is the law.
57 But thanks be to God! He gives us the victory through our Lord Jesus Christ.

Then why do I still mourn? I can only answer in human terms. I miss Joy's presence, her phone calls. I miss her laughter and joyous spirit. I miss our discussions. I have an abundance of memories that ever invade my daily thoughts, and those are precious memories. But in terms of eternity's eyes, I realize I see only through a dark glass, or as the NIV interprets, **". . . a poor reflection as in a mirror" (I Corinthians 13:12).** Yet Joy sees clearly, for she is now face to face with her LORD and Savior. Although I could selfishly wish for Joy's physical presence, I cannot deny her the ultimate joy of living in God's presence. That is my greatest comfort. She knows freedom and the total love of God. She has received His reward: "Well Done Good and Faithful Servant." What greater significance!

The morning of August 24, 2000, Joy's thirtieth birthday.
Mike took the picture of Joy and Picaboo. They look alike, don't you think?

XXII. A Happy Memory

This was Joy's last journal entry.

June 11, 2000

It has been almost one year now since Mike and I married! It's hard to believe. The days have gone so fast. What a gift marriage has been. Thank you, God, so much. I'll always treasure the birthdays, Christmases, Valentines, and holidays.

I treasure every day and look forward to the tomorrows. It is so amazing to me. Even though there are difficult days, I am grateful for being able to do what I can, to be where I am.

I want to make sure that if it's the last day I ever have, I will have left a happy memory in its place.

Today is a happy day. No! A Day of Joy!

Thank you, LORD, for your faithfulness in my life. I can't wait 'till tomorrow.

You are my Rock.

Deuteronomy 32:4

**The Rock! His work is perfect,
For all His ways are just;
A God of faithfulness and without injustice,
Righteous and upright is He.**

June 26, 1999
Gordon escorts Joy.

XXII. REFLECTIONS

"Why? Again!"

The infamous "why" question raised initially at Joy's diagnosis again lifted its head, but in a totally different context. The "why" demand moved from a fist raised in anger to a fallen knee in submission. The cursed "why" question had become the blessed *why* question. "Why, God, did you trust us to parent such an amazing life, one for which we could not claim credit?" Joy had blessed our lives. It was a mystery to me. We, as parents, had made our mistakes. Intellectually and spiritually Joy had become our role model. Our lives had been enriched. She modeled for us how to live, how to endure, how to suffer, how to hold on to God, how to reach out, how to minister, how to love, how to die. . . God had placed his hand on Joy. She had responded. In so doing God blessed us, through Joy.

"Thanks for the Memories," sermon, 1999

> *We struggle in deserts of life. My own desert has been that of ill health. I have constantly struggled with sickness and the loneliness that often brought. I remember one time in the hospital when I was particularly sick I wrote in my journal, 'On days like today, when I feel sad, lonely, or without joy, I ask questions of myself and my God. . .' As I worshiped tonight in song with Deb and Justin, and as I searched the Scripture for that word that would be comforting, a theme became prominent: I was relying on myself and my world rather than on God.*

> *Many times after illnesses, many deserts, I began to reflect back on God's work in my life. I've experienced bleeding, infection, a collapsed lung, but have been healed, protected from death. I have been protected by a powerful God and delivered by His outstretched arm. I constantly need to remember God who delivered me and know that He will continue to deliver and protect me. It is easy to feel overwhelmed in our deserts, in the pain and difficulty of the moment. It's human. We must never forget who it is that we need to turn to.*

March, 1997

> *With all that goes through my mind – my thoughts, fears, hopes, dreams – it is hard to know where life will take me, what choices I will need to make, or how my life will impact this world for Christ. As I talk and think through my fears and future, I have missed the essential ingredient, the sustenance of my heart!*

> *I have relied on things and relied on people to bring me sustenance, to fill me up. This was my error. Mike. I have based my happiness on his attention and presence. Mom and Dad. I have relied on them for support. I have relied on my classmates for support and care. With all these, yet I am not happy. I have not been satisfied.*

Each of these will add to my life, no doubt. But only One can sustain me and provide me the comfort, care, healing, and joy that will satisfy my heart and fears. My fears come from an over-reliance on the earthly world I live in. Reliance on Christ and my LORD will satisfy and sustain me, for his loving kindness is everlasting and satisfies my soul.

I can understand now the Psalmist. We talk about the form – the opening, the praise, the lament, then the closing – confidence in God. It's not just a form. It's a recognition of the ultimate, the ultimate peace that comes only when we leave the self-earthly-reliance to seek and accept the care of our LORD.

When talking with Sister Del Rae, she said she sees the LORD as her sustenance. Now, more than then, I truly understand the theme of looking to 2000. I believe unless we look to the LORD first for our sustenance and direction, any earthly scheme will come up lacking. More precious than the students, the programs, or the buildings is the LORD. Who will give themselves to Him?

Joy

A child was born and brought such joy
No matter if a girl or boy
Touched by God to bless us so
Enriched our lives as we watched her grow.

A special mission we would see
Like the child of God in Galilee
Given to us by God above
She blessed the world with His love.

Explained in Psalm 139
God's work for Joy he had in mind.
His message written upon her heart
She shared to all who desired a part.

Joy's burden for health to be denied
Urged His message before her demise.
She loved, she spoke, she inspired, she wrote,
She lived, she worked, she gave – all.

Joyce Harris
First stanza, an anonymous seminary student

EPILOGUE

Mike Speaks of Joy and Their Marriage

"We love because He first loved us." I think of this often when I remember and reflect on the time Joy and I shared together. Our life scripture was **First John 4:16.**

> **We know how much God loves us and we have put our trust in him. God is love and all who live in love live in God, and God lives in them. (NLT)**

It is actually very difficult to write about Joy. As I think about Joy, the incredible sense of missing her hits me hard. It is almost seven years since we said good-bye. During this time, there have been so many times I wished to have one more good-bye, to hear her voice and remember the love we shared.

Joy made such a huge impact in my life from day one. When I think of the book title, *Blessed by Joy*, it touches my heart, as this is so true for me. For you see, I know my life would be totally different if she had not reached out to me, accepted me as a person, and loved me. Joy never gave up on me. She entrusted me with her love. I remember asking myself so many times when she was sick or in the hospital, "Can I do this, am I capable of providing unconditional love to a very sick woman?" Yet, I was always swept by an overwhelming wave of, "Yes, I love her." I spent many nights and weekends hanging out at Avera McKennan Hospital prior to the transplant. When we did things, it was within Joy's capability. It's truly amazing that I accepted this, as I was a very active person.

Joy was alive in the Spirit. The laughter, love, and joy that she had for people was within her person. We were drawn to each other by God's hand. She once wrote in her journal that there was a spiritual connection between us. This is so true. It is amazing that this could happen since we came from completely different backgrounds and walks of life. One can give absolute credit to God and His guidance in our lives. Joy blessed me in every aspect of life. Her laughter and sense of humor always lifted my spirits.

Joy's passion for ministry and reaching others in need continues to impact my life. I remember so many times thinking how can she possibly do what she does with so little lung support. Many times, when Joy was scheduled to preach, I suggested she find someone else as she was feeling awful, barely able to just get up. Yet off we would go. She would deliver an incredible message. Wow, what amazing faith and trust in God! Despite all of her health concerns, and knowing that her years to live were limited, she remained faithful. She trusted God with all her heart and soul. How can this not affect me for the rest of my life? I am truly unable to describe the words I have for Joy. Whenever I think of her, it is that simple overwhelming sense of love that we shared from the time we met. I still miss her dearly.

It is amazing how one can feel after we lose someone we dearly love. The love Joy and I shared was brief, but the memories are fond and never leave. I struggled for a period of time. "Who am I?" "Who am I without Joy?" My struggle was gripping and painful. I was numb. I remember so many times sitting alone in our home . . . remembering . . . reflecting . . . crying. The tough part was that very few people asked me how I was doing especially around three months out.

It's now been almost seven years. I don't go to the cemetery as often as I used to, but the memories of Joy never slip away. Joy touched my life. I continue to reflect, but now the immense sorrow and pain are washed away. The memories are now precious, with thankfulness for the time we shared together.

A Son-in-Law, by Gordon

Mike Sauers has been an inspiration since I met him. As parents of a daughter with a chronic illness, we wondered if Joy's love would be fulfilled. She had so much to give and yet doubted her own strength and future. Mike was an answer to prayer in a way that I never would have imagined. I thought of him as a son and still enjoy being with him.

Mike had the wisdom to consult with his mother, Cheryl Sauers. She taught him to see value and strength in a frail human being. She also suffered from hip and leg pain and could advise him with wisdom learned from personal experience. She encouraged her son to love Joy fully. In an interview by Jill Callison published in the Argus Leader on February 4, 2001, Cheryl commented: "I told him the same thing I feel now. There are people who can be married forever and not have what you (Mike) have for a short time. If you are brave enough to fight along with what Joy is going through, it is worth it."

June 18, 1997

I struggle as Mike and I are close. I ask myself if this is right – if he is right for me. I pray about it. I pray for him and for me. I know I love him. I wouldn't ever want to hurt him. I just can't help but think how much more he could do, more he could be if he loved someone other than me. But, the LORD has brought us together for a purpose and for that I will see this through. The LORD's plan is perfect and he holds my life in his palm.

LORD, I release to you my love, my friends, my family, my life. LORD, your will alone is perfect and holy. May I but try to live according to your will and word. Guide me in this life endeavor.

Joy spoke of the realistic choices that Mike had to weigh.

August 28, 1997

Michael is an amazing man. We talk about my life and future, how undetermined it is. I live with uncertainty. I have no choice. Mike does, yet he chooses to come beside me, to enter into that uncertain world. What an amazing man to choose such a thing when so many opportunities and possibilities are available to him to do otherwise. I'm not sure I could ever bear to make the choice of a life or career without him. He means so much to me. I love him so. LORD, lead and guide both of us in the choices we'll make each tomorrow.

Joy

When Joy entered the darkness of the lung transplant, Mike joined us quickly at the hospital in Minneapolis. Mike stayed with us hour after hour through the troubling times when doctors questioned whether Joy would live through rejection and infection. Mike held our hands when we prayed for healing and protection as Joy's life swayed in the balance.

When Joy began the long therapy back to strength, she was skin and bones. Mike had to love her deeply to stay faithful through those difficult days. We talked frequently sharing our pain and concerns on our weekend trips to Minneapolis. We give credit fully to God for the way He brought the two together and provided the grace for them to love one another. God prepared Mike in a special way to come alongside Joy and to complete her.

I felt Mike's pain after Joy's death. Their house was a house of sorrow. The light that Joy always brought had gone out. Joy never got the opportunity to enjoy the remodeled kitchen she and Mike planned. That made the emptiness even harder to comprehend. Joy's dogs, Picaboo and Doozy, never recovered either. They could not speak, but the pain showed through their eyes. God's presence rescued all of us. Joy's spiritual journal left a legacy that brought sense to her pointless death.

God did not leave Mike hanging. Eventually, we began to notice Mike's step carried more spring. He became more conversant as we visited over evening meals. We suspected before we even met Ruth, that Mike had met a lovely young lady. God had done it again. We were extremely happy for them. Ruth is a deeply committed Christian. She mended Mike's broken heart and gave his life meaning. This was truly a blessing. Ruth is a perfect match for Mike. As Cheryl, Mike's mother, stated at their wedding, "God filled the loss of a Christian wife with another who is devoted to God." Now an addition has blessed their home with the birth of their precious little boy, Luke Michael. I know Joy is rejoicing in their family. God provides for His children who love and are committed to Him.

We still spend time with Mike, his wonderful wife and son. We pray daily for them. We can only thank God for all these blessings.

Love Forever, Jami

Jami is the sister who lived in the shadows, who spoke no harm to Joy, who accepted Joy. Joy was her role model. Jami's attachment to her sister could not easily be severed. Jami lingered at the grave site. She stood silently at Joy's coffin. We waited for her in the car, not understanding why she chose to remain. It was very cold. Jami finally, hesitantly, began to walk away.

A few weeks later, Jami and I were talking on the phone, and she explained why she stayed with Joy. She said it was very disturbing that people walked off, just walked away leaving Joy alone out there. I said, "Jami, Jami – Joy is not in that grave. That is only her earthly remains. Joy is alive, living with Jesus surrounded by God's love. She is free. She is in heaven. She will live eternally with God."

Two years later, Jami, Gordon, and I went to Joy's grave. Jami had written a letter to Joy. She pulled out four hand-written pages and read her very personal message. She spoke of her love for Joy, "First of all I want to tell you I love you, and I'm sorry I didn't tell you until almost too late. I miss you so much. I wish I could go back in time and do things over." Jami spoke of her admiration for Joy – her strength, her caring nature, her beauty. She talked of her regret for the past and asked for forgiveness. "Sometimes I still think I can call you – that you're really not gone. I wish I could just talk to you or see your face. I wish you could come visit me. You are a mystery to me. I miss you and love you."

Love Forever,
Jami

Gordon, Joyce and Jami

ADDITIONAL SUPPORT COMMENTS

A Text and Thesis
by **Hugh Litchfield**

Lamentations 3:17-26

Sir Robert Jones attended the funeral of his friend, Robert Browning, that great English poet. Afterwards he wrote that he was disappointed in it. "Such a funeral for him was entirely too sad. I would have given something for a banner or two to wave or if the chorister had come into the triforium and rent the air with the trumpet."

This is what we want to do today – to wave the banners and sound the trumpets to celebrate. This is what Joy would want us to do, what we want to do. But it is hard to do. What words can you say?

Through the years, I gave Joy several assignments – most of which she complained about. But last Friday, she gave me one. She told me what to tell you today. She gave the text and thesis for this moment.

I. The text – Lamentations 3

What a text! The word means "weeping." It is a book written in tears. The writer is standing in the midst of a Jerusalem that had been destroyed, of a Temple that had been destroyed. His life had fallen to pieces and he didn't know what to do. He cried out:

Lamentations 3:17-18 – My soul is bereft of peace; I have forgotten what happiness is; so I say, 'Gone is my glory, and all that I had hoped from the Lord'. (New Revised Standard Version)

In his despair and brokenness, it was a time for lamentations, for weeping.

I think all of us can understand that, for it seems as if our world has fallen apart, our lives have been broken. We feel like lamenting, and weeping, and I think Joy would tell us that it's okay. For it is a hard time. We cannot imagine the pain that this magnificent family is having to deal with, but we want to help you get through it. We care for you.

But we also want to know how we will get through it. For Joy was, well, Joy was ours! Our friend, our classmate, our colleague, our inspiration. What do we do now? For we had come to believe that Joy would always be around. She had come through so much – what's another miracle! We expected it. As many of you have said these past days, "I can't really believe it!" but it is so. We know how privileged we were to have been allowed to share in her life – so how do we go on?

We remember and tell our stories. Last night, we heard many stories of Joy and her influence on our lives. If you were standing where I am, you would add your own remembrances. As I have been reflecting on her life, there are memories I will carry with me.

I will remember her courage. She was a tough, feisty person – I hope you know that. All of her life, fighting against this sickness, walking with death very near. But she didn't let it control her life – she fought against it. In the end, death conquered her body, but never her spirit. I will remember her courage.

I will remember her honesty. When you know how precious the days are, you don't have time for idle chit-chat. She would always get to the point, not beat around the bush. You knew what she thought and felt. Sometimes you didn't particularly want to hear what she thought, but she would tell you anyway. Such honesty is refreshing.

And of course, I will remember her humor. Several said last night that you enjoyed teasing Joy. But let me tell you, she could give it as well as take it. As a Vikings fan, she was not above rubbing it in whenever the Vikings beat your favorite team. Laughter and a smile were always with her – she lived up to her name.

Although short in stature, I will remember Joy's heart – a heart so big it took in the whole world. No one was left out, especially those who lived on the fringes, who were strangers in our land, who were often forgotten. Her heart took in everyone.

And of course, I will remember her zest for life. As had been said, she lived life fully. There were places she wanted to go, things she wanted to do, and she went after them. If you tried to keep up with her as she went after life, you were the one who would run out of breath. There are others who will live much longer as far as age goes, but I know – I know – that no one will ever get more out of life than she did.

And on we could go. We will miss her. It is a time to lament. But I imagine Joy saying to me, "Enough of that. Get to the point. Tell them the thesis. Tell them what I told you to tell them."

II. Thesis: Great is God's Faithfulness

In the middle of his despair and tears, the writer remembered God, remembered how good God had been to them in the past. He began to dry his tears and take hope.

> **Lamentations 3:22-24 – The steadfast love of the LORD never ceases, his mercies never come to an end; they are new every morning, great is your faithfulness. The LORD is my portion, says my soul, therefore I will hope in him (ESV) .**

(The Holy Bible, English Standard Version Copyright © 2001 by Crossway Bibles, a division of Good News Publishers.)

He began to believe that God would not give up on them, that God would be faithful to the promises made to them, and that one day, Jerusalem would be rebuilt.

This is the word Joy wanted us to hear. For she had discovered through all the experiences of her life, that God was faithful to her. Through all the days living with this disease, through all those countless times in and out of the hospital – she discovered that God was faithful to her. Through the double-lung transplant, when she almost left us then, God got her through and she discovered that God was faithful. And in those three years since – how faithful God was to her. She married the love of her life; she graduated from seminary; she got a job and made positive contributions to the life of the seminary and she got to preach. She developed a passion for preaching. Quite often, I would get a call in the office: "Hi, this is Joy. I have a thesis and objective. What do you think?" I would then ask her where she was going to preach. Just a few weeks ago, she stood in the pulpit and preached about – the faithfulness of God.

And through me, she is still trying to preach to us that word. How are we going to make it through this moment and beyond? The same way Joy did – by depending on the faithfulness of God. I think Joy would say, "Don't you get it yet? God will help you do it." This God who came down to earth in the Person of Jesus, who sought us out to let us know that we are loved, who suffered and died on the cross – not for anything He had done, but for everything we had done – to forgive us. But God raised Jesus from the dead and is faithful to the promise given to us. **Whoever believes in Him will never die, but have life everlasting. John 3:15** (paraphrased) God will be faithful to us. God will get us through.

- This God will be faithful to take our tears of lamentations and turn them into shouts of celebration.

- This God will be faithful to take our broken and hurting spirits and bring us peace and calm.

- This God will be faithful to stoop down to us when we have fallen, and pick us up again and get us on the way. This God will be faithful to us.

It is like Hopeful in Bunyan's *Pilgrim's Progress*, standing in the midst of the rushing waters of the Jordan as he was crossing over into the Promised Land, calling out to those who would follow after, "Take heart. Be of good cheer. For I have felt the bottom, and it is sound!" Of course it is sound, for underneath are the everlasting, loving, faithful arms of God.

Well, Joy. I've tried to tell them your thesis – that the God who was faithful to you will be faithful to us. God won't fail us. When I think of that, I can see it in my imagination – those banners waving in the air, the sound of the trumpets, and the shouts of celebration. For it is true – while earth has lost a saint, heaven has gained one.

Great is God's faithfulness. It is a good word. It is the right word for this moment.

But I want to give you one more word, a word to take with you. It is a precious word, a magnificent word, a beautiful word.

- Every time you hear this word, I hope it will remind you of what we did here today.

- Every time you hear this word, I hope it will remind you of where our hope and comfort really is.

- Every time you hear this word, I hope it will remind you of how you are to live life from this moment on for all your days.

I hope you never forget this word. What is the word?

The word is – **JOY!** I know for me, it is a word I will never forget.

(Reprinted by permission, Hugh Litchfield, Distinguished Professor of Homiletics Emeritus, Sioux Falls Seminary, a North American Baptist Seminary, Sioux Falls, SD, November 9, 2000.)

MY MEMORIES OF JOY HARRIS SAUERS

I want to let you know the impact Joy had on my life. As a medical professional I took care of her for 22+ years, and, although many patients have had an impact on my life, none quite so like Joy.

I remember the little girl who had to go into the mist tent at night. I think there were a few "battles" between the respiratory therapists and Joy about when to go into the tent. I'm certain Joy won every "battle"! We learned early on who was in charge and some beautiful friendships began to develop. What a great fighting spirit she had even as a young child.

As she became a teenager, we learned not to wake her up too early in the morning for her breathing treatments. The beautiful friendships continued. What great conversations we had. It was so fun to chat with her; there was so much to learn from her. We watched her grow from a little girl with such a great spirit to become a wonderful woman. She was such a fighter. She possessed so many wonderful qualities – kindness, compassion, sense of humor, to name a few. What struck me most about her was her tremendous faith in God. She could have complained about her illness, but never did, instead facing it head-on. She may have questioned God, but never did, instead going out spreading His word and helping others. She was given that wonderful gift and never took it for granted, for she used it wisely the way God wanted her to. What a wonderful woman she was and I know you are so very proud of her. Many in her shoes would have given up, but not Joy!

She went through so much and was given so many gifts, a wonderful family, many, many friends and the chance to marry her best friend. What a happy time for her as she prepared for her wedding. It was such a pleasure to watch her marry Mike. I only met him a few times, but, through Joy, I know what a wonderful man he is. Their time together was too short, but their love for each other was so powerful. There was such a sparkle in her eyes when she spoke of him.

I will miss her warm smile, her infectious laugh and our conversations. She was such an important part of our pulmonary rehab program. We miss her deeply, but also know she is with us in spirit and is watching over us.

Her funeral was a beautiful tribute to a wonderful person who will never be gone from our hearts. I am so grateful to have been a part of her life. Watching her grow up, going through so much and never giving up is a tribute to her wonderful fighting spirit.

I have seen this many times and it makes me think of Joy:

God Saw You

God saw you were getting tired and a cure was not meant to be,
So He put His arms around you and whispered, "Come with Me."
With tearful eyes we watched you, and saw you pass away,
And though we love you dearly we could not make you stay.
A golden heart stopped beating, hard working hands to rest.
God broke our hearts to prove to us. . .
He only takes the best.

Joy, you are the best. Thank you for being a part of my life. I'll never forget you.

Rest in Peace, my friend.

Jean Snyders
Avera McKennan Hospital
Respiratory Care Services

SERMONS BY JOY

A Place Called Hope

Jeremiah 31:31-34

The phrase, "A Place Called Hope," came to mind as I studied the life and words of the prophet, Jeremiah. The Northern kingdom of Israel had already been destroyed by Assyria, and Babylon was coming to destroy what was left of the nation. Jerusalem, the Jews' sacred city and home, would soon be demolished. Jeremiah confirmed all the terrible prospects as he spoke of the impending destruction for the nation. But Jeremiah also prophesied a message of hope. Jeremiah basically said, "There is 'A Place Called Hope.'" It was God's promise for the nation of Israel and for us. God promised hope even when there seemed to be no hope for a nation and people in trouble.

Jeremiah was a man of the LORD, called into ministry to be a prophet when he was just a teenager. He served his entire life as a faithful servant of the LORD, never marrying or having children, an outcast in his community, hated by both the social and religious leaders of the time. Jeremiah was also called the weeping prophet. In spite of the harsh treatment he received from his people, he wept over Jerusalem and for his people as he cried to the LORD, "Is there no chance of healing for this nation?" Jeremiah felt deeply for his nation, for he knew they would be destroyed because of their disobedience. You see, Israel was spiritually lost and in trouble.

I. We are a people in trouble.

In chapter 7, Jeremiah spoke the LORD'S words against Israel for what the people had done. The people had been ignoring the covenant of the LORD. You can see Jeremiah checking off each offense as it was listed: injustice to the poor and weak, check; murder, check; adultery, check; stealing, check; lying, check; and the worship of other gods, check plus. Even the priests were in trouble. They overlooked the sins of the people while continuing to pretend all was well – in authentic worship. How dare they, the LORD said, come into the temple to worship while living such lives of disobedience. The nation of Israel had become a nation of spiritual adulterers giving their loyalty, worship and affection to false gods rather than to the LORD, their true Father. They had broken their covenant with God. Trouble! Exile and the destruction of Israel's land and way of life was coming. Israel was a nation in trouble.

Are we not also a people in trouble? Look at our schools – violence, drugs, and dropouts, kids in pursuit of the ultimate in money, attention, or the high life. Nations are financially broke, some are starving and near revolution. Idols of

Hollywood promote scientology, crystals, the spirit world. We may not worship the ancient fertility gods that Israel worshiped, but we have our TVs, sports, shopping malls, and our quest for the ultimate body. We may not steal or take advantage of the needy, but we fail to lend a hand to those we see in need. How many times this season will we race through the mall in our quest for the ultimate gift and breeze right past the Angel Tree where a simple Barbie Doll or Tonka truck would make a kid's Christmas? We buy the bigger-better-sportier car rather than a more modest one then donating the extra money to local charities, international relief organizations or our own church. Are we not a people in trouble just as Israel was in trouble? We are a people in trouble. As the LORD said, "Will you then come and stand before me in my house and say 'we are safe' and go on doing these abominations?"

There is a story of a Methodist missionary to Zambia, Colin Morris, who wrote a book titled, *Include Me Out,* and he was speaking of the church. He said, "I want to be included out of the church because I don't think it cares about people." The reason he said that was because he had to go to a budget meeting in one of the places in Zambia to decide what to do with the hundreds of thousands of dollars that had been given to the mission work in that area. He made his way to the building where the meeting was to be held, and there lying by the steps was a Zambian who had died of hunger. They discovered some pieces of dried leaves and a ball of grass in his stomach. Colin Morris thought that there is something wrong about a church meeting to discuss what to do with hundreds of thousands of dollars while at its very doorsteps, people are dying of hunger.

How can we say, "We love you LORD' yet ignore those whom the LORD has called us to love and minister to? How can we say, "We worship you LORD" if our actions and hearts do not reflect His Word? That was the problem with Israel. It is still happening today. We need to hear the words of the LORD. God promised there is 'A place called hope,' if you will turn to Me. "Turn!"

II. We can find hope if we turn to God.

Early in Jeremiah's ministry the LORD said to Israel, "Here is what I can give you – restoration. Turn to me. Return to your father." Time after time, prophecy after prophecy, Jeremiah used the word "turn" or "return" forty-eight times, but Israel, time and time again, responded "No" and continued to live lives of disobedience. You see, Israel refused to listen to the message, and because they did not hear or turn/return to God, Jeremiah gave them the bad news from the LORD, "I will send you out of my sight and destroy your land and cities. 'You will be EXILED.' All the people, animals, trees and land will burn when my anger and wrath come upon this place." Yet, Israel refused to return to the LORD. The people continued to rebel. Therefore, Israel suffered the consequences. The Babylonians came and destroyed the land of Israel and city of Jerusalem and took many into captivity. They had ignored the message to turn. They missed the message of hope. Only future generations would experience the "Place Called Hope."

They say men will never admit they are wrong, but I think most of us fit that description at some time or another. Some good friends of mine have a three - year-old little boy, Eli. They describe him as their strong-willed child. The other day Eli, while wrestling with Grandpa, cut open his head and had to have stitches. A week later, Eli was to go back to the doctor to have them removed. Before going, however, he decided to take all the books off his shelf and leave them lying on the floor. So, when they returned home, it was time to pick up the books. Dad said, "Eli, you need to put your books back on the shelf." "No!" was his reply – time out #1. After a few minutes, Dad tried again a couple times, "No!" was always the answer – time out #2, 3, and 4. So Dad tried a different approach. "Sit in the chair, and tell me when you are ready to clean up. When you are ready, I will help you and we'll pick up the toys together." Well, this was around 3:00 or 4:00 o'clock. When Mom came home at 6:00 o'clock, Eli was still sitting on the chair, singing to himself, talking, and saying, "Nope, still not ready, not yet." We can all relate to this child's attitude – nope, not going to cooperate, not ready. We go along singing, chatting, and passing the time like there is nothing wrong. This was Israel – stubborn and refusing to obey. We need to listen to that voice that says, "Join me and I will help you. Walk with me. We can do this together." God is calling us with similar words. He offered Israel hope. He offers us "A Place Called Hope" today, if we will just turn to Him.

III. We have hope in God's promises.

So what was this place called hope the LORD promised? Was it cities restored and land productive again? Maybe. Would Israel be an international leader and rule many lands as they had under King David? Maybe not. Would they be forever prosperous and never experience hardship again? No. God's promise of hope was not physical or material, it was spiritual and eternal.

The LORD first addressed the people with these words, "I have loved you with an everlasting love! Therefore, I have continued my faithfulness to you." He went on to explain what His love and faithfulness would mean in verses 31-34. The result of God's love and faithfulness was the new covenant. "I will make a new covenant with my people. This will be a covenant they cannot break. Everyone, all people, from the least to the most powerful, will know me and my laws. They won't have to teach people to 'Know the LORD,' because everyone will know Me within their hearts and their entire being. All sins will be forgiven and forgotten, forever." This promise of a New Covenant has been fulfilled for us today in the life, death, and resurrection of Jesus Christ. Over and over the

New Testament referred to Jesus as the new covenant. The new covenant referred to the body and blood Christ shed for our sins, forgiven, forever. It is through Him that we experience grace. What a promise, what hope. There will come a day when all will know and acknowledge God as Lord and He will rule forever. The hope of life eternal, God as LORD over all, is the promise we, as Christians, can hold onto for the future.

But the new covenant is not just about Jesus. It's about us, too. Israel refused to turn and return to the LORD and suffered the consequences. They could not understand the hope God had to offer, for they lived lives of disobedience and defiance to God's will. We in the church have Christ, but we still must live in his will. We must be willing to turn and return to the God who loves, is faithful, and forgives us when we are in trouble.

A particular Scottish preacher experienced first-hand the love and faithfulness of God and the hope He offers as he wrote a hymn based on the passage of Jeremiah 31. George Matheson was a well-known man, brilliant scholar and beloved pastor in Scotland in the late 1800s. He wrote these words to this hymn, "O Love That Will Not Let Me Go."

O Love that will not let me go,
I rest my weary soul in Thee;
I give thee back the life I owe,
That in Your ocean depths its flow
My richer fuller be.

O Joy that seekest me thru pain,
I cannot close my heart to Thee;
I trace the rainbow thru the rain,
And feel the promise is not in vain
That morn shall tearless be.

O Cross that liftest up my head,
I dare not ask to fly from Thee;
I lay in dust, life's glory dead
And from the ground there blossoms red
Life that shall endless be.

Many believe George wrote this piece as he was struggling with the loss of a promised marriage. George throughout his childhood had struggled with vision problems, but by the time he was in his early twenties, he had lost all his sight. His fiancé left him when she realized the reality that he would soon be totally blind. In the midst of his troubles, George knew who to turn to – his LORD – His love, faithfulness in His promises, and new life in the new covenant.

We, too, experience trouble. We are a people in trouble. We sometimes even create trouble. Like Israel, we stubbornly refuse to turn away from trouble. But there is a place to turn and return to in times of trouble, the LORD. We can experience the love and faithfulness God has declared to us. We have forgiveness and love exemplified in the new covenant, Jesus Christ. We have the promise of a future hope and eternal life, a time when all will know God and acknowledge Him as LORD. There is a "Place Called Hope," and it exists in the love, grace, and promises of the LORD.

The Real Wonder Bread

Text: John 6:35-40

As kids my sister and I were victims of television advertising. It was sad, but we always saw the Wonder Bread commercials and just knew that was the only bread to buy. It was the softest, tastiest, supposedly most nutritious bread, and every other kid had it in their sack lunch. Of course we needed it too. It was "Wonder Bread." Well, I never buy Wonder Bread now. Nevertheless I decided to look up some of the facts about Wonder Bread. Here they are:

> Wonder Bread went national in 1925. Today Wonder Bread is the best selling bread in the United States. Thousands of loaves of fresh Wonder Bread are distributed to store shelves on more than 7,000 delivery routes from Continental's 40 bakeries across the country.

> Elmer Cline, vice president of the baking company, was appointed to merchandise the one-and-a-half pound loaf bread. Attending the International Balloon race he was awed by the sight of the sky filled with hundreds of colorful hot-air balloons. The spectacular sight prompted Cline to name the new bread, Wonder Bread. The wrappers on that bread have featured colorful balloons ever since.

> In 1941, Continental Baking Company joined in the government-supported bread enrichment program, adding vitamins and minerals to Wonder Bread. Known as the "quiet miracle bread," the enrichment nearly eliminated beriberi and pellagra and brought essential nutrients to people who previously could not afford nutritious foods.

> Wonder Bread has been endorsed on television by Howdy Doody and Buffalo Bob, and was praised in song by the Happy Wonder Bakers quartet.

As humans we can do without many things – broccoli, pork chops, apple pie, but if we had nothing else, we could survive on bread and water. Bread has always been a staple in the diets of almost every people group throughout time.

We need bread. In this passage, Christ introduces to us a different image of bread, a bread of life. It doesn't come with the fancy color ballooned wrapper or advertising gimmicks. It is simply Christ. He is the bread of life, not physical life, but spiritual life. Only Christ can bring life to the spirit and life that will last into eternity. That is truly far more deserving of the name "Wonder Bread" than is the recipe of flour and water in the bright colored wrapper.

I. Jesus satisfies

Just before this passage in John, we read about the feeding of the 5,000 which probably was more like 12,000 when you include the women and children. Jesus had just fed all these people with enough fish and bread to satisfy everyone. It had been a real miracle and one that people were still talking about. In fact, many of those still following him had been following Jesus since that miracle. They were waiting for another miracle. They were waiting for something great – something more to satisfy their desires. They were asking Jesus to give them more signs, to enable them to do great miracles. They were seeking more. Jesus had fulfilled their physical needs, yet they were still needy.

Jesus' focus was something different. Jesus said, "I am the bread of life, whoever comes to me will never be hungry and whoever believes in me will never be thirsty." Jesus changes the image altogether. He moves from the physical to the spiritual. He knows the importance of bread as a physical necessity. He is the necessity for life. Jesus is life. That is what he was trying to get across to those who were following him. They wanted to be satisfied and thought that would happen through Christ's physical miracles. But Jesus was talking about being satisfied spiritually for eternal life. Jesus is the only source of satisfaction, the only source for life forever.

Do we really understand that thought or are we like Jesus' followers? I think a lot of people today, sometimes even us, look for satisfaction in our things. We look to be fulfilled in what we have, what we can get, what we want. There is a bumper sticker that says, "If you think money can't buy you happiness, you're shopping in the wrong place." Is that bumper sticker true? Does money really satisfy? No, it doesn't. If it did, the wealthy would be the happiest people in the world. Comedian Louie Anderson was once interviewed and told about his painful childhood and family life. He said he would have traded all his fame, all his money, all he had, to have had a positive family life. The wealth of his life was not satisfying. Though his home and bank account were full, his heart was empty. You see, your car will not be able to transport you into eternity. Designer clothes will not satisfy your need to feel good about who you are. Your spouse or friends cannot fill your spirit or your emotional needs. The world and its goods cannot satisfy. Wonder bread always touted that it had all the nutrition needed for a healthy meal. Maybe. Physically it provided nutrition. But only the real Wonder Bread, Jesus Christ, the bread of life, will satisfy your heart, your spirit, your life and for eternity.

Early in 1977, a coffee shop in Nashville, Tennessee, gained national attention when one of the cinnamon buns it sold reportedly looked like Mother Teresa. The popular press hailed it as a wonder. The coffee shop owner put the bun on display in a glass case and sold picture postcards of the "miracle bun." Business improved as tourists came to see and pay homage to this marvel. People weren't coming for the flour, water, and frosting on this piece of pastry. They were looking for something spiritual. It suggests that our hunger is not for bread but for a sense of God's presence. The hunger in our spirit is greater than our hunger for food. Sometimes we lack the discernment to discriminate between the real Bread of Life and cheap junk food.

What are you seeking? What will satisfy you? Food? Goods? Wealth? Beauty? Success? None of these truly satisfy and none lead to life. Only Jesus can satisfy. Jesus is the bread of life. Whoever comes to Christ will never hunger and whoever believes in him will never be thirsty. You will be satisfied.

III. Jesus saves.

John's whole purpose in writing about Jesus' life and miracles was to point people to who Jesus was – the Messiah. Jesus was God's son and his mission was to do the will of his Father. Jesus came to touch people, to save people for eternity. Jesus' mission was to bring people to himself, to faith, to salvation. And so Jesus ends this talk by saying, "All who see the Son and believe in him will have eternal life, and I will raise them up on the last day." Sounds simple, yet for many it was hard to believe. The Jewish leaders continued to argue with Jesus. How can he claim to be from God? They still did not understand the type of Savior and Messiah Jesus was going to be. Many of the people who were following Jesus at this time eventually fell away because they could not take the step of faith Jesus required. Many did not understand that Jesus could satisfy their soul. They left when he didn't continue to satisfy their wants.

But since that time, many have believed, many have come to know Christ. Christ calls all and accepts all who come to him, believing in him. Christ's mission was to save the world – to fulfill the plan of the Father for a Savior. Jesus saves and can save you today.

Who are you in this story? Are you like those who followed Jesus? Many of you today may be looking for satisfaction in the world, yet cannot find any. You may be seeking, yet are unfulfilled in your heart. Are you one who is searching for the satisfying bread of life and living water that comes from Jesus? Do you need to experience the miracle of salvation, healing, and a whole spirit? Jesus can satisfy your heart and spirit. Choose Jesus!

Maybe you are one of the Jewish leaders who questions Jesus' claims and motives as Messiah. You have seen how Jesus works and how he changes the lives of all who believe in him, yet you, yourself, have not believed. Maybe you have your own expectations of what Jesus should do or be. Jesus came to fulfill God's plan for salvation. Choose Jesus.

If you have already placed your faith in Christ, you are John, the author. You know the Savior and now the task is to point others toward him. The mission Jesus started is yours to continue. Point people to Jesus and take Jesus into your world.

The bottom line – Jesus gives life. He alone saves. Jesus accepts any and all who will come to him and believe. He is ready and waiting for us to take the step of faith. Though he is no longer on this earth, his mission of salvation continues. Maybe you haven't made the decision to accept Christ by faith. If you haven't and would like to talk with me or a deacon about accepting Christ, please do so, today. Choose Christ. He will never leave you empty.

II. Jesus came for all who might believe.

There were also the Jewish leaders who were following Christ, though more suspicious about what he was up to. They had seen and partaken in Christ's miracle of the feeding and were wondering what this miracle might mean. Expectations were high at this time that a Messiah was coming and they were watching. They were focused on Christ as the Messiah. But they had it wrong. They believed the one that would come from God would come with a sword and inaugurate a new Jewish nation. They wanted a Christ who would rule on the earth and overtake the governments that had control over the Jewish people. They were looking for a warrior who would satisfy their need for a kingdom on earth, for power and control. They were wrong.

Jesus had tried to show how his power was different. It wasn't about overtaking governments, but about meeting people's needs. Jesus ministry was to get to the heart, not to fight the great battle for power. Jesus said, "You have seen me, yet you still do not believe." The Jews and the people had seen Jesus' work and miracles, yet they still didn't get it. Jesus continues, "I have come down from heaven to do my Father's will and my Father's will is that I accept all who will come to me and raise them up on the last day." Jesus' task was not to conquer lands or armies, but to conquer lives and hearts for eternity. Jesus was on earth for all people, any who might accept him. The Jewish leaders could not understand this. They wanted a Jesus for them only, for their benefit and agenda. Their expectations were wrong. They missed the heart, the person and the mission of Jesus. Jesus came to all with the goal of saving all who believed.

What about our perceptions of Jesus? Do we see Jesus as who he really is? Who do we say he is? Do we recognize him as the one who is interested in saving peoples' lives, all people? We have expectations about who Jesus can minister to and save – certainly not the prostitute or AIDS victim. The mentally ill could not possibly understand or be included in God's plan. Or maybe we see a Jesus who will help us to be more successful, more popular. Sometimes we want Jesus to be the great one who acts when we ask. We have dreams about what Jesus will do for us. The Jews certainly did. They knew exactly who they wanted Jesus to be and what they wanted Jesus to do. But Jesus is not about fulfilling our wants or expectations. He knew his mission was the Father's and that mission was to reach any and all who would come to him. Are you like the Jewish leaders who questioned Jesus and his mission? Have you seen Jesus, the real Jesus, or are you looking for Jesus with false expectations?

Unfortunately we are often like the Jewish leaders. There was a story of an old man. This old man was brought to a hospital emergency room late in the evening – an apparent mugging victim. He looked like one of the homeless. He was poorly clothed, dirty, disheveled, battered, and apparently unconscious. One of the young medical students took one look at him and said, "What in the world should we do with this worthless wretch?" The old man opened his eyes slightly and in an amazingly strong voice said, "Call him not worthless for whom Christ died!"

We need to know Jesus as Jesus described himself – as the one who came to save all people, that "whosoever believes in him will have life." Christ came to minister to the hearts of people, to save people for eternity. Knowing that, we need to re-examine our understanding of Christ. Christ came for all who might believe.

If you already know Christ, the task is to continue the Father's mission, to take Christ to the world. Who do you know that is unsatisfied, not physically, but in spirit? Who do you know who does not understand Jesus and how Jesus longs to bring them into the kingdom of heaven? Will you take Christ to your neighbor?

<u>Conclusion: Believe in the real wonder bread of life.</u>

Jesus came to give life. He is truly the most wonderful bread you can choose to partake of. Those who come to him will never be hungry. Those who believe in him will never thirst. You will be satisfied – heart, mind, and soul. Those who believe in him will have eternal life. Amen

I chose two sermons to include in Joy's story. Joy loved to preach and sought opportunities for pulpit supply during the summer of 2000 when pastors were on vacation. She had eight more sermons.

The titles are as follows: Faith's Melodies
                                   Every Thorn Has Its Rose
                                   Show Me the Money
                                   Showdown at the Altar
                                   When Difficult Times Come – What Then?
                                   Loving the Blockheads of the World
                                   Thanks for the Memories
                                   Go Ahead, Make My Day

<u>If you would like any one or all of these sermons, please contact us at:</u>

www.gordon and joyce.net

OR

blessedbyjoy@gmail.com

<u>We ask only that a donation be made to</u>
<u>Sioux Falls Seminary at the following address:</u>

Leadership Foundation
Sioux Falls Seminary
1525 South Grange Avenue
Sioux Falls, South Dakota 57105

Acknowledgements

I mentioned to Joy during the last year of her life that she should write her story. She said nothing, only smiled. She knew then what we did not know. Her body was failing but not her will and spirit. That was the year she got to preach. She left us her sermons. She left her journal. She left us memories. She left us an example of a life committed to God. She left us inspiration and a legacy. She willed to us her story and trusted us to tell it like it is and was. She and God would be the author. She demonstrated to us that God can use a life that is committed to serving Him even if limited by health, strength, and years. It was up to us to tell the story, and it has taken almost seven years. I can hear her now saying, "What took you so long, Mom?"

So I first give thanks to God. I thank Him for entrusting Joy's life to us although we cannot take credit for her accomplishments. I thank Him for gifting Joy for ministry, for healing her time and again, for extending her life so that she could speak His Word.

I thank God for directing my fingers on the keyboard. He gave me clarity of words and memories. God has been evident throughout this entire process. If anything is out of place or misrepresented, the blame sits here in my heart and mind.

A simple thank you to those of you who have assisted me can never be fully defined. The encouragement of friends as I worked on this project was God's hand nudging me along. There are many people to whom I want to give credit. One of the first is Dr. Rhoda Carpenter who, in a spontaneous moment, affirmed my abilities as a writer. She stirred me to stop thinking about it and just get on with it. When I finally set my hands to the keyboard buttons, I pretended I was writing specifically to Rhoda. Thank you, Rhoda, for believing in me and speaking an inspired word when I needed it.

Gordon was serving as interim pastor at Bridgewater Mennonite Church. I mentioned to a few ladies that I was writing the story of our daughter, Joy. A week or so later, Dan and Martha Stahl offered the services of their daughter who is a writer and editor for on online agricultural magazine. Suzanne Stahl Kosec willingly and gently sat down with me and helped me understand the role of a writer, how to fill in details of a story, how to put myself into the moment and re-live the events and feelings. This at times was excruciatingly difficult but necessary. Thank you, Suzie.

I was searching google for an editor when the web page of Patricia Fry popped up. She is an author of twenty-four books and many articles. She also is an editor, and now "dedicated to hopeful authors everywhere" (*The Right Way to Write, Publish and Sell Your Book*). I emailed Patricia, and she answered within a few minutes. I ordered three of her books. Excellent books! I asked if she would edit my book. She asked me to send her only five pages of my manuscript, and she would respond. I needed someone experienced and skilled who could give an objective point of view without reservation. I was not disappointed. Through the trials of editorship, suggestions, rewriting, and re-organization, I came to appreciate this lady, her honesty, her professionalism, and her friendship. She was quick to pick up on details that needed clarification. But she would not rewrite. She made me do that. It was worth the pain.

I would still be in the throes of writing if it had not been for the North American Baptist Conference International Headquarters in Chicago. Gordon served as Interim Executive Director during this last year and a half. I often tagged along with him traveling from Sioux Falls, SD. The office in Chicago generously furnished me with a computer and desk. They were extremely patient with me. Believe me, when I say <u>patient</u>. They graciously ignored my tears when I would embarrassingly run to the nearby lady's room. They never called attention to my deep breathing and sighs. They always accommodated my pleas for help when I could not locate the socket to plug in the flash drive. They even shared their snacks. Thank you, Phil Bailey, for your help in many of my requests. The conference office was the perfect place to work uninterrupted by phone calls, laundry, cooking, errands, attention to Alley (my cat), volunteer work, etc. All of you in Chicago deserve a special commendation. I understand the burden of work you carry that is often unrecognized by the churches and conference you serve. You serve with dedication, excellence, and humility. Thank you!! Gordon and I treasure our friendships with you.

On our many trips to Chicago, Nancy and Fred Folkerts graciously opened their home to us. They cooked for us, took us on sight seeing excursions, allowed us to use their laundry, and saved us and the conference a "bundle" of money. We were not treated as guests but as family. We had fun. We rested. We shared in our many conversations. Your unselfish dedication to God's work will not go unrecognized. God has been good, and we value your friendship and wisdom. Many, many blessings to you in your new retirement home.

The Sioux Falls Seminary has been more than a place of employment for Gordon during the last 33 years. It has been a community of friendship, service and scholarship dedicated to the training of future leaders for the church. The seminary was where Joy discovered her spiritual gifts and her love of ministry. Within the confines of that school, Joy truly was inspired for leadership. The work of God's Spirit, the attention to worship, and the study of God's inspired Word fed and nourished Joy's thirst for knowledge and her passion for ministry. The Seminary – including faculty, administration, and students – can gratefully take credit for this book and for much of Joy's spiritual journey. The friendships that were formed created a network of support that filled a missing link in her life. Joy found blessings, love, and acceptance within that community of faith at Sioux Falls Seminary. On Joy's behalf, we give you recognition. Thank you!

What would we do without those amazing church secretaries? Darla Brinkhaus-Gross – that is you – secretary at Trinity Baptist Church. You have the intelligence and the social where-with-all to laugh and not wring your hands when my computer skills begged for help. It cost you time and effort to fix, but you willingly went the second and third mile. Your grammar, your word skills, your punctuation, your creative writing, not to mention your patience – these have contributed significantly to this book. I will not hesitate to give credit to you for the sub-title that you thoughtfully pulled out of your head. Through our work together, we have become dear friends, and yes, it was fun. But sorry, I cannot share any profits with you. It all goes to the seminary.

There are more – Krista Mournet, you have enthusiastically and perpetually inspired me in the completion of Joy's story. You always said, "I can't wait to read your book." So I pressed on. Thank you. Pat Asche – you willingly printed and printed again and again the pages of the manuscript. You are such a positive, exuberant, and masterful secretary at the seminary. Thank you and also to your husband, Chuck, the pastor, who mentored Joy in her supervised ministry.

CCW, Christian Coalition of Writers – our little group of writers in Sioux Falls – you have called me to accountability and always, always encouraged me with words and enthusiasm. Thank you, Lenore Lang, Joyce Heisler, Wanda Todd, Sherry Carson, and Darla Brinkhaus-Gross. You said this book would happen, and thanks be to God, it is now a reality. Thank you and love to you all. I look forward to all the next times.

Dr. Jacqueline Howell, "Jackie", you read the entire manuscript, not just the medical stuff – praises to you. You found "stuff" no one else could spot. Thank you for the medical words, spellings, and collection of information. Your intelligence and personal involvement with Joy and our family will always be appreciated. I will never forget Joy's first hospitalization in Sioux Falls (1975) that was so difficult. You came to sit with us and quietly, with your presence, brought a sense of calm and assurance. I don't think I ever thanked you, but I do now!

Barbie and Mike Hagan, you adopted us into your family when we felt alone during Thanksgiving holidays separated from family. Mike, professor of Biblical Hebrew and president of the seminary, you graciously tutored Joy in an extra semester of Hebrew. You eventually employed Joy at the seminary as Liaison in Long Distance Learning. Joy stated in her journal thankfulness for that "dream job." Thank you for the detailed reading of the manuscript, your suggestions and corrections. Barbie, you gave special attention to Jami. You enjoyed her spontaneity and realized she was the child left in the shadows. You took her in and gave special recognition to her. Our friendship all these years took on deeper meaning when you reached out to me after Joy's death. Both you and Mike have positively impacted our lives in ways we can never express. Thank you and we love you.

Pastor Ron Norman and our family of faith at Trinity Baptist Church – thank you, pastor, for reading the manuscript and for valued words of Joy's story and our family. Your affirmation means a great deal to me. Trinity Baptist Church – you have been our prayer warriors and our family of faith for more than 33 years. You have ministered to us in our darkest hours. Kelly Lashley, you were the spiritual guide for Joy and Jami during their youth. You had great fun with them and also served as their Bible teacher and role model. Their lives are a credit to you.

Pastor Daryl Dachtler, thank you for the prayers you led on behalf of Joy during those five months when she lay in a hospital bed in Minneapolis with little hope of recovery. God came through in amazing, miraculous ways. God is faithful.

The medical community who cared for Joy, who were touched by her life, who were instrumental in meeting Joy's life needs. Joy had a team of doctors, pharmacists, nurses, therapists between Avera McKennan in Sioux Falls and Fairview University Hospital in Minneapolis. Notable were Dr. Terry Lang, Joy's pediatrician, Dr. Rod Parry, lead pulmonologist, Dr. Wendell Hoffman, infectious disease. In Minneapolis, thank you, Dr. Bolman, lead surgeon of the transplant team, the man with gifted hands and big heart who said to Joy, "You are an amazing woman!"

Dr. Jordan Dunitz, Joy's primary pulmonologist at the hospital and clinic at Fairview University Hospital in Minneapolis. You gave Joy personal and skillful medical attention during and after her transplant. The numerous broncoscopys, the laser surgeries to inhibit the growth of scar tissue, the implant of stents in her lungs – you are a gifted physician with a heart for your patients. Thank you, Dr. Dunitz. You and Joy had a very special relationship. And a sincere thanks to your wife and family for giving you the freedom to devote to your profession. God bless them all.

We thank our pharmacists, Ron Park, followed by Eli and his wife, Carla. Eli, you came to our house week after week to personally deliver the many medications, once late in the evening during a bitter snow storm and sub-zero temperatures. I will never forget that night. Thank you. I pray that Joy's story will bless your life and give you gratification.

Russ and Cheryl Borchardt, owners of Crossroads Book and Music, you welcomed me back after a six month absence while I stayed with Joy in Minneapolis. You trusted me not knowing when I would return. Thank you all dear friends and colleagues at Crossroads. You have demonstrated integrity, love, and faithfulness.

An unusual thanks needs mentioning – Jill Callison, editor at the Argus Leader. You will never know the number of people who approached me, who called me, to tell how touched and blessed they were by the two front page articles you wrote with Joy and about Joy. Those articles were an example to the world that God loves and provides for His children. Our God cannot be undone.

Hugh Litchfield and your wife, Sarah, are long time friends of 45 years. You earned the title of Distinguished Professor of Homiletics Emeritus at Sioux Falls Seminary. But we remember you best for fulfilling Joy's dying request. You proclaimed a message of hope from the scripture that she assigned to you to preach. You knew her well, and your words skillfully characterized the meaning and spirit of Joy's life. I still love to read it. You taught her to love the preaching of God's Word, and you sent her off well to claim that "Good and Faithful Reward." Thank you, dear friends.

A grateful thanks to both Ron Sisk and Hugh Litchfield for reading Joy's sermon manuscripts. Your comments and corrections were a necessary element for sharing Joy's sermons with the public.

Jami, the cover of this book is your gift to Joy. You designed a beautiful and elegant cover that captures the spirit and image of Joy. God has gifted you, and He takes delight in your creative work, after all He is the Great Creator. Thank you to your friends, Sarah Fuscia and Ryan. Especially appreciated is Walter Johnson for the computer graphics he composed. Gordon and I thank Ryan Stander for the back cover photograph and Shanda Stricherz for translating it from her computer onto a disc.

Finally, I thank Ted and Marietta Faszer. You opened your home to Joy and her Bible study groups. Those studies and relationships were precious. Joy discovered a heart for ministry and preaching through the opportunities to teach. The gift of hospitality will not go unnoticed. God rewards.

Thank you, Doris and Peter Fehr, Marge and Harold Lang, for providing a place of rest for our body and soul during five months of spiritual and physical struggle as Joy's life hung in the balance. You were our rescue team.

So many, many people who prayed – missionaries, churches, students, friends, family, strangers, professionals – God knows who you are and honored your prayers with Joy's life who gave a witness of Him to the world.

I leave this story with you, the readers, so that you may experience God's amazing touch. I pray that you may be open to listen for His voice, be willing to respond, be inspired to continue the story of His love, be committed to do His work and to live recklessly for the salvation of others. There will not be another Joy, but there will always be you and the presence of God's hand upon your heart and life. May you go forward with joy and singing to the LORD, serving Him with faithfulness and love.

To God be all glory!
Joyce Behm Harris

BLESSED BY *Joy*